# CAREER MATCH

## Connecting Who You Are with What You'll Love to Do

**Shoya Zichy**
**with Ann Bidou**

AMACOM

American Management Association

New York ◆ Atlanta ◆ Brussels ◆ Chicago ◆ Mexico City ◆ San Francisco
Shanghai ◆ Tokyo ◆ Toronto ◆ Washington, D. C.

# To Mother, Charles, Sheila, and Fiona
# My own living color laboratory!

Special discounts on bulk quantities of AMACOM books are
available to corporations, professional associations, and other
organizations. For details, contact Special Sales Department,
AMACOM, a division of American Management Association,
1601 Broadway, New York, NY 10019.
Tel: 212-903-8316. Fax: 212-903-8083.
E-mail: specialsls@amanet.org
Website: www.amacombooks.org/go/specialsales
To view all AMACOM titles go to: www.amacombooks.org

*This publication is designed to provide accurate and authoritative information
in regard to the subject matter covered. It is sold with the understanding that
the publisher is not engaged in rendering legal, accounting, or other
professional service. If legal advice or other expert assistance is required, the
services of a competent professional person should be sought.*

*Library of Congress Cataloging-in-Publication Data*

Zichy, Shoya.
    Career match: connecting who you are with what you'll love to do /
Shoya Zichy, with Ann Bidou.
        p.   cm.
    Includes bibliographical references and index.
    ISBN-10: 0-8144-7364-4
    ISBN-13: 978-0-8144-7364-1
    1. Vocational guidance.   2. Personality and occupation.   I. Bidou,
Ann.   II. Title.
    HF5381.Z467   2007
    650.14—DC22

                                                                    2006031850

Printing number

10   9   8   7   6   5   4   3

# Contents

# Introduction
# and Acknowledgments

## Where It All Began

On a muggy night in May I sat stranded in an Asian airport. Only the floor sweepers punctuated the late night desolation. It was the end of a long, very overscheduled business trip—one of the many I took each year in the search for new banking clients. In the midst of a large pile of waiting room debris, I noticed a book. Dog-eared and well-used, it caught my attention. I picked it up, and my view of the world was altered forever.

"If a man does not keep pace with others, perhaps it is because he hears a different drummer," it began with the oft-quoted Henry David Thoreau. The book, an obscure and since-discontinued interpretation of Swiss psychologist Carl Jung's theories, outlined the seemingly obvious differences in the way people take in information and make decisions. Some of this I knew intuitively. Yet the information hinted at a new way to deal with my clients and associates.

On returning to my Hong Kong office, I set out to color code each of my customers based on their Jungian behavioral profiles. Each file contained brief instructions for support staff to follow in the event of my absence. "When a Gold comes in, make sure all statements are up to date and organized in date-sequential order. If a Blue makes an appointment, call our investment guys in New York and get three new ideas." And so it continued, outlining a strategy for each of four color groups.

It proved uncannily effective. Almost overnight, our new business increased by 60 percent. But there was more. I began to enjoy my clients more, my stress level went down, and, in time, my relationships with others outside of work began to improve as well.

For some ten years, I continued to use this technique. The bank sent me back to the United States, and the clients grew more diverse—white-robed sheiks in Abu Dhabi, shipping magnates in Athens, or aristocratic landowners in Spain—the same color-coding instructions dotted their files. What's more, they worked—for men, for women, old and young, widely varying ethnicities.

In that decade, I never met another individual who spoke of Jung—at least not in terms of applying his concepts to marketing. Then in 1990 I joined some friends in Maine to escape from burnout and institutional re-organization. I needed to rethink my career.

The small Port Clyde Inn sparkled in the crisp October sunlight, and on the front porch sat a man reading a book. We began to chat and he spoke of the author Isabel Myers and her new applications for the work of Carl Jung, a system called the Myers-Briggs Type Indicator®. It was the conversation I had been looking for.

Over the next few years, I would discover a hidden universe of books, seminars, tapes, and associations involving hundreds of people around the world. I had a new, strong sense of internal direction. Suddenly, things just began to happen; the right people and events began to materialize. Jung would have called it "synchronicity."

It would be a couple of years before I could undertake my own research, but eventually my life became focused on the business applications for personality styles. The material that follows sums up the information provided by over 10,000 people who have attended my seminars and the written works of "personality type" experts who for the last two decades have laid the intellectual groundwork that serves as the basis of this book. Very few of the principles are my own; however, as my client list can attest, I have pioneered unique ways of applying these ideas to the workplace.

For the sake of simplicity, I have adopted my own color-coding system of earlier times, which I call Color Q. "When you meet a Gold, make sure that…" It served me well for many years, and it will serve you well, too.

## The Purpose of This Book

Many of us share the fantasy that we can do anything and be anyone . . . with just a little more effort. This is an illusion that blocks real development. Growth does NOT require significant change, or that we emulate "role models" because we are somehow innately inadequate. It does require that we understand and accept the dynamics of our own GENUINE style—its unique strengths and weaknesses. It also means that, in time, we tone down some of our blind spots.

There are many systems for understanding people. This is the one I have found that probes most deeply into the core of human behavior. It confirms that each personality style is natural, equal, observable, and predictable, and that each can be equally effective at work.

Truly exceptional people always do so much more than is required. The only way to do that without severe burnout is from passion born of confidence. You are the right person doing the right thing in the right place and enjoying it! Sound impossible? Not at all, for those who are true to themselves in spite of naysayers, parental expectations, and societal pressures. Use this book to reveal your road to being exceptional.

## What Color Q Is Not

Color Q is not the answer to all career problems. It is not a painless shortcut to maturity and wisdom. Most of all, it does not measure the impact of education, intelligence, mental health, special talents, economic status, motivation, drive, or environmental influences on the core personality type. There are billions of unique people on our planet and only four Color groups. If you wonder what that leaves, I say only the deepest, most important part of you – the part that ALWAYS knows what it really wants, and won't be happy until it gets respect!

The framework is not gender specific. It works equally well for males and females. Both men and women are found in each personality style, though in some groups the percentages differ.

Finally, Color Q is NOT a complete, in-depth Myers-Briggs evaluation. It is a ten-minute self-assessment designed to acquaint you with concepts that are applicable to your career. If, after reading this book, you are intrigued enough to take the whole Myers-Briggs Type Indicator, check the website www.colorQProfiles.com, and you will be matched with an appropriate professional for assessment and feedback.

## What Color Q Is

Color Q is about coding people—ourselves and others. We do it all the time. "He is shrewd and entrepreneurial." "She is energetic and artistic." This helps us to group our impressions mentally and store them in the appropriate synapse of our brain for future use.

Color Q is also a tool for understanding the sometimes incomprehensible behaviors of bosses and co-workers (and even friends, dates, and mates!). Since so much career advancement depends on your "people skills," you'll find your increased ability to "read people" perhaps the most valuable outcome of reading this book.

Enjoy this journey!

## Acknowledgments

I've been blessed to connect with so many people who share my passion for the study of personality differences. I am particularly grateful to the following:

- Peter and Katharine Myers for continuing to support new applications of personality type.
- David Keirsey, whose book *Please Understand Me* started me on my journey, and Linda Berens whose ongoing research continues to enrich our understanding of temperaments.
- MBTI specialists who have written on personality and careers, in particular, Allen Hammer, whose *MBTI Career Reports* provided a rich array of insights. Paul Tieger, Donna Dunning, Charles Martin, and Otto Kroeger have provided valuable contributions to this area as well.
- The individuals profiled in the book and the thousands who have participated in my seminars. Your life stories have brought my model to life.
- Linda Konner, our agent, for seeing the potential of the manuscript and providing steadfast focus, support, and wisdom.
- The vibrant AMACOM team Andrew Ambraziejus, Ellen Kadin, and Vera Sarkanj, for their professionalism and dedication to the publishing and marketing of this book. Barry Richardson, for his editing savvy, and Kathy Whittier, for copyediting and production coordination. Marie Corbett, my Citibank colleague of many years, for helping organize the resource section.
- Denise Seegovian, Lene Skou, and the student advisors, Yan Kuznetsov, Faith Serrano, Ally Tubis, and Alexandria White for their ongoing marketing advice.
- My interns Debra Asfour and Mary Li for taking time out of their graduate studies to transcribe tapes and find new marketing technologies.
- Russ Cohen *russ@russcohen.com* for his innovative cartoons.
- And last, but certainly not least, thanks to my family, Mother, Charles, Sheila, and Fiona for always being the cheerleaders.

**From Ann Bidou:**
Thanks to Katy Libby, who did the grunt work in Toymakers Café so I could write.

This is for my niece, Libiann—spend your life trying all the stuff you think, or they say, you can't do. I believe in you.

To everyone in the Norwalk and Huntington groups, and especially to Michel Corey. Thanks for your insights.

And finally, to Greg, my husband, thank you for your invaluable support, encouragement and belief, for sure, for sure.

# People Profiled

## In Order of Appearance

**GREENS:**   **Diane Sawyer**, journalist, ABC News; **Frank McCourt**, best-selling author; **Laura Ziskin**, film producer; **Angelina Jolie**, actress; **Bono**, musician; **Alexandra Lebenthal**, financial executive; **Terry McGuinness**, human resource director; **Maggie Hoffman**, public relations manager; **Lonnie Carter**, playwright and professor; **Michele Frank**, clinical social worker; **Gregory J. Marion**, business consultant; **Gloria Parker**, model, actress, interior designer, berry farmer; **Oldrich Teply**, fine and commercial artist, teacher; **Dan Shaw,** writer; **Anne Thayer**, conference planner; **Phyllis Rosen**, stock trader, career coach.

**REDS:**   **Donald Trump**, real estate tycoon; **Christie Todd Whitman**, consultant, former governor of New Jersey; **Peter Tanous**, author, owner/investment consulting firm; **Marla Kreindler**, attorney/employee benefits and financial services; **Charles Nemes,** owner, Barbizon modeling school; **Stan Waring**, manufacturing executive; **Gregory Bidou**, entrepreneur/restaurant and mail order businesses; **Lilliana Goldberg**, veterinarian; **Joyce Jenkins**, internal coach, Citigroup; **Christopher L. Dutton**, President and CEO, Green Mountain Power, **Bud Murdock**, innkeeper.

**BLUES:**   **Hillary Rodham Clinton**, United States Senator, D-New York; **Charles Schwab**, Founder/Chairman/CEO, The Charles Schwab Corporation; **Rehana Farrell**, Chief Financial Officer, Merrill Lynch;

Michael Isaacs, Chief Executive Officer, U.S. Balloon Company; Kathlene Burke, law student, Jeannette Hobson, Vistage Chair, coach, small and medium-sized businesses; Glenn Frontera, producer/director, Multimedia Production, MTA New York City Transit; Joshua Stone, music composer, Alger B. ("Duke") Chapman, Senior Advisor, Cambridge Group, former CEO, Chicago Board of Options; Charles M. "Chuck" Sheaff, surgeon; Chuck Wardell, managing director, executive recruiting; Jack Rubinstein, small business advisor, Bruce Terman, Ph.D., medical research scientist; Ari Levy, hedge fund manager.

**GOLDS:**    Kay Bailey Hutchison, United States Senator, R-Texas; Joan Shapiro Green, board member; Alan "Ace" Greenberg, Chairman of the Executive Committee, Bear Stearns; Mellody Hobson, President, Ariel Capital Management; Linda Konner, literary agent; Kathleen Waldron, Ph.D., President, Baruch College; Sergio I. de Araujo, Managing Director and Senior Investment Officer, U.S. Trust Company; Martin Deeg, chemical engineer and manufacturing company owner; Linda Chavez-Thompson, Executive Vice President, AFL-CIO, Princess Fazilé Ibrahim, philanthropist; Eric Nichols, Ph.D., psychologist and professor; Mary Waite, small business president.

**ENTREPRENEURS;**    Trisha Rooney Alden and Phillip Rooney: father/daughter entrepreneurial team, R4 Services; Helen Glunz, Glunz Family Winery & Cellars; Nordhal Brue, Bruegger's Bagels; Carla Hall, Carla Hall Design Group.

**MONEY & COMPENSATION:**    Betsy Howie, author.

# THE JUMP START
*Defining Yourself and Others*

# CHAPTER 1

# Don't Read the Whole Book . . .

**THIS IS NOT YOUR TYPICAL** career book. The Color Q system doesn't change people, but it does change how they view themselves. You will not be told to be more organized, to assert yourself, imitate your boss, or emulate some celebrity CEO. You will not even have to change how you dress. Instead, every word will move you to operate from your deepest, most natural talents, fueling the passion that separates good workers from great achievers. You just need to recognize your strengths and use them on a daily basis.

Sound easy? It's not. Most of us come loaded down with guilt and parental/societal expectations that push us in unnatural directions. Did pressures like money, prestige, educational opportunity, or family desires force you into making more "practical" choices? If doing so hasn't made you happy, then what will?

You need to get back to your core and make it work in the workplace. Define this core by taking the Color Q Self-Assessment in Chapter 2 and being bluntly honest. For many of you, it will be career-altering, IF you answer as you really are. Please note that a preference is NOT "I generally work with piles, but I'd prefer if I kept my desk clean." What you actually *do* is what you prefer.

You do not need to read the whole book, unless you want to explore all sixteen Color Q personality types. Learning a little about other people's styles, however, will help you in:

- Job or promotion interviews.
- Team projects.
- Salary/contract negotiations.
- Sales.
- Boss/co-worker conflicts.
- Dates.
- Family relations.

The theory behind the Color Q system has been tested for decades on millions of people worldwide. It has changed lives and altered careers, including those of both authors of this book. If it changes your life, as we think it will, we'd like to know. Your story is as significant as the ones included in this book. Email me at *Zichy@earthlink.net* and check out my website at www.ColorQProfiles.com.

# CHAPTER 2

# The Color Q Personality Style Self-Assessment

## Instructions: Part I

In the Color Q personality profiling system, you have a primary personality Color. This is who you are at your core. You also have a backup Color—a strong secondary influence. Finally, you have an Introvert or Extrovert tendency. Color Q describes people, for example, as Green/Red Introverts. This ten-minute either/or self-assessment will reveal all three aspects of your personality.

Select one of the two choices in *each* line according to your first impulse, which is usually correct; but choose as you *are*, not as you would *like* to be. Don't overanalyze your choice. There are no "right" or "wrong" answers. Think of this like your left or right hand. While you can use both, you have a preference for one over the other, and you use that hand with less effort and better results. If you are truly torn between the two choices, it may mean you either feel guilty about your honest answer, or feel pressured to function in a certain way.

First, fill out Section I, choosing what YOU (not your boss, mate, parents, or anyone else) prefer. Choose from Column A or B. Each A or B choice must be filled in, choosing the statement that describes you at least 51 percent of the time. You *should wind up with nine checkmarks total in this section.*

## Section I

- Be sure **to answer every question.** Total each column, and then follow instructions to Sections II or III.

**At least 51 percent of the time I tend to:**

| Column A | | Column B |
|---|---|---|
| ☐ value accuracy more | or | ☐ value insights more |
| ☐ be interested in concrete issues | or | ☐ be interested in abstract ideas |
| ☐ prefer people who speak plainly | or | ☐ prefer unusual ways of expression |
| ☐ remember many details | or | ☐ be vague about details |
| ☐ be down to earth | or | ☐ be complex |
| ☐ focus on the present | or | ☐ focus on future possibilities |
| ☐ be valued for my common sense | or | ☐ be valued for seeing new trends |
| ☐ be realistic and pragmatic | or | ☐ be theoretical and imaginative |
| ☐ be trusting of the facts | or | ☐ be trusting of my intuition |

**If you have chosen more items in Column A, please <u>go directly to Section III</u>.**
**If you have chosen more items in Column B, please <u>go to Section II</u>.**

Count the number of checks in each column. Then move on to Section II or III depending on your results. Assess your primary Color now.

## Section II

**At least 51 percent of the time I tend to be *more*:**

| Column 1 | | Column 2 |
|---|---|---|
| ☐ frank and direct | or | ☐ tactful and diplomatic |
| ☐ skeptical at first | or | ☐ accepting at first |
| ☐ unemotional | or | ☐ emotional |
| ☐ analytical | or | ☐ empathetic |
| ☐ apt to meet conflict head on | or | ☐ apt to avoid conflict where possible |
| ☐ principled | or | ☐ sympathetic |
| ☐ objective when criticized | or | ☐ apt to take things personally |
| ☐ impartial | or | ☐ compassionate |
| ☐ competitive | or | ☐ supportive |

**If you have chosen more items in the left column 1, <u>you are a Blue</u>.**
**If you answered more items in the right column 2, <u>you are a Green</u>.**

## Section III

**At least 51 percent of the time I tend to:**

| Column @ | | Column # |
|---|---|---|
| ☐ meet deadlines early | or | ☐ meet deadlines at the last minute |
| ☐ make detailed plans before I start | or | ☐ handle problems as they arise |
| ☐ be punctual and sometimes early | or | ☐ be leisurely, sometimes late |
| ☐ like to be scheduled | or | ☐ prefer to be spontaneous |
| ☐ like clear guidelines | or | ☐ like flexibility |
| ☐ feel settled | or | ☐ often feel restless |
| ☐ have a tidy workplace | or | ☐ have a workplace with many piles/papers |
| ☐ be deliberate | or | ☐ be carefree |
| ☐ like to make plans | or | ☐ like to wait and see |

**If you answered more items in the left column @, <u>you are a Gold</u>.**
**If you answered more items in the right column #, <u>you are a Red</u>.**

## Instructions: Part II

Now read the short overview of you primary Color below. Does it ring true? If yes, continue to Part III. If not, skip down to Part V, "What to Do If This Doesn't Ring True for You."

### GOLDS     (46% of population)

**Grounded, realistic, and accountable,** Golds are the backbone of institutions of all kinds—corporate and public. **They are society's protectors and administrators who value procedures, respect the chain of command, and have finely tuned systems for everything**, from raising children to running large divisions. Golds get involved in details and are known for following through and mobilizing others to achieve concrete goals. They are the most effective in making lists, planning in advance, and dealing with what has worked in the past.

### BLUES     (10% of population)

**Theoretical, competitive, and always driven to acquire more knowledge and competence,** Blues are **unequaled when it comes to dealing with complex, theoretical issues and designing new systems.** As natural skeptics, their first reaction is to criticize and set their benchmarks against which they measure everyone and everything. They are highly precise in thought and language and future oriented, trusting only logic, *not* the rules or procedures of the past. Blues are visionary and do best in positions requiring strategic thinking. Then they move on with little interest in maintenance.

### REDS     (27% of population)

**Action-oriented, spontaneous, and focused on "now,"** Reds need freedom to follow their impulses, which they trust over the judgment of others. Cool-headed and ever courageous, they **get things done and handle a crisis better than most.** Found in careers that provide freedom, action, variety, and the unexpected, they bring excitement and a sense of expediency. Work must be fun and the environment collegiate. Reds resist schedules and hierarchies. Long-term planning is a low priority as each day brings it own agenda.

| **GREENS** | **(17% of population)** |
|---|---|

**Empathetic, humanistic, and creative,** Greens need an environment that is supportive and egalitarian and that provides the chance to impact the lives of others. Gifted in their understanding of people's motivation, they have **an unusual ability to influence and draw the best out of others. They also excel in verbal and written communications and in the ability to position ideas.** Greens are enthusiastic spokespersons for the organizations or causes of their choice, creating a unique, charismatic quality that sweeps others into their causes.

## Instructions: Part III

*Now that you have determined your primary style,* go back to the assessment and fill out the section *you originally left out* (**Section II or III**). This will provide you with your backup style. You should share about 40 to 50 percent of the characteristics of your backup style. The backup style refines your primary style.

If your primary is Gold or Red, *your backup would be Blue or Green.*
If your primary is Blue or Green, *your backup would be Gold or Red.*

Your Backup style is_____

## INSTRUCTIONS: Part IV

From each pair of statements, choose one statement from the left or right column. You should wind up with seven checkmarks in this section.

**At least 51 percent of the time I tend to:**

| Column (e) | | Column (i) |
|---|---|---|
| ☐ like to talk | or | ☐ prefer to listen |
| ☐ become bored when alone too much | or | ☐ need time alone to recharge batteries |
| ☐ prefer to work with a group | or | ☐ prefer to work alone or with one other |
| ☐ speak first—then reflect | or | ☐ reflect first—then speak |
| ☐ be more interactive & energetic | or | ☐ be more reflective and thoughtful |
| ☐ know a little about many topics | or | ☐ know a few topics in depth |
| ☐ initiate conversations at social gatherings | or | ☐ wait to be approached at social gatherings |

**If you answered more items on the left, you are an Extrovert (drawing energy from group activity).**

**If you answered more items on the right, you are an Introvert (drawing energy from your own inner resources).**

**Note your full style here: Primary Color_____**

**Backup Style_____Extrovert or Introvert_____**

## More about the Extrovert and Introvert

Since the Extrovert/Introvert dimension is often misunderstood, it is worth explaining further. First of all, it appears to be biologically based and has nothing to do with liking people or being socially adept.

Extroverts (which Jung and the Myers-Briggs community spell as "extraverts") get their energy from being with people and doing group activities. If they have to spend too much time alone or doing tasks that require solitude, they quickly become tired, bored, and dispirited. Introverts get energized from their inner resources—that is, from spending time alone to recharge their internal batteries. Even if they like being with people, which most Introverts do, interacting too much can drain their energy.

The population divides fairly equally between Extroverts and Introverts, and many hide their natural preference well. An Introvert who needs to socialize for business can appear as an Extrovert to those who do not know him or her well. We all use both, but not at the same time. Also, as your score will indicate, you may be mild or pronounced in this dimension. Relationships between the two are often tense, until this dimension is understood and valued.

## Next Step

If your Overview sounds right, read about your primary Color first: Greens in Chapter 5, Reds in Chapter 10, Blues in Chapter 15, and Golds in Chapter 20. Then read your individual chapter, which is one of the four immediately following your primary Color.

If you want to delve deeper, read about your backup Color. For skeptical Blues, reading Chapter 3, A Quick History of Personality Typing, might be your first stop so you don't feel you're wasting your time on an unproven methodology. Greens may want to skip straight to their individual chapter, and then into Chapter 4, A Tour of the Prism Company, to learn about all the other Colors. That's okay, too. Golds will prefer to follow the recommendations above, and reading one chapter a day will allow you to absorb and review this material. Reds, we know the self-assessment wasn't all that much fun, but your individual chapter will be! Go there now and skim it; you'll see it can be quite entertaining.

## What to Do If This Doesn't Ring True for You: Part V

Your personality Color is simply who you really are WHEN NOT PRESSURED by family, friends, or work life. But if the majority of characteristics do not ring true, you may belong to another group.

Go back to the Self-Assessment and check the section where you had close scores. Did you answer the way others need you to be? Or as you feel you ought (instead of prefer) to be? That creates false results. Choose the opposite column and follow instructions to a new Color. If that fits better, go up to Section III and continue.

Or see if a family member or someone who knows you well agrees with your self-assessment. You might be very surprised, as one lawyer was when her friend of thirty years completely corrected her answers to most of the self-assessment! The lawyer didn't want to admit to her real preferences for a messy workplace and last-minute deadline rushes. Remember, we're not judging you here, or even suggesting you need to change. And what you categorize as a "weakness" actually might be a strength; for example, the ability to operate effectively in chaotic conditions.

People are multifaceted. Though everyone has a predominant type, people may be one of several shades of that style. A person may be a strong Gold with a Blue backup. Another might be a slight Gold and hence not as pronounced. Also, as you get older, you develop the nonpreferred parts of your personality and may appear less Gold than in younger years.

If you currently are going through catastrophic life changes, or have been dissatisfied with your life for some time, scores can reflect your survival skills and not your real preferences. You may have "forgotten" your real preferences, although unhappiness is a signal that they're being denied. Try answering as if, right now, you lived in the world of your choice. If your personality Color still seems wrong, wait until things have stabilized and retest yourself.

# CHAPTER 3

# A Quick History of Personality Typing

CATEGORIZING PERSONALITIES into types—an activity called "typology"—has been embraced by major civilizations since ancient times. For more than twenty centuries, scientists and scholars have recognized that, while individual people are unique, there are predictable patterns of human behavior. Around 400 B.C. the Greeks, most notably Aristotle, Hippocrates, and Galen, believed human behaviors fell into four groups, or "humors"—sanguine, melancholic, phlegmatic, and choleric.[1]

In the 1920s the pioneering Swiss psychologist Carl Gustav Jung, who had been a favorite student of Freud's,[2] split away and developed his own typology. According to Jung, human beings' four ways of intersecting with reality were thinking, feeling, sensation, and intuition, which he outlined in his book *Psychological Types,* published in 1921. He called these the four "functions."

Jung spent most of his life studying how people are similar and different. He concluded that certain inborn or early-emerging preferences become the steadfast core of our likes and dislikes about other humans and the physical world. He further described each of these functions as being used in ei-

[1]www.ancienthistory.about.com/cs/hippocrates/a/hippocraticmeds.htm?rd=1
[2]Norman Winski, *Understanding Jung* (Los Angeles: Sherbourne Press, 1971), p. 10.

ther the outer or inner world and hence in different ways, concluding that each person has one of eight mental processes as the most preferred or dominant.

Jung's theories were very abstract. Fortunately, in the 1940s, a mother and daughter team would begin to provide a practical key to unlocking his work. These two U.S. women, Isabel Myers and her mother Katharine Briggs, individually and together would spend the next forty years testing Jung's ideas by observing the people around them. They quantified their observations, then rigorously tested and validated them. They created the most extensively tested personality typing system ever developed, the Myers-Briggs Type Indicator® Inventory (MBTI® assessment)[3], which to date has been administered to more than 50 million people worldwide.

In the 1950s, another typology enthusiast, David Keirsey, did work that overlaid the Greek humors onto the Jungian/Myers-Briggs types. In his book *Please Understand Me*, he outlined four temperament groups, which serve as the basis of the Color Q model in this book. Since then his work has been expanded by his longtime student Linda Berens, president of Inter-strength™ Associates, who continues to provide a rich array of new insights.

Today, work on the MBTI is continued by the next generation, Peter and Katharine Myers, co-trustees of the MBTI Trust. Katharine D. Myers, whose work with the instrument began in 1942, became the first President of APT, the Association for Psychological Type, the leading membership organization of the "type" community. Twenty years later the Myers' strong sense of stewardship remains in evidence. They are mentors to those seeking new insights and applications. The aspirations of young people and their career satisfaction is an area of ongoing interest. Peter Myers is Chairman of the Myers-Briggs Foundation and continues to develop the work of his mother Isabel Myers by promoting new research and keeping the assessment on the cutting edge. He believes the most important contribution of the Myers-Briggs model is the insight that "successful human endeavor results from the development of effective perception and decision-making," emphasizing once again that understanding and working with one's own natural preferences, regardless of what they are, creates success.

"The Jungian model is an excellent nonthreatening tool for developing career goals," said Katharine Myers in a recent interview. "Extensive research shows that certain types more than others are drawn to each career. However, since every type is found in every field, no one should be told not to go into any specific career. If an individual is strongly drawn to a profession, he or she needs to be clear on the tasks inherent in the job and then

---

[3]Myers-Briggs Type Indicator® and MBTI® are trademarks of the Myers-Briggs Type Indicator Trust in the United States and other countries.

evaluate what their skills will contribute." It is not uncommon for people to create special niches in areas dominated by other types.

Myers is a Green, as defined Chapter 5. And like many in her group she excels at fostering the growth of others. "My passion for what I do is so great that I'm still working at 80, which I never planned to do," she says.

Meanwhile, modern brain imaging technology has validated many of MBTI's theories by showing how chemicals and activity in different parts of the brain impact behavior. Most importantly, it has been demonstrated that Jung was indeed correct. While each person is unique, there is a part of them—a core, if you will—that is solid and steady. It is that core that the MBTI, and the Color Q system, define and apply to a multitude of life issues.

I developed Color Q as a quick introduction to the concepts of "personality typing" and the more complex Myers-Briggs model. When running team-building and leadership seminars for my corporate clients like ABN AMBO, Northern Trust, Merrill Lynch, The U.S. Treasury, and Prudential Insurance, I also began to ask participants to fill out an investment questionnaire. From this pool of knowledge emerged the Money Q profiles, which explain how different personality types approach money and compensation. Several results of this proprietary research are presented in Chapter 27, which sheds light on how different individuals approach the financial negotiation aspects of their job search.

# CHAPTER 4

# A Tour of the Prism Company

*An Overview of the Four Color Groups*

**YOU'LL GET THE MOST OUT OF** this book if you learn how to recognize people of other Color types. This tour of the (fictitious) Prism Company offers clues to help Color code your boss, co-workers, dates, mates, friends, and family.

## The Gold Department

At the Gold department entrance, a motion-sensor-activated sign lights up when you approach, requesting your visitor's pass. A card swipe machine reads all your data—name, reason for visit, time of entry—and unlocks the door.

Inside is a reception area with elegant wood paneling, several classical oil paintings, and immaculate deep pile carpet. The tone is hushed. Behind a large, raised desk is a receptionist wearing a crisp business suit. Her desk has her name and title on a square wood and brass plate, next to a discreet bouquet of mixed flowers. She nods you into the department corridor for your tour. It has taken you less than a minute to start your visit.

On your right is a bulletin board with the slogan "Responsibility and Accountability Lead to Money and Security" displayed across the top. Although the sounds of work are all around you, everything seems hushed and well under control. All employees are wearing tailored suits, and most are at their desks doing paperwork. Computer screens flicker with spreadsheets or accounting software.

Down the corridor, each employee has an office, all of which are decorated in tasteful muted color schemes. No one seems to be absent, yet no desk has any clutter on it. Apart from family photos, nothing but the current moment's work is evident anywhere. Filing cabinets predominate, which reveal highly organized files with plenty of room to spare. Everyone's clock, you notice, is set to precisely the same time.

People greet you in a dignified, well-mannered way, but stay focused on their tasks. You notice functions like business analysis, accounting, budgets, customer service, production scheduling, and manufacturing project planning.

A conference room near the middle holds a large oval table of impeccably shined mahogany. A schedule of the week's meetings is posted in a frame next to the door. Someone of good and traditional taste has designed this room. Pens are in holders on the center of the table. The well-hidden wastebasket is empty. Windows behind the velvet curtains are crystal clean.

You've been allotted twenty minutes for your tour of the Gold Department, and your time is almost up. You are once again asked to swipe your visitor's pass to record the time of your exit.

You leave with the impression that the Gold Department has its tasks well under control, and its employees are not only well-disciplined, but proud of it.

## The Blue Department

You now stand facing a stark blue door. It gives the impression you are about to embark on an interstellar journey. This notion builds as your forefinger is requested for a fingerprint ID and your right eye for a retinal scan. Your magnetic-striped visitor's pass now seems quaint and unnecessary.

The door suddenly opens in four different directions to create an entry port. The receptionist is wearing a plain but well-made blue suit. His jacket is off and the sleeves of his white shirt are rolled up. His demeanor is that of a college professor—serious, distracted, attempting to be helpful while multitasking.

Digital images flash around the reception area walls. Several feeds of science and history channels run across multiple video screens. There is an antiseptic smell in the air that reminds one of a laboratory. One full wall is devoted to highly technical, leather-bound print reference materials.

While your Blue Department tour is open-ended in terms of time, the receptionist instructs you to "keep simplistic and obvious questions to a minimum" when talking to employees, "so as not to disturb those in strategic or problem-solving modes."

Above their bulletin board is a slogan that says "Pushing the Boundaries." Thinking you are about to encounter characters like Data in *Star Trek*, you are surprised to see a man in a cashmere suit wearing a silk tie of muted colors. He introduces himself as the Head of Product Trend Research. He pulls you into a meeting being held in an open "Brainstorming Room" and the group there asks you several questions to be answered "from the viewpoint of an average person."

Each answer you give elicits intense and pointed debate among the brainstormers. As they refer to you in the third person, you feel a bit bewildered; they don't even notice as you slip back out into the corridor to continue your tour.

Some cubicles are crowded with piles of research materials. Some are neat, some are not.

Everyone seems to be pushing his or her intellects to the limit to prove some point. Scientific and high-tech jokes and puns elicit short barks of laughter. Mostly, employees' eyes glitter from the stimulation of new and far-reaching concepts. You find it odd that half the employees are dressed in expensive designer outfits while the other half look quite academic and understated; most all suit jackets hang off the backs of chairs.

The conference room is as high tech as the reception area. A large screen for videoconferencing and computer presentations dominates one end of the room; laptop computers, all wired into the middle of the table, are available at each seat. The seats seem to be experiments in ergonomics, with fantastic shapes and very lightweight materials. You are startled to see Nobel Prizes displayed here; you've never seen one before.

You walk out into the corridor, past more cubicles. One reveals a man with an intensely knitted brow, staring up at the ceiling, fingers touching in a pyramid on his desk. An empty piece of paper and a pencil await. As you pass, he springs to life, frantically recording ideas that seem to be coming all too fast. His function reads Strategic Planning. Other departments you see are research, long-term marketing, computer programming, analytics, science lab, or abstract reasoning.

You are left with the impression that when Prism Company needs a new idea, research, or long-term strategy, they are in excellent hands here. But unless you are intellectually quick, this department is an intimidating place to be.

You fingerprint and retinal scan yourself out of the Blue Department. It has taken you an hour to complete your tour here.

## The Green Department

As you search your pockets for the almost-forgotten visitors' pass, you bump unexpectedly into a tall, wise-looking woman in a black turtleneck.

Her suit is a tapestry of rich jewel tones. Her eyes are deep and gently inquiring. You and she are standing right outside the entrance to the Green Department.

"I'm presuming you are looking for your pass?" she asks. "They can be a nuisance to find." You finally locate it and she smiles. "So, we have an official visitor now! Lovely, lovely!" She looks deeply into your eyes; you get the feeling that she has seen into your soul and taken the measure of your character through your handshake.

"The Blue Corridor unsettled you, didn't it?" she asks, rhetorically. "Well, you seem like a safe enough person to admit in here. Come in and I'll arrange for some tea."

She opens the Green Department's entry door, which wasn't locked. This reception area is the lushest yet. Curved couches and deeply cushy silk-covered chairs in beautiful rich hues are arranged in several conversation areas. Sculptures of crystal and iron sit in the center of low coffee tables. Beautifully arranged modern paintings hang alongside ones of mythical theme.

"We have a guest!" the lady at the Green door calls. She smiles at you as she heads back out. You realize she is actually the security person for this department, intuitively judging if someone should be admitted.

"Well, hello, welcome! I'm the Department Head, and these are my Section Motivators! And you are…?" The Department Head shakes your hand warmly as you exchange introductions; you are impressed and flattered to be greeted by top brass, although you wonder briefly what a Section Motivator is.

The Department Head guides you to her office. Behind her glass desk is framed the slogan "Productivity Happens with Motivation and Collaboration."

"If there's anything you want to ask as we go, certainly feel free. We don't limit your questions or your time here! I really believe we have something to learn from everyone who walks through here." All the Section Motivators smile and you feel more relaxed than you did when trying to self-censor stupid questions in the Blue Department.

You sit with her on an antique Victorian sofa. A Section Motivator brings you a generous mug of hot water and a basket of fine teas.

As you steep your chosen brew, the Section Motivators introduce themselves—Client Management, Human Resources and Training, Communications/Public Relations, Graphic Arts, Organizational Development, Marketing/Sales. When you ask what a Section Motivator is, the Public Relations person explains that each section is egalitarian and the Motivators, who would be Section Heads in other departments, have the sole role of motivating all workers in their areas. You nod, wondering how they do that. Their confident smiles indicate they not only know how, but do it well *and* enjoy it.

You turn down offers of fruit and nuts, curious to explore this very different department. The corridor is crowded full with talking employees. Laughter is everywhere. Sometimes, people look at you with such friendly interest that they bump into someone else! Then they laugh, apologize, and continue on.

Flowers, plants, aquariums, and miniature water fountains leave only small open spaces for work. Walls and furniture feature interesting, sometimes avant garde, color combinations. Clocks are either fast, slow, or have stopped altogether.

Computers are mostly off; those that are on feature email or graphics programs or word processing in the writers' offices.

The conference room is packed with employees, some in designer outfits and some in bohemian dress. The conference table is round, and no one appears to be leading the conversation, yet consensus seems to happen naturally. They are working out an issue of miscommunication with a client on a video screen, and all are working hard to achieve harmony. You slip past, wishing all businesses would be that concerned about their customers.

You get to the end of the corridor and walk through an impressive display of notable Prism Company graphic pieces framed on the walls. You hear someone giving a younger employee constructive mentor-style feedback and see that workers here are very into what they're doing.

The mentor looks your way as you head toward the exit. "Hope you enjoyed your visit with us!" An outstretched handshake and sincere smile accompany this farewell as you walk out the exit door, two hours after entering.

You are left feeling that the Prism Company enjoys a glowing public image. The Green Department's interpersonal skills turn negative interchanges into opportunities to create award-winning customer service. The productivity and continuing revenue streams it creates, although hard to measure, are believed to be quite significant.

## The Red Department

At the Red Department you see a video monitor on the right side of the door. A professionally done internal company news program engages your interest. You are startled when the screen flickers and a female face appears. "Hello! Do you have your visitor's pass?"

After a moment to collect yourself, you fumble for the pass and hold it toward the screen. "Thanks! I'm clicking you in!" The screen flickers back to the news feed. You wonder where the camera was that sent your image back and what other surprises await you.

The Red reception area seems like a private club. Most of its walls contain leather-bound books of history or technical reference titles. One corner is devoted to glass cases full of sports trophies. Several pieces by world-renowned sculptors stand on pedestals. Original framed comic art pieces by Harvey Kurtzman and others take pride of place on conspicuous wall areas, along with the Reds' framed slogan "Chaos Contained! Let's Do It Now!" One Baccarat crystal ashtray holds the cold remains of an expensive cigar. In the center is an aquarium teeming with exotic specimens.

There doesn't appear to be a receptionist. The woman who requested your pass walks in, dressed in a colorful designer suit. "Go on in, ask anybody anything," she says with a wave of her hand and a quick grin. She strides athletically down the hall without waiting for you.

You notice it's not a corridor at all; after a short row of private offices it's an open bullpen with many desks. Most of the private offices have their doors shut; their occupants all appear deep in thought with notes or mechanical objects the focus of their concentration.

In the bullpen, some people have their feet up on their desks. They look like they're amusing themselves while waiting for something. Desks are decidedly messy with piles, sports memorabilia, family photos, and souvenirs from exotic vacations. One impatient and frustrated person is bravely cleaning out an overstuffed file cabinet. His discard pile is a breeding ground for paper airplanes, constructed apparently to tease him by co-workers not burdened with filing duties. "My turn to file," he grumbles to you. "We all hate it, so we take turns. My lucky day."

"We've got a network crash, people, let's go, let's go!" someone shouts, and in the space of thirty seconds a quarter of the Red Department whips on their jackets and heads for the door. You see functional titles like Crisis Manager, Network Integration Specialist, and Computer Repair on the vacated desks. "Saved by the crash! This is great!" says the file cleaner and, dropping everything, rushes to join them. Everyone looks energized and eager as they exit.

Computers left behind flicker with frozen video games and entrepreneurial business plan software. The only working clocks you see are in the upper corners of those computer screens. But a number of remaining employees, you notice, wear expensive watches.

You become curious about the three large enclosed rooms that exist in this department. One is the Video Department from which the news feed emanates. Another is right next to the desks of people with the titles Contract Negotiator and Manager of Short-Term Marketing. You go inside this one to find a gourmet kitchen and well-appointed executive dining room. A chef is busy making shrimp canapés. "Important client coming in for a contract signing," he explains. "Little shrimp for the big fish!" He grins, and you laugh at his deadpan humor.

You begin to notice that everybody here talks in short, crisp sentences. Nor do they sit still for long.

The third big room is the Red conference room. Inside, a well-appointed leather couch and a number of leather club chairs, all on well-hidden wheels, allow for any number of meeting arrangements. It would be difficult for a prospective client not to be impressed by the effortlessly upscale comfort and flexible arrangements afforded by this room. Within seconds, it could accommodate a meeting of 25 or an intimate gathering of two or three.

A well-dressed woman wearing a Promotion Director title badge walks in. "Sorry I wasn't around when you came in," she says extending her hand. "I was discovering a network crash! Now I can let the experts enjoy their crisis."

She briefly describes some of the functions of the Red Department—negotiations, franchising, contracting, investigations, computer services, and manufacturing. "We prefer our problems short-term and tangible!" she says. "We leave the long-term stuff to the Greens and Blues."

Heading out the door, you see a group of people up ahead engaged in a heated conversation. "Take the risk, Jones! What are you, some kind of conformist wuss? There's no room for that here. I'll bet you anything that my widget beats your ball bearing any day in Wiley's application! Let's put it on the line and see!" You step around them gingerly as they get more competitive with each other, but you sense there's camaraderie behind the challenges.

As you approach the exit door two and a half hours after entering, there is another video monitor showing the corporate news feed. The same face flickers on, requesting that you put your pass in the slot below. As you do, you thank the person for a very enjoyable and fascinating visit. She smiles a quick smile and says, "You're welcome!" before the news feed returns. You're out the door and into the parking lot with a lot of impressions to sort out about the diverse and fascinating Prism Company.

You can see why the Prism Company is such a successful enterprise. No one seems to be working in a job he or she hates; the departmental environments all seem to bring out the best in those who work there. You decide if you ever start a company, you will try to follow the example of the Prism Company, and maximize productivity through the best placement of natural talent.

Most companies don't run like the Prism Company. But that should not detract you from finding your own best "department," with the help of Chapter 2's self-assessment questionnaire and your personality profile chapter.

The Prism Company can help you figure out the Colors of others as you walk into their work spaces. You can tell a lot by how they dress; what is, or is not, on their desks. Try it with your boss and read about his or her Color; your interactions should improve immediately.

# PART 2

# GREENS
## *"Let's Humanize It"*

Greens thrive in a work environment that supports personal development and feels like an extended family.

**CHAPTER 5**

Greens Overall

**CHAPTER 6**

Green/Gold Extroverts

**CHAPTER 7**

Green/Gold Introverts

**CHAPTER 8**

Green/Red Extroverts

**CHAPTER 9**

Green/Red Introverts

# Greens Overall

**GREENS REPRESENT APPROXIMATELY** 17 percent of the overall world population. If you're not a Green but would like to learn how to identify and communicate with one, go to Figure 5–1 on page 25.

## News Personality Diane Sawyer

ABC News television journalist Diane Sawyer is one the best-known Greens in the United States. She epitomizes many of the group's artistic and interpersonal skills. For most of her early adolescence, she recalls being nonconformist, klutzy, and "tediously serious." She and her friends would go off to a creek to read Emerson and Thoreau. They called themselves the "reincarnated transcendentalists." "My sister was the elegant one," she recalls laughingly. "I was the one who kept falling down the stairs."

But others remember that in high school she won the U.S. Junior Miss pageant and after college moved to Washington, DC to serve as assistant to Nixon White House press secretary Ron Ziegler.

In 1978 she took a job with CBS, but Dan Rather and other senior figures were very vocal about the presence of someone tainted by Watergate. She ultimately won over her colleagues with her incredible stamina, spending a week at the State Department during the Iranian hostage crisis, sleeping no more than an hour a day. They also were disarmed by her typical Green charm and ability to let her ego go for the sake of the story.

Working with, instead of against, her natural Green core traits led to a string of successes. In 1981 she was promoted to the *CBS Morning News*

## Figure 5–1   How to Recognize a Green

- ☐ Big picture thinker.
- ☐ Informal and warm.
- ☐ Diplomatic.
- ☐ Unusual ability to influence by persuasion.
- ☐ Bridge-builder; resolves conflicting views.
- ☐ Draws the best out of people.
- ☐ Idealistic.
- ☐ Verbally fluent and metaphoric.
- ☐ Intent listener.
- ☐ Sensitive to criticism.
- ☐ Avoids confrontation.
- ☐ Chic, flamboyant, or careless dress.

HOW TO COMMUNICATE WITH A GREEN

- ✔ Pick a harmonious environment for meetings.
- ✔ Personalize the relationship—ask about family, hobbies, and pets.
- ✔ Listen empathetically.
- ✔ Be insightful and idea-driven.
- ✔ Encourage creative freedom and input.
- ✔ Expect nonsequential discussions that eventually return to the main point.
- ✔ Stress any opportunity for personal growth.
- ✔ Stress solutions that are innovative and future-oriented.
- ✔ Use inspiring and positive phrases.
- ✔ Limit mundane support facts.
- ✔ Eliminate conflict and competitiveness; be collaborative.
- ✔ Give all feedback diplomatically.

*Show;* in 1984 she became the first female correspondent on the prestigious *60 Minutes.* She became recognized for her interviewing skills, which she modestly attributed to being prepared. Others said she had an intuitive ability to surgically get under the skin of her subjects "without drawing blood." Greens are among the most intuitive of all the Color types. In 1989, she jumped to ABC to co-anchor the news magazine *Prime Time Live,* which became *20/20.*

Diane Sawyer evinces the typical polarities of the Green personality—the ability to be earnest and irreverent, intense and funny, authoritative and vulnerable. She is known as an intellectual who also excels at portraying glitz. Most of all, she is both intensely private and genuinely interested in people. True to her type, she prefers quality to quantity in her relationships.

Sawyer's group, the Greens, need opportunities to use their creativity and to impact the lives of others. They excel in verbal and written communications and are heavily represented among writers, TV anchors, and biographers. In corporate settings, they excel in sales, marketing, and public relations. Whatever the work setting, they thrive when their uniqueness is recognized. Harmony and authenticity bring out a Green's best.

Pulitzer Prize winner Frank McCourt, author of *Angela's Ashes, Tis,* and *Teacher Man,* expresses Green characteristics through his teaching and writings. For thirty years he taught high school English in New York City, continuously seeking to engage students while battling administrators and bewildered parents. Defying established guidelines, he found ingenious ways to motivate kids: using a pen to teach parts of the sentence and cookbook recipes to spark creativity. Most of all, he turned his own poverty-soaked background in the slums of Ireland into a valuable lesson plan. He described the smell of one toilet shared by an entire street; the fleas in his mattress; and the roaming rats, along with the antics of his alcoholic father and depressed mother, without losing his humor or sense of compassion. In so doing, he formed a powerful bond with his students and actually learned to enjoy his job.

Hollywood producer Laura Ziskin demonstrates how far a Green can go in a creative industry. Several years ago, in a move that shocked the industry, she stepped away from a position of significant power as President of Fox 2000 to return to what she loves doing best—producing films. Leadership in business usually means building institutions—a natural goal for Golds and Blues. It is not a meaningful goal for Greens. They prefer leading small creative organizations that downplay hierarchy and rules and promote originality and fun.

"The most difficult thing about the film culture," she says, "is that the main value is greed. My daily quest is to find things that will stimulate, excite, and keep people engaged while still providing the necessary profits." About the financial aspects of filmmaking, "I look at it as an algebra problem. I like the deal-making part, which is creative," she says. "The rest I can't get too excited about." Day-to-day management of expenses gets delegated to others.

Laura has put her stamp on U.S. popular culture, producing films such as *A Star is Born, Pretty Woman, What About Bob? The Thin Red Line,* and the recently widely acclaimed *Spider-Man.*

Greens often are found at the forefront of human interest causes. Two probable Green celebrities well-known for their humanitarian works are actress

Angelina Jolie and U2 frontman Bono. Jolie is goodwill ambassador for the United Nations High Commissioner for Refugees. She has traveled worldwide in her role as spokesperson for war-traumatized children and refugees. She is known for her work "on the ground," spending far more time in actual refugee camps than ordinarily required. Her multimillion dollar relief donations go well beyond ordinary celebrity charitable efforts. She was recognized in 2005 with the United Nations Global Humanitarian Action Award. Making a difference in the world is paramount for the Green personality.

Bono toured Africa in 2003 with Secretary of the Treasury Paul O'Neill to try to raise governmental awareness of the AIDS epidemic there. (That year, Congress appropriated $350 million toward the Global Fund for AIDS, Tuberculosis and Malaria.) Bono has called upon the United States to donate an additional 1 percent of the federal budget to help the poor worldwide. He has plans at this writing to sell fashion accessories with proceeds going to AIDS research and relief. He is encouraging credit card companies to include charitable giving as an option for reward points. Bono has a Green's desire to live a meaningful life and improve the world any way he can. His creativity in accomplishing these goals shows a core Green characteristic.

Besides Diane Sawyer, Angelina Jolie, and Bono, other famous Greens in the entertainment world are Oprah Winfrey and Jane Fonda. Mahatma Gandhi, Mikhail Gorbachev, and Eleanor Roosevelt illustrate the Green leadership style in politics. Ralph Waldo Emerson was a well-known Green writer; Abraham Maslow a Green psychologist; and Pope John Paul XXIII was a prominent Green in the religious field.

This chapter will help you determine if you've tested your primary and backup personality Color correctly. It also will help you identify Greens among people you know, as will Chapter 4, A Tour of the Prism Company/The Green Department, and Chapter 25, Adjusting to the Styles of Others.

If the self-assessment at the beginning of the book has scored you as a Green, you are brilliant with people and communications issues, like Diane Sawyer. More than the other three Colors, you will enjoy this book because it will help you learn even more about people. You are likely to Color code everyone you know and test the tips supplied in here for communicating with them.

Of all the Colors, your skills are more often (unfairly) considered "soft." This book will show how they can be put to economic advantage. Your highly developed marketing abilities make you a top choice for creating lasting product brands. Your people skills calm turbulent teams and departments in record time. Staff turnover can be staunched by putting a Green in charge; and productivity spikes when a Green is in charge of a team.

Go to your specific profile now to discover your most natural path to professional satisfaction and success.

# CHAPTER 6

# Green/Gold Extroverts

**YOU'RE NOT ONLY A GREEN,** you also have strong secondary characteristics of the Gold personality. And you have tested as a Color Q Extrovert, which means you recharge your batteries by being with others, rather than being alone. You are compassionate, persuasive, loyal, and have a talent for predicting future trends.

## You Overall

You are outgoing, sociable, warm, and articulate. Green/Gold Extroverts are gifted communicators with an unusual ability to influence. Those you admire receive your deep loyalty. In return, you expect equal appreciation. This can lead to frustration and disappointment.

You have an abundance of innate "emotional intelligence" and interact well with most Color types. You operate best in harmonious groups. Driven by intuition, foresight, and compassion, you excel at leading others to achieve their potential. You are exceptionally skilled at projecting the trends and pitfalls of the future.

People who are rude or bully others are a major irritant. You respond well to praise, but are easily hurt by criticism. This makes you appear touchy, as even the most well-intentioned criticism may fluster you. Actual conflict disturbs you (except when standing up to rude bullies, which you do with steely strength).

You are enthusiastic, with the energy to work on several projects at once. Decisive and often in a hurry, you can be more than a little impatient with anyone who slows you down. While it is your nature to be supportive, you can be both critical and confrontational when your standards are not being met.

Your interest in others is so strong that you run the risk of not giving enough time to yourself. In both personal and professional relationships, you make others feel valued and liked.

case study one
_____

## Financial Executive

Until December, 2005 Alexandra Lebenthal was President of Lebenthal and Company, a highly respected Wall Street institution. Formerly known as a conservative bond house, it expanded under Alexandra's big-picture vision into mutual funds, estate planning, and insurance.

Alexandra earned her position after her grandmother Sayra, who founded and ran the firm for over 60 years, groomed her to take over. Despite an earlier interest in becoming an actress, at age 31 she became the youngest ever female president of a brokerage firm.

She got high marks from her Wall Street peers, particularly for the quality of her advertising and brand positioning. Green/Golds are creative abstract thinkers and gifted at positioning products and ideas. Alexandra says, "We came up with a commercial that announced, 'I have a mission to make you a customer for life, and all I have to do is put your needs first.'" Treating clients like members of the family differentiated her firm's client service and satisfied Alexandra's Green side.

She enjoyed creating the vision for Lebenthal and Company and looks forward to starting her own financial services firm in 2007. Her natural Green/Gold ability to predict future trends serves her well. It was this ability that alerted Alexandra to offer new products that kept Lebenthal and Company strong, profitable, and ultimately marketable. They sold to Advest Group in 2001 for $25 million. In 2005 Merrill Lynch acquired Advest and laid the Lebenthal brand name to rest. Alexandra's noncompete clause expired in mid-2006.

When heading a firm, she embodies the typical democratic management style of her Color. "I want the people who report to me to feel that they are a meaningful part of shaping the company," she says, "and shaping me as a leader." Today she has teamed up with Israel Discount Bank to open a new municipal bond firm and continues to be a guiding hand for investors.

# You on the Job
## As a Leader

A people-centered, idealistic vision drives your enthusiastic style. You respect the needs and opinions of staff at all levels, influencing with persuasion rather than control. Consensus and cooperation are your goals. You provide your people sensitive and appropriate support through personal difficulties.

Your Gold side introduces structure and organization and initiates action. You are usually upbeat, accepting setbacks as new challenges rather than defeats.

## As a Team Player

If a team is stalled by interpersonal conflict, you are the bridge builder. Others understand you merely want to achieve stated objectives. Rather than being dictatorial, you energize the team with enthusiasm and a warm sense of humor. You inspire former combatants to their best combined efforts. As focused and results-oriented as you are, it's rare that your team misses a deadline.

Look at Figure 6–1 for a list of your natural work-related strengths.

Now see how another Green/Gold Extrovert uses his strengths in a very different field.

# Ideal Work Environment

Alexandra and Terry each gravitated to environments where they have control of products or services that contribute in some way to the well-being of society. These are key elements of Green/Gold Extrovert satisfaction.

When a job offer is made, leverage as much as you can from the list in Figure 6–2 on page 33.

The WORST type of work culture for an Extroverted Green/Gold is tense, overly competitive, and highly political. It is secretive about critical information, rewarding power plays over productivity. The atmosphere is impersonal among management, staff, and co-workers. The company compromises your core values; it exploits both its workers and its customers.

While Green/Gold Extroverts can progress in such corporate cultures, your interpersonal talents usually must remain low key in order to survive.

## Figure 6-1   Natural Work-Related Strengths

Approximately 80 percent of these attributes will apply to you. Check off those that do and use them in your resume and interviews. This will set you apart from the canned responses of others. You:

☐ Excite others with high-quality ideas and enthusiasm.
☐ Organize people and resources.
☐ Build morale, loyalty, and productivity.
☐ Mentor others well, exponentially increasing your value to the firm.
☐ Create harmonious teams; turn around troubled departments.
☐ Think creatively; see future trends.
☐ Communicate in memorable ways using colorful words and graphics.

Productivity and accomplishment are stunted, and career achievements become an uphill climb.

case study two

## Human Resource Director

Terry McGuinness is Managing Director of an international investment management conglomerate. He manages 98 human resource professionals worldwide, overseeing a broad range of services from hiring to employee relations.

He sees his greatest accomplishment as having led the implementation of a new organizational structure to better align Human Resources services with the goals of the company's different business groups. Having key staff members report both to him and the business executives makes these HR executives more responsive to the business issues. This, in turn, increases their value to the organization, bringing them more respect, responsibility, and compensation. Terry also took the results of an employee survey and made those criteria part of the annual performance reviews and bonus allocations of management, thereby improving overall morale and productivity.

Working on global issues is also of high interest to Greens, who easily understand the big picture. Dealing with people in many countries enables Terry to stay on top of international trends, customs, and the most effective HR practices.

Known for his facilitation skills, he is usually called on to run meetings at the most senior level. He introduces and runs sophisticated training programs for all levels of managers, enabling him to experiment with the latest in adult learning theories.

When it is time to let people go, he also is known for his skill at walking terminated executives through their situations and explaining the benefits of their severance packages in a positive way. He stays close to them and monitors their cases until they are hired by another company. Many actually return to thank him once they find new jobs!

## The Extroverted Green/Gold's Ideal Boss

Even a great job can be frustrating under the wrong boss; a mediocre job under a great boss is pretty hard to leave. Green/Golds get on especially well with other Greens. But bosses of the Color types who possess the skills in Figure 6–3 on page 34 also can be good mentors.

## Careers That Attract Green/Gold Extroverts

As Alexandra's and Terry's stories illustrate, you have deep personal values and care about the needs of others (on the Green side) and value organization (on the Gold side).

*Please note that not all* the following careers will appeal to you, but recognize that each, in some way, draws on the strengths of your style and appeals to a significant number of your Color group. This is not a comprehensive list, but it will show underlying patterns of preference. If unlisted careers offer similar patterns, your chances of success increase. Copy in parentheses highlights the Color style characteristics that create success.

In addition, two codes indicate those jobs that are currently predicted to have an above-average salary and growth potential. This information is based on the continuously revised data provided by the U.S. Department of Labor and Bureau of Labor Statistics available on the O*NET website, *http://online.onetcenter.org/.*

## Figure 6–2   The Ideal Green/Gold Extrovert Work Environment

Compare your current work environment to the description below. Don't be deceived if these descriptions seem "obvious." It confirms you've tested your individual Color correctly. Other Colors, especially Golds, would find this environment uncomfortable and unproductive. The optimal Green/Gold Extrovert work environment:

- ☐ Is harmonious, with people who can be trusted. Backbiting and internal competition are discouraged and viewed as unproductive.
- ☐ Has strong values that align with your own. Its mission is to produce products and services that contribute to the well-being of society.
- ☐ Makes good use of your well-developed organizational skills. Your projects draw on your people, communications, and organizational skills simultaneously.
- ☐ Allows responsibility for one's own projects. You see a big picture and possess the ability to excite others about it. When you work too long on someone else's project, his or her constraints may leave you feeling frustrated and unfulfilled.
- ☐ Provides ongoing new learning experiences. You are energized by company training or outside schooling. On the job, you're enthused by assignments that publicize new products or services, learn or teach new technologies, create promotional strategies, discover new markets, or require continuing education.
- ☐ A corporate culture integrating the above elements is fertile soil for your career advancement.

**Bold** indicates that the career is considered to be among the top **100 best-paying jobs** based on the average or median salary paid to individuals *with five years of experience.* Excluded are jobs where salary statistics are not available, such as "business owner," or not indicative such as "actor.")

*Italics* identifies the jobs that are predicted to benefit from an above-average growth rate over the next several years.

***Bold and italics*** indicates jobs that will benefit from both **higher pay** and *high growth potential.*

Note there are successful people of all Color styles in all occupations. In nonideal jobs you can still shine by creating your own niche.

**Figure 6-3    The Green/Gold Extrovert's Ideal Boss**

Check off if your boss:

☐ Is insightful.

☐ Asks you about your vision for the project, the company, or your career.

☐ Gives positive feedback and stresses areas where he or she agrees with you.

☐ Is organized and delivers on commitments—a good role model.

☐ Shares the same values of improving the world.

## Arts/Communications/Computer/Promotion

*advertising and promotions manager* ◆ **art director** ◆ artist ◆ *desktop publisher* ◆ book publishing professional ◆ **corporate communication director** ◆ *exhibit designer* ◆ *film editor/producer* ◆ *graphic artist/designer* ◆ *interior decorator* ◆ *Internet marketing manager* ◆ literary agent ◆ media planner ◆ *merchandise displayer* ◆ *multimedia specialist* ◆ museum director ◆ **public relations director/*specialist*** ◆ *set/costume/exhibit designer* ◆ TV/stage producer ◆ **website editor/art director** (involvement with media, draws on superior language skills, communication through graphic presentation, manages the corporate image).

## Business/Management

account executive ◆ *consultative salesperson/**manager*** ◆ **corporate communications director** ◆ *diversity manager* ◆ ***human resources manager*** ◆ **industrial psychologist** ◆ ***marketing specialist*** (ideas/services) ◆ ***group/unit manager*** ◆ **organizational development consultant** ◆ *employment interviewer* ◆ *training and development specialist* (fosters relationship essential for your company, develop colleagues, use communication and facilitation skills).

## Education

***educational administrator*** ◆ guidance counselor ◆ *instructional coordinator* ◆ *school psychologist/teacher/ professor* [all levels—art, drama, English, humanities, languages, special education] ◆ *school social worker* (helping others reach their potential, patient one-on-one influencing).

## Health Science/Psychology

*alternative health care practitioner* ◆ *clinical psychologist/**psychiatrist*** ◆ ***general practitioner*** ◆ *home health aide* ◆ ***internist/medical researcher*** ◆ **optometrist**

◆ *pediatrician* ◆ *physician assistant* ◆ *speech pathologist* ◆ *therapist* [marriage, occupational, substance abuse] (environment congruent with values, insights into others, see new ways to solve problems, patient one-on-one influencing).

## Law

*lawyer* [children, communication & media, domestic relations, environmental, intellectual property, trust & estates] ◆ *mediator* (understanding of human motivation).

## Social Services

*coach* [business, life] ◆ *counselor* [career, child welfare, outplacement, pastoral, substance abuse] ◆ fundraiser/institutional solicitor ◆ **philanthropic director**/consultant ◆ *religious leader/educator* ◆ senior day care director ◆ *social worker/community services manager* (need for good organizational skills, goal setting, and using all resources, helping people who need it, work congruent with your values, improving the world).

case study three

## When a Career Isn't Working

Buddy Coleman (a composite of the author's clients) sold insurance for fifteen years for a leading company. He really enjoyed dealing with customers and took pride that he was helping them shape their futures in positive ways.

After fifteen years, this was no longer enough. The amount of paperwork had increased over the years, something that Green/Gold Extroverts find suffocating. Dealing with concrete events and practical rules-based questions had burned him out. He craved something (anything!) that would engage his Green/Gold's preferred focus on the big picture.

At a meeting of his professional insurance sales organization he was intrigued to hear that the long-time director was retiring, and a search was on to replace her. Buddy immediately expressed his interest to an attending board member and was strongly encouraged to submit a resume. Today, he directs the efforts of twelve volunteers and flexes his Green/Gold creativity writing a monthly Future Trends column for the organization's glossy newsletter. He has increased the number of membership events by 50 percent and attends each one personally, providing the people contact this Green/Gold always enjoyed.

## Your Personality's Challenges

Green/Gold Extroverts have a unique set of potential work-related blind spots. Some below you have, others you don't. Tone down a blind spot by focusing on it, then choose more productive actions and make them habits. (Suggestions for doing so are in parentheses below.) You:

- Avoid conflicts and confrontations. (You take conflict and criticism very personally and protect yourself by avoidance. Instead, face it. Build a thicker skin by repeated exposure, on your terms.)
- Tend not to recognize underperforming workers or manipulative friends/relatives. (Don't shove aside that little alarm bell inside. Memorize this phrase and speak up immediately: "I see you [are/are not] doing X. I want to say something now so you don't think I'm OK with this going forward.")
- Base important decisions too much on likes and dislikes and not enough on facts, figures, and research. (With your next important decision, guide yourself as usual by your likes and dislikes. Then force yourself to do some research—just a little! Assemble a few facts and figures. See what happens when you consider this new input.)
- Can irritate others by being moralistic. (If you're pontificating, stop yourself with this phrase: "And now, I'll get off my soapbox! But do you agree? How would you handle it?")

## Your Job Search—the Good, the Bad, and the Ugly

Green/Gold Extroverts have outstanding people skills. Many interviewers are Greens, with whom you'll feel an immediate rapport. But with interviewers of other Colors, you need to rehearse different communications styles.

Your natural strengths easily allow you to:

- Organize and execute a comprehensive job search campaign.
- Network widely to get leads.
- Impress your interviewer with your verbal skills and confidence.
- Project your past experience into new fields or functions.

In order to avoid your blind spots, you need to:

- Thoroughly check out the facts about a position rather than rely on intuition.

◆ Slow down in making decisions until there has been sufficient reflection.
◆ Not take rejection personally.
◆ Not be too accommodating in discussing your compensation package. Treat the process as a chess game to increase both respect and compensation.

## The Green/Gold Extrovert's Interviewing Style

You'll feel immediate rapport with an interviewer whose Color is close to your own. However, if your interviewer seems to have a significantly different style, use the suggestions in parentheses.

In following your natural style, you will:

◆ Express yourself with warmth and passion. (Tone it down with a cooler type of interviewer.)
◆ Stress the big picture first and place less emphasis on the details of your experience and goals. (Some interviewers prefer sequential or chronological presentations. Let them lead; note if the interviewer is more concrete and practical. If so, avoid brainstorming and metaphoric language.)
◆ Try to personalize the relationship as quickly as possible. (If the interviewer greets you warmly and has many personal photos around his or her office, go with your natural style. If you are greeted coolly and the interviewer seem analyzing and detached, be formal. Focus ONLY on answering the questions succinctly.)
◆ Avoid subjects that cause conflict. (Rehearse difficult questions ahead of time, such as: Why did you leave your last job? What are your weaknesses? What would your former boss say about you? Do you have budgeting skills?)
◆ Have trouble negotiating salary and other financial issues. (Research comparable pay and standard benefits. If you have a strong resume, don't hesitate to ask for more, saying, "With my qualifications, I'm expecting X." If they still lowball you, leave. You'll respect yourself, and you may get a counter offer.)
◆ Think on your feet and respond quickly; talk more than listen. (Active listening is essential to understand the interviewer's priorities. Prepare a list of questions important to you, and listen closely to the answers.)

Okay, go do something family-oriented now. Later, check out Chapter 20, Golds Overall, first, then carefully read Chapter 4, Tour of the Prism Company, to learn about the strengths of other Colors. Like all Colors, you need the strengths of others, and you can put them to work for you if you know where to look and how to ask. Read Chapter 25 to learn how to recognize the Colors who can best assist you.

# CHAPTER 7

# Green/Gold Introverts

**YOU'RE NOT ONLY A GREEN,** you also have strong secondary characteristics of the Gold personality. And you have tested as a Color Q Introvert, which means you recharge your batteries by being alone, rather than being with people. Your Color group's members are a curious combination of warmth and reserve. Sharing primarily with those closest to you, you don't reveal much to others until trust is established. You have deep insights into people and enjoy helping them grow. Although an idealist, you also are good at organizing and following through on projects.

## You Overall

Intuition, foresight, and compassion drive Green/Gold Introverts, who excel at understanding and motivating others to achieve their greatest potential. You have a deep need for empathetic relationships, but your intimate group is small. Appearing cool and detached outwardly, you harbor strong feelings about your loved ones and your values. When those values are violated or those people threatened, you surprise people by shedding your easy-going nature and becoming tough, demanding, and aggressive.

Because you are a keen and penetrating observer, you know what motivates others. You have a good handle on the cosmic drama around you. Routine stifles you, but you take life as it comes and do what you must.

A harmonious environment, where your originality and interpersonal skills are used to organize and inspire, is a necessity. You enjoy exercising your considerable "emotional intelligence" in circumstances where it is appreciated. Very loyal to individuals, causes, and institutions you admire, you expect a high degree of loyalty and support in return.

Others see you as patient, creative, committed, stubborn, and somewhat enigmatic. In relationships, you are supportive and affirming, making people you care about feel valued and liked. Conflicts both at home and work are problematic and will be ignored as long as possible.

Green/Gold Introverts are tactful, complex, and articulate. Some of the words that describe your work ethic are conscientious, goal-oriented, orderly, serious, hardworking, and ambitious. You are decisive and often in a hurry, impatient with anyone who slows you down in achieving objectives. You can be so ambitious that you'll actually do more than the task requires.

Creative and full of penetrating insights, you are gifted at predicting trends. This also allows you to solve problems in new ways.

As an Introvert, you get fatigued and cranky working in open office settings or when your privacy is not respected. Yet your interest in others is so strong that you run the risk of not giving yourself that all-important time alone to recharge.

The people who irritate you most are superficial, rude, or invade your privacy. When angered, you become both critical and confrontational. In the second half of your life you handle these folks better, using your superior verbal abilities to extricate yourself from the web of their agendas. You realize that you are not obligated to help everyone who needs it.

## case study one

## Senior Vice President, Public Relations, Health Care

Maggie Hoffman is a master in the management of perception. Her public relations savvy is brought into play every day at New York-based PR firm Porter Novelli, assessing and managing the opinions of important groups and individuals for her clients. Though her job is to make her clients look good, Maggie didn't mention one of the measures of her own success—we had to hear it from her subordinates. They call themselves MITs—"Maggies In Training."

In keeping with her Green/Gold personality, Maggie does three things very well. She discerns future trends and does quality research to back up her predictions. She is a superior communicator with both clients and staff. Finally, she stays focused on maximizing both billable hours and productivity while avoiding costly staff burnout.

"She is very structured both in how she produces work and how she thinks things through," note those who work with her. These are the qualities of her Gold component. Of her Green side, Maggie says, "Most satisfying to me is knowing people on my teams are engaged, challenged, and happy."

Her associates say Maggie is the go-to person on their team for clients seeking business advice and resources. This is unusual in the public relations industry and speaks to her professional credibility.

Maggie stresses out when involved in group activities that are not well-orchestrated. Cold calling and prospecting, functioning under huge time crunches and managing people during crisis phases are her least favorite work situations. But when she nails the right strategy for a particular client or brand, she feels deeply energized.

# You on the Job

## As a Leader

"Work hard to convert ideals into reality" is your mantra. You see an idealized vision of the future (usually farther out than most can envision) and strive to make it happen. Building consensus and cooperation through persuasion rather than control is the Green/Gold Introvert's hallmark. You give all opinions an airing, bringing out people's best through appreciation and support.

Naturally and almost fiercely committed to your work, you have integrity about what you do. You are an outstanding role model, inspiring others to great heights. But you don't just sit in your office and dream; you get out there, putting real-world structures and organization into place to achieve your goals. Accepting setbacks as simply new challenges, you sometimes find startlingly new and better ways to meet goals. When staffers have professional or personal difficulties, you are there for them in appropriate ways.

## As a Team Player

Since your goal is harmony, you build bridges (often with humor) between conflicting factions. The focus is on results and providing the structure to achieve them. You brainstorm multiple ideas, get people laughing about the one that really will work, and inspire their best efforts before they finish chuckling.

## Figure 7–1   Natural Work-Related Strengths

Approximately 80 percent of these attributes will apply to you. Check off those that do and use them in your resume and interviews. This will set you apart from the canned responses of others. You:

- ☐ Are visionary; you can see trends and far-reaching potentials of situations.
- ☐ Coach and mentor others well, giving diplomatic feedback.
- ☐ Organize projects well and ensure timely follow-through.
- ☐ Recognize the right people for the right task.
- ☐ See new ways to solve problems and express solutions in a clear way.

Although you navigate emotional territory well, you have your practical side. You meet deadlines and ensure that human and material resources are not wasted.

You may irritate teammates by sticking to ideas not shared by the rest of the team.

Look at Figure 7–1 for a list of your natural work-related strengths.

Now see how some Green/Gold Introverts use these strengths in very different fields.

case study two

## Playwright and College Professor

Lonnie Carter has been a professional playwright since 1969 when he graduated from the Yale School of Drama in New Haven, Connecticut. He saw his first live play at age 19, a Tennessee Williams work that formed a lasting impression of the theater. "I liked what language did in plays," he recalls. "I felt I could do something, if not similar, then complementary, with the use of language. It makes me feel good; I have fun doing it."

Lonnie also teaches acting and playwriting at New York University, where he is energized by his contact with the students (unlike some colleagues who find this draining). "Students will suck you dry," Lonnie admits. "But I like my students; some I like enormously. I love hearing from a student five years down the road saying, 'I'm in a play in San Diego that's a great success; thank you.' That's thrilling."

Although he never experienced overnight success as a playwright, he recently won a Village Voice OBIE Award (off-Broadway theater's highest honor) for his work "The Romance of Magno Rubio." He attributes his success to persistence. "Each year was just another step in the process," Lonnie says. "Then it was thirty years of steps." Now he is so busy going from one production to another that "I seem to write in moving vehicles more than anything else!"

Lonnie does not like the air travel that cuts into his creative time or the bureaucracy of working within a large university structure. "Luckily, I don't have to do many meetings at the university any more," he says.

case study three

## Self-Employed, Private Practice

Michele Frank is a New York City-based licensed clinical social worker in private practice. For eleven years she has been focusing on helping couples and individuals deal with anxiety, depression, and relationship issues.

Michele particularly likes listening to clients and feeling connected with them—a core Green/Gold value. She finds it meaningful to help others solve their problems using her well-developed intuition. "It's very gratifying," she says, "when they relate that they feel extremely understood and safe in the therapy process with me. I feel affirmed that my intuition has so much value." Using her empathetic skills to help clients see new solutions to problems is intrinsically very satisfying for her; Green/Golds by nature gravitate toward anything that helps others reach their fullest potential.

Typical of her Color, Michele dislikes administrative work. Being a managed care provider, she finds the detailed, fact-focused, and repetitive nature of the paperwork stressful but has used her Gold strengths to organize and focus.

# Ideal Work Environment

Your ideal work environment allows you to contribute in some way to the well-being of society, like Michele Frank. Other than that, you're flexible!

When a job offer is made, leverage as much as you can from the list in Figure 7–2.

The WORST type of work culture for a Green/Gold Introvert is tense, overly competitive, and highly political. Here the creative drive is crushed, and Green/Gold Introverts become critical and defensive. Any work culture where products or services exploit both staff efforts and customer vulnerabilities is intolerable to the Green/Gold Introvert. You desire deeply to contribute positively to the world. Requiring focus on too many details or being too hierarchical and status-conscious also are work cultures that destroy your creativity and productivity.

When Green/Gold Introverts work in such nonideal corporate cultures, productivity is stunted and career achievements become an uphill climb.

## Figure 7–2   The Ideal Green/Gold Introvert Work Environment

Compare your current work environment to the description below. Check all that ring true for you. Don't be deceived if these descriptions seem "obvious." It confirms you've tested your individual color correctly. Other Colors, especially Blues, would find this environment uncomfortable and unproductive. The optimal Green/Gold Introvert work environment:

☐ Is egalitarian, predictable, and orderly.
☐ Has people who can be trusted.
☐ Rewards creativity.
☐ Is a culture with strong values and a willingness to invest in staff development.
☐ Produces products and services that contribute to the well-being of society.
☐ Provides opportunity to work on a variety of activities.
☐ Offers control of and responsibility for your own projects.
☐ Rewards your well-developed organizational skills.
☐ Does not impose purposeless paperwork.
☐ Allows for quiet time, reflection, and private work space.

**Figure 7–3 The Green/Gold Introvert's Ideal Boss**

Check off if your boss:

☐ Has high integrity.
☐ Shares your values.
☐ Personalizes your relationship.
☐ Supports staff through obstacles.
☐ Protects you from office politics.

## The Green/Gold Introvert's Ideal Boss

Even a great job can be frustrating under the wrong boss; a mediocre job under a wonderful boss is pretty hard to leave. Green/Golds get along especially well with other Greens. But bosses of other Color types who possess the characteristics in Figure 7–3 also can be good mentors.

## Careers That Attract Green/Gold Introverts

Like Lonnie and Michele, you are most attracted to careers that provide recognition for your creativity or that help others grow and develop. Green/Gold Introverts need to work with people who can be trusted. Working alone or in small groups is best, ideally allowing for private space and quiet time.

*Please note that not all* the following careers will appeal to you, but recognize that each, in some way, draws on the strengths of your style and appeals to a significant number of your Color group. This is not a comprehensive list but it will show underlying patterns of preference. If unlisted careers offer similar patterns, your chances of success increase. Copy in parentheses highlights the Color style characteristics that create success.

In addition, two codes indicate those jobs that are currently predicted to have an above-average salary and growth potential. This information is based on the continuously revised data provided by the U.S. Department of Labor and Bureau of Labor Statistics available on the O*NET website, *http://online.onetcenter.org/*.

**Bold** indicates that the career is considered to be among the top **100 best-paying jobs** based on the average or median salary paid to individuals *with five years of experience.* Excluded are jobs where salary statistics are not available, such as "business owner," or not indicative such as "actor."

*Italics* identifies the jobs that are predicted to benefit from an above-average growth rate over the next several years.

***Bold and italics*** indicates jobs that will benefit from both **higher pay** and *high growth potential*.

Note there are successful people of all Color styles in all occupations. In nonideal jobs you can still shine by creating your own niche.

## Arts/Communications/Computer

*advertising and promotions manager* ◆ **art director** ◆ artist ◆ book publishing professional ◆ *desktop publisher* ◆ *exhibit designer* ◆ film editor ◆ *graphic artist/designer* ◆ *interior decorator* ◆ ***Internet marketing manager/customer relations*** ◆ *literary agent* ◆ media planner ◆ *merchandise displayer* ◆ *multimedia specialist* ◆ museum director ◆ music composer/director ◆ novelist ◆ ***public relations director/specialist*** ◆ *set/costume designer* ◆ translator ◆ TV producer ◆ ***website editor/art director*** ◆ writer/playwright/*journalist* (involvement with media, often work alone, creativity rewarded, superior language skills needed).

## Business/Management

**communications director** ◆ consultative salesperson (ideas more than tangible products) ◆ *diversity manager* ◆ *employment interviewer* ◆ *human resources manager* ◆ **industrial psychologist** ◆ job analyst ◆ marketer (ideas/services) ◆ **organizational development consultant** ◆ *training and development specialist* (help others achieve their potential, need for tact).

## Education

*educational administrator* ◆ *instructional coordinator* ◆ librarian ◆ *teacher* [*all levels*—art, drama, English, humanities, languages, social studies, special education] ◆ university professor (helping others reach their potential, patient one-on-one influencing).

## Health Science/Psychology

*alternative healthcare practitioner* ◆ *clinical psychologist/**psychiatrist*** ◆ *general practitioner* ◆ **optometrist** ◆ *pediatrician* ◆ *physician assistant* ◆ *speech pathologist* ◆ *therapist* [marriage, occupational, substance, abuse] (environment congruent with values, insights into others, see new ways to solve problems, patient one-on-one influencing).

## Law

*lawyer* [children, estate, communication and media, environmental, intellectual property, poverty law] ◆ mediator (organizational abilities, helping others, making the world a better place).

## Social Services

*coach* [business, life] ◆ *counselor* [career, child welfare, outplacement, pastoral, substance abuse] ◆ fundraiser/institutional solicitor ◆ **philanthropic consultant/director** ◆ *religious leader/educator* ◆ senior day care director ◆ social scientist ◆ *social worker/community services manager* (need for good organizational skills, goal setting, and using all resources, helping people who need it, work congruent with your values, improving the world).

---

### Case study four

## When a Career Isn't Working

Mikao (a fictional composite of the author's clients) grew up in a family that did daily yoga and hiked on weekends. From an early age, she enjoyed outdoor activities and decided to become a fitness instructor after graduating high school. As a Green/Gold, she was enthused by the opportunity to help others reach their fullest potentials.

Mikao enrolled in fitness certification classes at her local community college. Green/Gold Introverts tend to enjoy school, though her abstract thinker's mind wandered as they discussed the concrete details of anatomy. Still, she attained certification and got a job quickly.

After a year of full-time fitness instruction, Mikao was burned out. The exercises had become irritatingly repetitive—anathema to creative Green/Golds. As she led her classes, she dreamed of futures she had abandoned and now longed to reclaim. Green/Golds are futuristic, big-picture thinkers; Mikao felt trapped in the here-and-now.

One of Mikao's students was a social worker who spoke passionately about his job. Mikao became inspired to get a social work degree. Five years later, she is far more energized at the end of a day handling her family crisis job than she ever was as a fitness instructor.

---

## Your Personality's Challenges

Green/Gold Introverts have a unique set of potential work-related blind spots. Some below you have, others you don't. Tone down a blind spot by focusing on it, then choose more productive actions and make them habits. (Suggestions for doing so are in parentheses below.) You:

- Can be too idealistic and ignore bottom line consequences. (There is a practical side to making an ideal real. The benefits you envision may be prohibitively expensive. Consult Golds and Blues about processes and costs.)
- Don't have a talent for politics. (Find a boss or other superior who can shield you from such things. If you become embroiled, just re- fuse to play—walk away. Strangely, that works most of the time.)
- Avoid conflicts, confrontations, and underlying problems. (These bring up strong emotions that you would rather not reveal. Don't wait until things boil over; it's easier—and quicker—to address these problems when everyone is calm.)
- Overpersonalize criticism. (You see criticism as a seismic rift in a rela- tionship. Next time a friend criticizes you, ask if he or she still likes you. Will you be surprised if they say, "Of course!"? Much criticism is well-meaning. Getting a thicker skin makes your day easier!)
- Go off on unrealistic tangents. (What's possible in five years excites you. But it won't tell a Red what to do today, a Gold how to admin- ister today, or a Blue how to strategize the way there. Ask them, "What should I do now to achieve this later?" You'll get a lot more buy-in for your five-year plans.)

## Your Job Search—the Good, the Bad, and the Ugly

Green/Gold Introverts need to be recognized for their unique creative ideas, even during their job search. You find fun ways to rise to the top of the resume pile. With some interviewers, particularly Greens and Golds, you will feel a comfortable rapport. But for other Colors, you need to prepare responses.

Your natural strengths easily allow you to:

- Cull leads from a small but trusted network of friends and former as- sociates.
- Create a master plan using both facts and intuition.
- Open yourself to new fields and unusual opportunities.
- Brainstorm trends and creative solutions, which can lead to new po- sitions created for you.
- Follow through on calls and leads.
- Create cover letters, resumes, and thank-you notes with superior writing skills.
- Keep paperwork organized.
- Present yourself as committed and competent.
- Read the interviewer well.

In order to tone down your blind spots, you need to:

- Network with friends first; work up to contacting people you don't know.
- Do deeper research on prospective companies.
- Research and understand a job's compensation range (find a willing Gold to help).
- Talk more; sell your accomplishments.
- Stay practical about costs and the bottom line.
- De-emphasize the needs of others; prioritize your own.
- Practice your salary negotiation with a willing Red.
- Take rejection less personally (find another Green for encouragement).

## The Green/Gold Introvert's Interviewing Style

If your interviewer seems to have a significantly different personality style, use the suggestions in parentheses. Mercilessly exploit these natural abilities of yours and get more job offers!

In following your natural style, you:

- See the big picture and typically present that first. (Great if you're interviewing for a senior level position, irritating if for a junior slot. No boss wants a subordinate who sees more on the horizon than he or she does. Share only if asked, do not volunteer.)
- Listen well with an unusual capacity to understand the viewpoints of others. (This impresses many interviewers. Some, though, want to see the tough professional. Focus on your viability for the job.)
- Present in an orderly way. (Be prepared to show the pros and cons of your background and goals. Use practical language; downplay metaphors or abstractions with interviewers who speak concretely.)
- Use personal experiences to make your points. (If your interviewer seems uncomfortable or breaks eye contact, cut it short.)

Okay, go do something cultural now. Later, check out Chapter 20, Golds Overall, first, then carefully read Chapter 4, A Tour of the Prism Company, to learn about the strengths of other Colors. Like all Colors, your blind spots can be complemented by the strengths of others if you know where to look and how to ask. Invest time learning how to recognize the Colors who can best assist you; it honestly will make your life a whole lot easier. If you are actively engaging in a job search, jot notes in the Roadmap in Chapter 28. Recording your strengths and strategies will keep you organized and on-track, and provide a creative springboard for your networking.

# CHAPTER 8

# Green/Red Extroverts

**YOU'RE NOT ONLY A GREEN,** you also have strong secondary characteristics of the Red personality. And you have tested as a Color Q Extrovert, which means you recharge your batteries by being with people, rather than being alone. Green/Red Extroverts are warm, free spirits who often feel forced to conform to norms of practicality set by other Colors. You'll likely have more career changes than other Colors, not because you're unfocused, but because you are gifted, curious, and flexible.

## You Overall

Energized by new ideas, you're intrigued by the unusual. Your deepest satisfaction is to be acknowledged for your originality and unique contributions. A free spirit, you are unconventional and admire the bravely creative.

A keen and penetrating observer, you know what motivates others. You're aware of what's going on at any moment in the cosmic drama around you. You love challenges that require you to be ingenious. Routine is a drag, but you take life as it comes and do what you must.

If you're not changing careers frequently, you definitely are changing projects and goals more often than other Colors. While you fear others may see you as a flake, in reality they think of you as dynamic and highly skilled at juggling lots of people and events . . . often simultaneously.

Have you taken up writing or public speaking yet? If not, you probably want to. Your verbal and written skills are superior. You can convince employers that you can do the job, even if you've never done it before, and by the way, do it better and more innovatively than anyone else!

You are a gleeful warrior against bureaucracy. It is imperative that you be allowed creative freedom, or you wither.

A need for empathetic relationships is another driving force. Warm and insightful, you establish rapport quickly by being genuine and nonjudgmental.

The trends and pitfalls of the future spread themselves out like a feast on the banquet table of your intuition. Intuition drives you into many areas of interest, almost against your will. Most impact people or are of global concern.

The people who irritate you most are manipulative or controlling. In the second half of your life, you'll move toward a more objective and logical approach to these people. You'll use your superior verbal abilities to extricate yourself from the web of their agendas.

## case study one

## Business Consultant

Gregory J. Marion is a typical Green/Red Extrovert who has carved out a niche in an atypical field. In senior management of a leading strategy consulting firm he has found success emphasizing the creative and relationship-building aspects of the work.

Not surprisingly, Greg says, "It's always been the hardest job for me to be an analyst relentlessly focusing on detailed facts. I prefer the 80/20 rule," he says, "Find the key facts but don't overdwell, then move on trusting your intuition."

Greg is in charge of managing a team whose goal he describes as "leading the client through change, which requires a strong point of view, persuasive skills, and building trust."

His biggest stress is having to act as an expert when he doesn't feel like one, since Green/Reds revere authenticity. He prefers long-term assignments; it takes him about twelve months to really talk his clients' talk with ease.

Building relationships with staff and clients energizes him most, as it does for most Green/Reds. He especially enjoys seeing ads and products from clients he has helped. "I want to actually touch the products on the shelf and bring them home and say, 'I was part of this.'"

Greg describes his top three strengths as "motivating others, coaching, and building relationships." These are core Green/Red Extrovert strengths.

Also typical are his dreams for the future. He'd like to be a published poet (most Green/Red Extroverts turn to writing at some point in their lives), a small business owner, a photographer, or a nonprofit manager. Drawn to artistic and socially relevant endeavors, Green/Red Extroverts also love working in groups small enough to know everyone well.

# You on the Job

## As a Leader

"Bringing out the best in people" is your real gift. During the startup phase of a company or project, you are a strong leader (particularly if conditions are chaotic). You inspire confidence and support, literally able to rally others to achieve impossible goals. Your understanding of what motivates people allows you to create unwaveringly loyalty from your staff. Inviting everyone from all levels to make suggestions brings forth unique ways to solve problems. You then motivate with positive and constructive feedback during implementation.

## As a Team Player

Brainstorming is your bread and butter, and you're better at it than almost anyone. Contributing idea after idea, no matter how outrageous, you eventually find those tremendously creative ideas that put your company on the cutting edge.

### Figure 8–1   Natural Work-Related Strengths

Approximately 80 percent of these attributes will apply to you. Check off those that do and use them in your resume and interviews. This will set you apart from the canned responses of others. You:

- ☐ Inspire others.
- ☐ Express yourself in interesting and colorful ways.
- ☐ Have ideas ahead of their time and can predict future trends by making unusual connections.
- ☐ Establish rapport quickly.
- ☐ Build effective and loyal teams by respecting different points of view.
- ☐ Network well within the organization.
- ☐ Are flexible, accommodating, and embrace change.

Others are at ease around your warmth, humor, and empowering "can-do" attitude. They then generate ideas and offer resources that otherwise would have been left dormant.

You may irritate teammates by talking too much and going off on tangents. Look at Figure 8–1 on page 51 for a list of your natural work-related strengths.

Now see how some Green/Red Extroverts use their strengths in very different fields.

## case study two

### Model, Actress, Writer, Interior Designer, Berry Farmer

Gloria Parker's face may be familiar to you—she was Oleg Cassini's top model and has appeared in numerous movies, television shows, and commercials. If not her face, you may know her name as writer for television series like *Murphy's Law* and *Tour of Duty*. Perhaps you bought high-end furniture from her upscale store on Montana Avenue in Los Angeles. If you were lucky enough, you hired her to decorate your house, as Meg Ryan, Tom Hanks and Rita Wilson, Pierce Brosnan, and Arnold Schwarzenegger did.

"I loved being on stage, making people laugh and cry," says Gloria of her early career. "It opened a world to me I might not ever have walked into."

When her acting career wound down, Gloria in typical Green/Red Extrovert fashion followed her heart and opened a furniture store, leveraging her show business contacts to sell and create a custom interior design clientele. "I enjoyed the artistic part, and I am really good at sales," she says.

Green/Red Extroverts build extensive personal networks, and Gloria's helped her crack open the screenwriting world. "The first play I did ("Women's Gym") got produced and sold to television!" she recalls with her natural enthusiasm.

Green/Red Extroverts love to be in the middle of things. Gloria is an especially good example. "It's really exciting when TV shows are interviewing you, you're in the public eye, you're young, and the world is at your feet." she says. "My store—the hottest people in California were coming to see me. And when my first play was produced, there was so much attention—the reviews were calling me brilliant and genius!"

Gloria eventually burned out on the LA scene and, once again, followed her heart. It led her to 26 acres on a quiet New England river where she continues to write and is building a berry farm.

Although to other Colors Gloria's many careers bewilder, for her they were a natural progression. "My deepest satisfaction is when something is completed and beautiful and it gives pleasure to other people."

When Green/Red Extroverts have done as much as they can enthusiastically and interest wanes in one career, they move on to the next exciting thing. They are merely following their artistic core, which leads them like a beacon to the next hot thing.

Green/Red Extroverts are starters, not administrators. Gloria, like most of her Color type, hates paperwork and accounting. She does it as a necessary evil and delegates it whenever possible. Owning a store with thirty employees was especially difficult, but her caring Green personality and natural Extroversion inspired deep loyalty in her employees.

case study three

## Fine Artist, Commercial Artist, Art Teacher

Oldrich Teply is one of the envied men who make art their living. His corporate graphic work, fine art, and teaching fulfill him on many levels. Most energizing to Oldrich is his teaching work at the renowned Art Students League in New York City. Handling classes of fifty painting students, he gently and diplomatically corrects errors in proportion, drawing, composition, or color. Green/Red Extrovert teachers are known for their inspiring ways, and they love the contact they have with their students. Oldrich can respond to different ages, backgrounds, and skill levels with equal ease. He has the Green/Red core desire to develop potential in others, and is most pleased when a student begins to show his or her own style.

For corporations, for example, he creates watercolors showcasing new high-rise condominiums. Such assignments can involve studying blueprints and conferring with architects and designers. Greens are particularly skilled at pulling together diverse data to create one compelling visual that communicates the spirit of a project.

At the request of Lou Gerstner, then-CEO of Nabisco, Oldrich drew twenty-eight caricature portraits of the company's new management team to ease their transition. At the annual meeting, as the pictures flashed onscreen, the humor Oldrich captured broke the tension surrounding the impending changes. Humor is one tool Green/Reds use to create harmony.

The variety and creative freedom of his work are deeply fulfilling to Oldrich, as is his minimal exposure to rules and bureaucracy.

## Ideal Work Environment

For Greg Marion, it's important that his clients know his heart is in the right place and he truly wants to be of service. Wherever Green/Red Extroverts work, if high value is placed on human well-being, they are happy. Green/Reds like Gloria Parker crave creativity and idea generation in a lively, fast-paced world.

When a job offer is made, leverage as much as you can from the list in Figure 8–2.

The WORST type of work culture for an Extroverted Green/Red emphasizes routine and details, like the paperwork and accounting tasks Gloria hates. Rules and procedures dominate, against which Green/Reds can't help but rebel. Highly political atmospheres destroy the creative freedom and trust necessary for Green/Reds to contribute their best.

When Extroverted Green/Reds work in nonideal corporate cultures, productivity is stunted and career achievements become an uphill climb.

## The Green/Red Extrovert's Ideal Boss

Even a great job can be frustrating under the wrong boss; a mediocre job under a wonderful boss is pretty hard to leave. Green/Reds get along especially well with other Greens. But bosses of other Color types who possess the characteristics in Figure 8–3 on page 56 also can be good mentors.

## Careers That Attract Green/Red Extroverts

Like Gloria and Greg, you are most attracted to careers that provide recognition for your creativity and versatility. Or you may be attracted to professions that involve teaching and helping others. Others will include those listed below.

## Figure 8–2   The Ideal Green/Red Extrovert Work Environment

Compare your current work environment to the boxed description below. Check all that ring true for you. Don't be deceived if these descriptions seem "obvious." It confirms you've tested your individual Color correctly. Other Colors, especially Golds, would find this environment uncomfortable and unproductive. The optimal Green/Red Extrovert work environment:

☐ Is democratic and informal. Your title is less important than your ideas and contributions.

☐ Encourages creativity and idea generation. Rewards you for your core talents rather than labeling you as "free spirit" or "too far out."

☐ Provides freedom to work at your own pace and explore new ideas. The more you are controlled, the less productive you become.

☐ Is lively, energetic, and fast-moving. You are energized by the new.

☐ Rewards humor and fun. A good laugh relaxes you and makes you want to contribute more.

☐ Places high value on the well-being of staff and clients. Companies that disrespect the human side make you fight rather than contribute productively.

☐ Offers variety and change. You don't handle routine well because it's not in your nature to do so.

☐ Focuses on the startup stage rather than maintenance. You will find ingenious ways to divest yourself of administrative details.

☐ Fosters cooperation and trust. Backstabbing and politics drain so much energy from the task at hand. You have no patience for these.

☐ Provides good training and development opportunities. Self-improvement is both your hobby and a lifelong pursuit.

*Please note that not all* the following careers will appeal to you, but recognize that each, in some way, draws on the strengths of your style and appeals to a significant number of your Color group. This is not a comprehensive list but it will show underlying patterns of preference. If unlisted careers offer similar patterns, your chances of success increase. Copy in parentheses highlights the Color style characteristics that create success.

## Figure 8–3    The Green/Red Extrovert's Ideal Boss

Check off if your boss:

☐ Is flexible.
☐ Appreciates your authenticity and energy.
☐ Has a sense of humor.
☐ Personalizes your relationship.
☐ Likes brainstorming new ideas and exploring new areas.
☐ Provides frequent feedback.
☐ Does not micromanage you.

In addition, two codes indicate those jobs that are currently predicted to have an above average salary and growth potential. This information is based on the continuously revised data provided by the U.S. Department of Labor and Bureau of Labor Statistics available on the O*NET website, *http://online.onetcenter.org/*.

**Bold** indicates that the career is considered to be among the top **100 best-paying jobs** based on the average or median salary paid to individuals *with five years of experience.* Excluded are jobs where salary statistics are not available, such as "business owner," or not indicative such as "actor."

*Italics* identifies the jobs that are predicted to benefit from an above-average growth rate over the next several years.

***Bold and italics*** indicates jobs that will benefit from both **higher pay** and *high growth potential.*

Note there are successful people of all Color styles in all occupations. In nonideal jobs you can still shine by creating your own niche.

## Arts/Design

art director ◆ *creative director multimedia team* ◆ *desktop publisher* ◆ designer [interior decorator, set, wardrobe] ◆ fine artist ◆ *graphic artist/designer* ◆ *landscape designer* ◆ *multimedia specialist* ◆ *web designer* (encourages originality and uniqueness).

## Business/Communications/Human Resources

account executive ◆ *conference programmer* ◆ *consultative salesperson* ◆ **corporate communications director** ◆ *corporate trainer diversity manager* ◆ *employment interviewer* ◆ ***human resources generalist/specialist*** ◆ **industrial** psychologist ◆ organization development consultant ◆ *strategic partnership developer* (brainstorming ability and relationship building, strong verbal and written skills, good mediator).

## Communications/Entertainment ◆ Media

actor ◆ *agent/manager* [artists, performers] ◆ columnist ◆ editor [book, film] ◆ *film producer* ◆ journalist ◆ *literary agent* ◆ model ◆ motivational speaker ◆ playwright/screenwriter ◆ translator ◆ TV anchor/newscaster (superior verbal and written skills, going from one glamorous project to the next).

## Education

*adult literacy specialist* ◆ educational consultant ◆ *guidance counselor* ◆ *instructional coordinator* ◆ *teachers at all levels* [plus art, drama, music, special education] (enjoy continuing education, establish rapport).

## Health Science/Psychology

dietitian ◆ *family practitioner* ◆ nurse ◆ *pediatrician* ◆ *psychologists of all types* ◆ public health educator ◆ *therapist* [physical, massage, speech, occupational] (relationship building, empathy, juggling lots of people).

## Law/Human Services

*counselor of all sorts* [career, crisis, high school guidance, substance abuse, etc.] ◆ fundraiser/institutional solicitor ◆ *lawyer* [intellectual property, environment, nonprofit] ◆ legal mediator ◆ philanthropic consultant ◆ religious leader ◆ *school psychologist* ◆ social scientist ◆ *social worker* [child family, school] (understanding human motivation, relationship building, good people/project juggling skills).

## Marketing/Public Relations

*advertising account executive/manager* ◆ *advertising creative director* ◆ *marketing specialist/consultant* ◆ media planner ◆ publicist ◆ publicity writer ◆ *public relations director/specialist* (product positioning and understanding human motivation).

case study four

### When a Career Isn't Working

At age 52, Glen, a New York attorney, had just about achieved all his major goals. Partner of a prestigious Wall Street law firm, Glen was respected and lavishly compensated. His cases were high profile, the envy of his peers. Yet for some reason he could not understand, Glen was finding it increasingly difficult to get up in the morning. He visited a therapist three times a week, seeking answers without knowing the questions.

It turned out Glen had a classic case of burnout—a condition that results when the job does not fit the needs of the personality. Glen had sailed through law school on his smarts, fueled with the idealism that a law career could make big differences in the world (something important to Green/Reds).

In his early years at the firm he worked long hours, energized by the camaraderie with his colleagues, as often is the case with this Color. Extroverted Green/Reds recharge their batteries through supportive interaction at work. This kept Glen going through the tough cases of his junior years. His outstanding ability to make clients feel special and well-served (another Green/Red core aptitude) earned him an early partnership. This put him in high demand; ample and excellent word-of-mouth recommendations attracted career-making cases.

Yet, at the top of his game, his reward was loss of interest and constant fatigue. A brief introduction to his Color style brought several things to light. As a Green, he disliked confrontation, the basis of most prominent cases. The relentless drive for high-stakes settlements and the pressure of outwitting opponents was draining rather than satisfying, as it would be to a Blue.

Glen resigned, much to the surprise of family, friends, and colleagues. He enrolled in a university to earn a Ph.D. in psychology. Now, several years later and brimming with energy, Glen is hanging up his shingle as a therapist for lawyers.

## Your Personality's Challenges

Green/Red Extroverts have a unique set of potential work-related blind spots. Some listed below you have, others you don't.

Tone down a blind spot by focusing on it, then choose more productive actions and make them habits. (Suggestions for doing so are in parentheses below.) You:

- Pay too little attention to rules you feel are obstacles to creativity. (Try to understand whose anxiety a rule addresses. Remember, genuine creativity can work around, and *through*, the rules.)
- Can talk too much, going off on tangents during group discussions. (You think holistically; hence, all topics addressed in any order are relevant. Be considerate of your fellow Colors who need linear thought and get jangled when the lines aren't straight!)
- Are too sensitive to criticism. (Because relationships are top priority to you, criticism feels like condemnation when it's not. Dare to ask your critics if they still like you. Most likely, they do.)
- Avoid conflict; often delaying dealing with the issue. (Enjoy the realization that conflict worked through to conclusion actually *strengthens* relationships. If you are a young Green/Red, this is a very hard lesson to learn. A thicker skin will bring you more and deeper relationships in the long run.)
- Get excited by new projects and then don't complete old ones. (Most projects get "old" before they're complete, leaving unfinished business. *Just finish or delegate* so your energy is totally free to devote to the new.)
- Make errors of fact. (Gut feelings have always gotten you to the right place at the right time; decisions based on facts often have led you astray. Start intuitively, then *prove yourself right*. Other Colors need facts and will devalue your ideas if they contain errors.)

## Your Job Search—the Good, the Bad, and the Ugly

Green/Red Extroverts love making a splash and impressing others. With some interviewers, particularly Greens and Reds, you blow away all competitors. With other Colors, you need a different strategy.

Your natural strengths easily allow you to:

- Actively network through a broad range of people for referrals.
- Enjoy exploring new options.
- Interview with enthusiasm.
- Establish quick rapport.
- Convince an employer to create a new job for you.
- Come across as adaptable, a quick learner, and a team player.

In order to tone down your blind spots, you need to:

- Role-play negotiating salary and financial issues (find a willing Gold or Blue to help).
- Do more research on prospective companies.

- Subdue wardrobe, hairstyle, and manner in interviews to counterbalance seeming lack of seriousness.
- Talk less in interviews and ask more questions.
- Hold back ideas on which you have not done cost research.
- Require yourself to make a minimum number of contacts each day of your job search.
- Do a realistic budget for your job search time.
- Instead of jumping at a job offer, say "This sounds great, but I need some reflection time. Can you allow me one or two days?"

## The Green/Red Extrovert's Interviewing Style

With an interviewer whose Color is close to your own, you will feel immediate rapport. However, if your interviewer seems to have a significantly different style, use the suggestions in parentheses. Mercilessly exploit these natural abilities of yours, and get more job offers!

In following your natural style, you:

- Speak with geniality, fluency, and energy. (You can overwhelm more subdued interviewers. Try to operate from an energy level only one notch higher than your interviewer, not ten!)
- Think on your feet and reply quickly. (Don't think this *always* makes you look good. It's possible to be too peppy. Mix it up—make some replies slow and thoughtful.)
- Make your points through lively and vivid imagery, personal stories, and humor. (With an interviewer who keeps his or her distance, replace imagery with facts—role play with a willing Gold, if possible. Use personal stories only when interviewers maintain eye contact. If humor falls flat the first time, don't keep trying! Let the interviewer set the tone.)
- See the big picture and typically present that first. (Great if you're interviewing for a senior level position, irritating if for a junior slot. No boss wants a subordinate who sees more on the horizon than he or she does. Share only if asked.)

Okay, go do something new now. Or continuing reading Chapter 10, Reds Overall. Then learn how to Color-code bosses and co-workers by reading Chapter 4, A Tour of the Prism Company, and Chapter 25, Adjusting to the Styles of Other Colors. The greatest value of this book really is learning how to interact with, appreciate, and use the strengths of other Colors. If you're doing a job search, jot down notes in Chapter 28, A Roadmap—it will keep you focused.

# Green/Red Introverts

YOU'RE NOT ONLY A GREEN, you also have strong secondary characteristics of the Red personality. And you have tested as a Color Q Introvert, which means you recharge your batteries by being alone, rather than being with people. Your Color group has warm, free spirits who typically feel forced to conform to norms of practicality and seriousness. You may have more career changes than other Colors, not because you are flawed, but because you are multitalented, curious, and flexible. The drive to write is more intense in you than in most other Colors and is a part of most of your jobs.

## You Overall

Thoughtful, insightful, intuitive, and complex, you do not usually impose your ideas on others. You prefer a small intimate group of friends, even though you have a deep need for empathetic relationships. Outwardly cool and detached, inwardly you harbor strong feelings about people and values. When your values are violated or those people threatened, you surprise others by shedding your easy-going nature and becoming tough, demanding, and aggressive.

Your deepest satisfaction is to be acknowledged for your originality and unique contributions. You are unconventional and admire other nonconformists.

Because you are a keen and penetrating observer, you have a good handle on what's going on in the cosmic drama around you. You enjoy helping others, not out of guilt but of a desire to assist. Life's challenges find you optimistic, adaptable, and ingenious. Routine saps your energy, but your adaptability helps you do what you must.

Projecting the trends and pitfalls of the future is one of your greatest gifts. A big picture thinker, you take in everything, focusing on what impacts people and has global ramifications.

You are a gleeful warrior against bureaucracy. It is imperative that you be allowed creative freedom, or you become a saboteur. While you are flexible and accommodating to work with, you get fatigued and cranky working in open office settings or when your privacy is not respected.

Others see you as insightful and an excellent listener. In relationships, you establish rapport by being genuine and nonjudgmental. But the true intensity of your feelings is revealed only to those who know you well.

The people who irritate you most are intrusive, controlling, and overly critical of others. In the second half of your life, as you move toward a more objective and logical approach to others, you will handle these folks better. Your superior verbal abilities extricate you from the web of their agendas.

## case study one

### Author and Editor

Dan Shaw is a talented author with a long, well-credentialed resume mostly in the home design field. He has written and/or edited for the *New York Times, House and Garden,* and *O At Home,* among many others. The majority of the time he lived and worked in New York City.

Today, he calls a very small New England town home. "I went to an office for twenty years," says Dan. "I like not going to an office right now. The type of life change I wanted was spiritually oriented." Dan created that opportunity for himself on a deeply forested piece of land by a river. Green/Red Introverts enjoy working at home more than most.

He describes working at magazines as being "all about the social interactions," normally a stressor to Introverts. But Dan liked this part of his job. "It was easy for me because it was part of the work structure, and I did not have to initiate social interactions," Dan says.

He brought many Green gifts to his work: "I see things very well—the unfamiliar in the familiar," he says. "I am confident in what I do, and I am a good writer who's done serious journalism. So I have very high standards." Green/Reds are perfectionists, an advantage in writers.

Typical of a Green, money and success are only two of many equal motivators. When asked about them, Dan replied, "I wouldn't mind having money, but it doesn't pull me." He explained his choice to freelance, saying, "I attained the number two position at a couple of magazines, and realized I did not have the ambition in me to be number one."

Today, Dan is developing two coffee table books, both of which he expects to publish within a year or two. He's in his home office five to ten hours a day researching, writing, or arranging new, exciting projects. "When I am writing, I get lost in it—not looking at the clock," he says. Working at home, sometimes he chooses to chop firewood or make stew: "That's the nice part of it," this Introvert admits.

# You on the Job

## As a Leader

"Dogged consensus builder" describes the Green/Red Introvert leadership style. You work doggedly to achieve what is important to you, especially treating colleagues and staff well. Ethical, supportive, motivating, creatively encouraging, sensitive, and patient are all words your people would use to describe you at the helm. A keen observer of people, you understand what motivates others, and you use that to draw the best out of them.

You build consensus by encouraging openness, giving positive feedback, being generous with time and resources, and being patient with "process" issues. Personalizing your relationships with staff and colleagues ensures support. You build extremely loyal teams by encouraging rather than commanding.

## As a Team Player

You have deep and accurate insights into your team members because you hear what is really being said. Warmth and acceptance put them at ease.

Defining common goals is your gift to the team, drawing people together. Matching people to appropriate tasks is another talent; you may find yourself suggesting who should do what even if you're not the leader.

Your forward thinking and provocative ideas frequently "get the juices flowing" in others. The team often credits you with breaking them out of creative log jams.

## Figure 9-1   Natural Work-Related Strengths

Approximately 80 percent of these attributes will apply to you. Check off those that do and use them in your resume and interviews. This will set you apart from the canned responses of others. You:

☐ Like to explore new possibilities, solving problems in an original way.
☐ Support the development of others.
☐ Understand how underlying emotions impact productivity.
☐ Get right to the guts of an issue.
☐ Can concentrate and work for long periods alone.
☐ Work without much supervision.

You may irritate teammates by becoming too attached to a value not shared by the rest of the team.

Look at Figure 9–1 for a list of your natural work-related strengths.

Now see how some Green/Red Introverts use these strengths in very different fields.

case study two

## Business Conference Planner

Anne Thayer is one of the 5 percent of Greens who work within the Wall Street community. She has carved out a niche in relationship-building financial conferences. Seemingly going against her artistic, Introverted nature, Anne nonetheless enjoys the creative aspects of the planning process. She writes the program, gets the speakers, and produces the program brochure. On conference days, she brings her acting skills to the conference podium.

As an Introvert, Anne is challenged by the fifty-plus cold calls she makes each day. Fortunately, she has a private office. When she needs a break, she closes her door and does the Five Tibetan Rites of yoga for a quick recharge. Afterward, she eats a simple bowl of bean soup, and she's ready to rock and roll. Her colleagues, who enjoy her warmth and empathy, discreetly hold her calls.

A theater major in college, Anne drifted into popular culture event planning to support her studies. She found she was more skilled and better paid behind the scenes than onstage, and a career in conference planning blossomed.

Conference planning offers Anne the opportunity to use her relationship-building and writing skills and get well paid for them. The financial concepts she must master, though, can be onerous for her; Greens rarely choose financial careers.

Conference planning involves three very Green areas—relationship-building, writing, and showcasing the leading ideas of the field. Anne loves to see people engaged in enthusiastic shop talk. She feels proud that her programs have paved the way for multimillion-dollar deals.

She also enjoys writing the programs and event brochures. Many Green/Red Introverts take up writing at some point, and Anne is fortunate that's part of her job. She enjoys being on-stage emceeing her programs.

Cold calls, constant networking, and after-hours socializing leave her exhausted. If forced to work a weekend she would normally spend recharging, she frequently runs down her immune system and catches a cold. When she can get enough alone time, however, she enjoys her work.

## Ideal Work Environment

Green/Red Introverts do best when not bombarded by the demands of an office; they make excellent telecommuters. You need reflective time and the control of a home environment, like Dan Shaw has.

When a job offer is made, leverage as much as you can from the list in Figure 9–2 on page 66.

The WORST type of work culture for an Green/Red Introvert emphasizes routine and details. Highly political atmospheres and power struggles destroy the creative freedom and trust necessary for Green/Reds to flourish. Tight deadlines impose pressure that is anything but motivating to them.

When Introverted Green/Reds work in nonideal corporate cultures, productivity is stunted and career achievements become an uphill climb.

## The Green/Red Introvert's Ideal Boss

Even a great job can be frustrating under the wrong boss; a mediocre job under a wonderful boss is pretty hard to leave. Green/Reds get along es-

## Figure 9-2    The Ideal Green/Red Introvert Work Environment

Compare your current work environment to the description below. Don't be deceived if these descriptions seem "obvious." It confirms you've tested your individual color correctly. Other Colors, especially Golds, would find this environment uncomfortable and unproductive. The optimal Green/Red Introvert work environment:

- ☐ Is democratic and informal. You function best with a minimum of rules, paperwork, and supervision. Rank and status are fluid.
- ☐ Is supportive and harmonious, fostering cooperation and trust. Backstabbing, confrontation, and malicious gossip really irritate and distract you from the task at hand.
- ☐ Encourages creativity and idea generation.
- ☐ Recognizes individual needs of both staff and clients. Seek companies that encourage work/life balance and high levels of customer service.
- ☐ Is in synch with personal values. Companies that violate your values will soon see you gone. You don't tolerate this.
- ☐ Allows for private space. As an Introvert, your batteries get drained when dealing with people, even if your people skills are superb. You recharge alone. You think and perform better in a private space where you can reflect on projects; insist on one as a condition of employment if at all possible.
- ☐ A corporate culture integrating the above elements is fertile soil for your career advancement.

pecially well with other Greens. But bosses of other Color types who possess the characteristics in Figure 9-3 also can be good mentors.

## Careers That Attract Green/Red Introverts

Like Anne, you are most attracted to careers that provide recognition for your creativity in writing and the visual and performing arts or your interest in helping others grow and develop. Green/Red Introverts need to work with people who have a personal interest in them and express appreciation. Working alone or in small groups is best for their productivity, especially if they are focusing on solutions that enhance the lives of others. The atmosphere ideally is casual and informal, like Dan's home office. Often

**Figure 9–3    The Green/Red Introvert's Ideal Boss**

Check off if your boss:

☐ Is flexible.
☐ Does not micromanage you.
☐ Takes a personal interest in you and your development.
☐ Protects you from professional intrigue and politics.
☐ Values innovation.
☐ Shares similar values to you.
☐ Has a high level of integrity.

Green/Red Introverts will change careers many times before finding something in which they believe.

*Please note that not all* the following careers will appeal to you, but recognize that each, in some way, draws on the strengths of your style and appeals to a significant number of your Color group. This is not a comprehensive list but it will show underlying patterns of preference. If unlisted careers offer similar patterns, your chances of success increase. Copy in parentheses highlights the Color style characteristics that create success.

In addition, two codes indicate those jobs that are currently predicted to have an above-average salary and growth potential. This information is based on the continuously revised data provided by the U.S. Department of Labor and Bureau of Labor Statistics available on the O*NET website, *http://online.onetcenter.org/*.

**Bold** indicates that the career is considered to be among the top **100 best-paying jobs** based on the average or median salary paid to individuals *with five years of experience.* Excluded are jobs where salary statistics are not available, such as "business owner," or not indicative such as "actor."

*Italics* identifies the jobs that are predicted to benefit from an above average growth rate over the next several years.

***Bold and italics*** indicates jobs that will benefit from both **higher pay** and *high growth potential.*

Note there are successful people of all Color styles in all occupations. In nonideal jobs you can still shine by creating your own niche.

## Arts/Design

art director ◆ *advertising creative director* ◆ **creative director multimedia team** ◆ *desktop publisher* ◆ designer [decorator, set, wardrobe] ◆ fine artist ◆ *graphic artist/designer* ◆ *multimedia specialist* ◆ *web designer* (uses originality and uniqueness, works alone or in small teams).

## Business/Human Resources/Marketing

*diversity manager* ◆ *conference programming* ◆ *employment interviewer* ◆ **human resources generalist/specialist** ◆ **industrial psychologist** ◆ *marketing consultant* ◆ **organization development specialist** ◆ *public relations specialist* ◆ publicity writer ◆ **strategic partnership developer** (good listening, understanding of human motivation, relationship building, strong written skills).

## Communications/Entertainment/Media

actor ◆ columnist ◆ editor [book, film] ◆ *film editor/producer* ◆ journalist ◆ *literary agent* ◆ writers of all types [playwright, screenwriter, novelist, biographer, poet, etc.] ◆ translator (involvement with media, often works alone; language skills, creativity, and written skills rewarded).

## Education

*adult literacy specialist* ◆ college professor ◆ educational consultant ◆ guidance counselor ◆ *instructional coordinator* ◆ *teachers at all levels* [plus art, drama, foreign language, music, special education] ◆ school psychologist (enjoys continuing education, helping others reach potential).

## Health Science/Psychology

*chiropractor/alternative health care specialist* ◆ dietitian ◆ **family practitioner** ◆ *therapist* [physical/massage/speech/occupational] ◆ *personal trainer* ◆ **psychiatrist/psychologists of all types** ◆ *veterinarian assistant* (empathy, excellent listener, keen observer of others).

## Law/Human Services

*lawyer* [intellectual property, environment, nonprofit] ◆ legal mediator ◆ philanthropic consultant ◆ religious leader ◆ school psychologist ◆ social scientist ◆ *social worker* (deeply held values, intuitive understanding of human motivation, relationship building).

case study three

## When a Career Isn't Working

Financial trading desks are notorious for their "frat house" culture. Those who thrive enjoy the adrenalin rush of making instant multimillion-dollar decisions. In the process they also scream, hurl obscenities at each other, and occasionally throw food across the room. And for the most part, colleagues do not take offense. Later they will all go out, share a few drinks, and wipe the slate clean.

Enter Phyllis Rosen. Riding the wave of the women's rights movement, she landed a plum job on the trading desk of a giant Wall Street brokerage firm when the company came under pressure to bring women into management.

"The trading desk was the center of everything," Phyllis says. "Whatever happened somewhere in the world had an immediate reaction on Wall Street. I became an information junkie." She also became an adrenaline junkie, her Red side loving the fast pace and the exhilaration of making good trades.

The rushes came at the expense of her Green side. Few Greens enter Wall Street, an arena that rewards risk-taking and virtually ignores the emotional component. Her male co-workers were her biggest source of stress. "In those days, they treated each other crudely," she says, "and went for blood when they smelled a weakness."

Not all trades go well, and Phyllis found it very stressful when she lost money for her clients. After a while, the pressures became greater than the adrenaline rushes, and Phyllis had to make some hard decisions about what else to do. After twenty years on Wall Street, she became a career counselor based in New York City. Although she still has some stress in having to replenish clients constantly, she says, "I'm energized by this work because I feel I make a difference, I'm good at it, and I satisfy my curiosity about people and the choices they make."

## Your Personality's Challenges

Green/Red Introverts have a unique set of potential work-related blind spots. Some you have, others you don't. Tone down a blind spot by focusing on it, then choose more productive actions and make them habits. (Suggestions for doing so are in parentheses below.) You:

◆ Can be too idealistic and ignore bottom line consequences. (Making an ideal real can be prohibitively expensive. Consult Golds and Blues about processes and costs.)

◆ Don't speak up enough and appear disengaged. (Few know how much energy it takes to listen, and you listen intently. Your concentration, however, comes across as aloofness. Just throw in a few comments to let others know you're present—humor counts.)

◆ Don't prioritize and appear disorganized. (You have only one priority a day—sit down and prioritize that day's activities. You can handle that, right?!!)

◆ Consider your own values superior. (Others may compromise or be more realistic, but your ideals are *ideal*. Once you recognize the strengths of other Colors, though, this tendency will mellow.)

◆ May miss deadlines because you are a perfectionist. (Being perfect means meeting the deadline. Your boss feels that way, so prioritize that career-important deadline over less important details.)

◆ Can be too reserved to be effective. (The more cautious you are to speak up, the more valuable your insight is likely to be. Give yourself the opportunity for positive reinforcement.)

## Your Job Search—the Good, the Bad, and the Ugly

Green/Red Introverts need to process information. With some interviewers, particularly Greens and Reds, you will feel a comfortable rapport. But with those of other Colors, you need a response strategy.

Your natural strengths easily allow you to:

◆ Get excited by new fields and unusual opportunities.
◆ Brainstorm creatively.
◆ Create cover letters and resumes with excellent writing skills.
◆ Present yourself as adaptable, committed, easy to work with, and a quick study.
◆ Create a master plan for your search with hard research and soul searching.

In order to tone down your blind spots, you need to:

- Network a little more, even if it feels phony to you.
- Stick with your objectives; don't change course on a whim.
- Role play compensation negotiations (find a willing Gold or Red to help).
- Talk more and sell your accomplishments.
- Hold back ideas on which you have not done cost research.

## The Green/Red Introvert's Interviewing Style

With an interviewer whose Color is close to your own, you will feel immediate rapport. However, if your interviewer seems to have a significantly different style, use the suggestions in parentheses.

In following your natural style, you:

- Are quiet and calm. (This can look like disinterest—most interviewers expect a certain amount of nervousness. Make sure to speak more than you normally do, especially at first.)
- Listen well. (This impresses many interviewers. But you may miss opportunities to sell your accomplishments. Role-play with a willing Red.)
- Share values and feelings with only a few people. (You may be able to open up to a Green interviewer who puts you at ease. With others, prepared statements about yourself will keep you looking confident.)
- Are global and metaphoric in speech. (With interviewers who look skeptical or confused, read straight off your resume for a while.)
- Present information and schedules as tentative and adaptable. (But don't be vague about when you can start a job—give an exact date!)
- See the big picture and present that first. (Great if you're interviewing for a senior level position, irritating if for a junior slot. No boss wants a subordinate who sees more on the horizon than he or she does. Share only if asked; do not volunteer.)

Okay, go do something fun but nonfattening now. Later, read Chapter 10, Reds Overall, first, then carefully read Chapter 4, A Tour of the Prism Company, to learn about the strengths of other Colors. Chapter 25, Adjusting to the Styles of Others, will help you identify different Colors and use their strengths collaboratively . . . you just have to know where to look and how to ask. If you are actively engaging in a job search, jot notes in the Roadmap in Chapter 28. Recording your strengths and strategies feels supportive and encouraging.

# PART 3

# REDS
## "Let's Do It Now"

Reds do best in fields that provide variety and change and the opportunity to rise to the challenge of a crisis.

# CHAPTER 10

# Reds Overall

Reds represent approximately 27 percent of the overall world population. If you are not a Red, but would like to learn how to identify and communicate with one, go to Figure 10–1 on page 75.

Reds are the most adventurous and exciting Color group. Perhaps the best-known Red in the United States is Donald Trump, a highly skilled, self-promoting, and flamboyant real estate dealmaker. Frequently referred to merely as "the Donald," he stars in his own reality television show, *The Apprentice*, which first appeared in 2004. (Mr. Trump has not taken the Color Q test, but his Color has been determined by the Myers-Briggs community.)

"Deals are my art form," Trump said in his 1988 best-seller *Trump/The Art of the Deal*. "Other people paint beautiful pictures on canvas or write wonderful poetry. I like making deals, preferably big deals; that's how I get my kicks."[4] Kicks are a prime motivator for Reds, who will scan the universe 24 hours a day to find the next exciting thing. "Money was never a big motivation for me except as a way to keep score," Trump added in his book. "The real excitement is playing the game."[5]

So it is also for Christie Todd Whitman, Management Consultant and former Governor of New Jersey. Born into a very politically active family, it was probably inevitable that Christie Todd Whitman would achieve politi-

---

[4]Donald Trump and Tony Schwartz, *Trump/The Art of the Deal* (New York: Random House, 1987), p. 1.

[5]*Ibid.*, p. 40.

## Figure 10-1   How to Recognize a Red

☐ Interested in the external world—sports, tools, architecture, motorized vehicles of all kinds.
☐ Concrete vocabulary.
☐ Desk has many piles.
☐ Casual manner.
☐ Constantly in motion.
☐ Spontaneous.
☐ Often late.
☐ Great sense of humor.
☐ Seek excitement and adventure, preferring activity to conversation.
☐ Know food and wine.

HOW TO COMMUNICATE WITH A RED

✔ Be stimulating.
✔ Avoid meetings or schedule them in fun places.
✔ Make presentations brief; use action verbs like "attack," "challenge," "stimulate," or "enjoy."
✔ Hands-on demonstrations are best.
✔ Avoid theories, get to the point, stay in the concrete here-and-now.
✔ Be very flexible and open-ended in conversation and plans.
✔ Stress immediacy of solutions—this will help "right now, today."
✔ Acknowledge and appreciate their crisis-calming skills.
✔ Allow them to follow their instincts, give them freedom to do so.
✔ If you make it fun, they respond.
✔ Accept that "timing" is everything.
✔ Be ready to go with "fly by the seat of your pants" decisions.

cal noteworthiness. But it helped immensely that she was a Red. Reds are outgoing risk-takers who prefer a hands-on approach to their work. All these attributes catapulted her from an unknown county board member in 1982 to Governor of the State of New Jersey a mere decade later.

What distinguishes Reds as children are competitiveness, love of physical activity, and a deep affinity for animals. Little Christie Todd had ample opportunity to exercise all these traits on her family's 232-acre farm in the rolling hills of western New Jersey. Here she made good use of the swimming pool and tennis courts. It was a working farm, replete with all the cows, sheep, pigs, and chickens with which a young girl could be fascinated. Christie recalls herself as a tomboy who loved to ride her horse, search for snakes, and go fishing.

Her father, Webster B. Todd, was a contractor whose family firm built Rockefeller Center in New York and restored Williamsburg in Virginia. At 50 he retired and turned to his true passion, Republican politics. His wife Eleanor joined him, attending every Republican convention from 1940 to 1976 in an official capacity. Christie had experiences of which few children could boast— at age 6 presenting dolls to Mrs. Nixon for her daughters Julie and Tricia; at age 9, attending her first national convention and presenting Dwight Eisenhower with a leather pouch for his golf balls that she had made herself.

She graduated from Wheaton College in Massachusetts in 1968. In 1973, needing a date to Richard Nixon's inaugural ball, she invited a banker, John Whitman, whose grandfather had once been governor of New York. They married a year later.

In 1990, Christie made a move that lower risk personality types would have dismissed as sheer folly. She plunged into the limelight by running against incumbent Senator Bill Bradley. Her own party did not support her, figuring she was sure to lose to Bradley, an All-American Rhodes scholar, a former star forward of the New York Knicks, and formidable fundraiser. He spent $12 million; she spent $1 million. She lost, but only by 2 percent. The gamble had worked; people took notice. "I knew it was a long shot," Whitman says today, "but I saw an opportunity to gain statewide exposure." She did, in typical Red calculated risk-taking fashion.

Reds enjoy camaraderie, and Christie's next steps maximized this preference. To position herself in three years' time as a viable gubernatorial candidate, Christie hosted a talk show, wrote a column, formed a political action committee, and spearheaded the Neighborhood Leadership Initiative, designed to identify and train grassroots leaders. But what got her the most attention, and gave her the most mileage during her campaign, was an extended bus tour designed to meet as many New Jersey citizens as possible. She beat her opponent Jim Florio in 1993 by 1 percent of the vote.

Reds overflow with physical and mental energy, as well as competitiveness. Many stories about Governor Whitman's energy and challenges to those around her to keep up abound. It was said during her tenure that the state troopers assigned to follow her around and guard her ended up in better physical shape than they ever were before.[6] She would set aside several days a week as road days, talking to people around the state.

[6]Patricia Beard, *Growing Up Republican* (New York: HarperCollins, 1996), pp. 196–197.

Politics did not blunt her love of animals. Her position allowed her to join park rangers in freezing midwinter weather to observe as they placed ear tags on newly born bear cubs. Christie would cuddle the cubs in her jacket as rangers tranquilized the mothers.

Reds are bold and not afraid of controversy, an asset in the political arena. Christie gained recognition for donning a bulletproof vest and going undercover with state troopers to see firsthand the drug dealing in her state's urban communities in order to help set policy.

These are the actions of a Red, whose shirtsleeve management style is easygoing, down-to-earth, and expedient. Reds are flexible, spontaneous, and have the ability to relate to and persuade other people. Politics is high on the list of most satisfying occupations for a Red personality. More than any other type, Reds love risk and thrive in chaotic situations, moving in to bring order and focus. Christie finds energizing "interfacing with people, hearing their concerns, doing the challenging back-and-forth, always being on your toes . . . working through knotty problems and building a consensus to support sensible solutions."

Reds love variety and action. Competition energizes Christie. Reds bring fun, humor, and empathy into the lives of others. She conveys a genuine interest in what you are doing, an ability to listen and be truly present.

Christie, like Reds in the corporate world, leads by keeping close to the grassroots, encouraging personal responsibility, seeking quick results, and focusing on personal goals. She is informal, action-oriented, and collaborative, viewing emergencies as interesting challenges rather than intrusions.

Her fun-loving, nervy, and nonconforming personality was an asset in her role as governor, but helped her less when she was tapped as head of the Environmental Protection Agency by President George W. Bush in 2001. In this job she lasted only two years and resigned frustrated by pressure on her office from the September 11 attacks and need for more time with her family.[7]

Today, Christie Todd Whitman keeps herself visible by running the Whitman Strategy Group, and environmentally oriented management consulting and strategic planning firm with offices in New Jersey and Washington, DC. This allows her to "work with constant variety, always going up the learning curve" of the environmental issues about which she cares deeply. She does a lot of speaking engagements and promotes her book, *It's My Party, Too*, which she wrote "to support an effort to change political discourse in this country."

Christie Todd Whitman embodies the typical traits of the Red personality—a "let's do it now," "can-do," "live and let live" super-realist who thrives from daring and an ability to handle a crisis better than any other

[7]www.wikipedia.org/wiki/Christine_Todd_Whitman

Color. She is known as someone who lives each day to the fullest. True to her type, she is genuinely interested in people, and her style is fraternal and chummy.

Whitman's group, the Reds, comprise 27 percent of the world's population. They do not respond well to theories or abstract concepts, preferring instead to focus on today's reality. Their view of the world is what they can see, touch, taste, smell, and hear for themselves. Reds need freedom and independence and hate to feel trapped in either work or relationships. Guilt, obligation, and duty rarely motivate them. They are loyal to friends and family, but loathe being tied down to schedules and routines not of their own choosing. The pursuit of action drives many Reds to try new experiences, adventures, activities, or foods. They work in order to spend, rather than to save or invest. "He who dies having worn out the most toys wins" is typical of the Red mentality.

Other famous Reds in the political arena are George W. Bush, Lyndon Johnson, John F. Kennedy, Franklin D. Roosevelt, and Winston Churchill. J. Paul Getty and Donald Trump represent Reds in the corporate world. Michael Jordan illustrates the Red style in sports, George Patton in the military, and Madonna in the field of entertainment.

This chapter will help you determine if you've tested your primary and backup personality color correctly. It also will help you identify Reds among people you know, as will Chapter 4, A Tour of the Prism Company/The Red Department.

If the self-assessment at the beginning of the book has scored you as a Red, congratulations! You are one of the most fun people in the known universe. You will also be impatient about reading a book like this, preferring instead to get on with things more real and less abstract. However, if you are interested in reading more about yourself, or you want to impress someone who thinks this is a great book and you should read it, go to your specific Color's chapter. We know you're going to skim it. Just be sure to read the section about your most satisfying careers, or you'll miss the most practical part!

# CHAPTER 11

# Red/Blue Extroverts

**YOU'RE NOT ONLY A RED,** you also have strong secondary characteristics of the Blue personality. And you have tested as a Color Q Extrovert, which means you recharge your batteries by being with people, rather than being alone. It's likely you have little patience for this book, and are just reading this to please someone. So we'll keep this realistic, or we know you're out of here!

## You Overall

High energy, good humor, and optimism are hallmarks of Red/Blue Extroverts. Unusually effective in times of crisis and change, you seek and revel in the unexpected. Active and independent, you function best in small collegial teams where hierarchy is secondary to getting the job done. Variety makes you happy, as does operating outside the norms followed by others.

Realistic and pragmatic, you trust only what you have personally observed. A particularly acute visual memory makes you exceptional at remembering details. You want the facts, but enjoy humorous anecdotes.

Your communication style is blunt and direct, which you find efficient. Others, however, may be put off by your style, and this confuses you. Though very attentive in the moment, you have a short attention span.

You resist making decisions under pressure. You like to keep all options open as long as possible. When ready, however, you decide with the speed of light.

Unusually adept at sizing up problems, you move in quickly for solutions. You trust your own instincts first, bureaucracy last, and often bypass rules and procedures. While adept at handling immediate problems, you have a hard time staying focused on long-term challenges.

Others see you as a gifted negotiator who can make logical and difficult decisions. Although you are very tolerant of most folks, you get annoyed by bossy people who insist on "doing things the right way," or whose emotionalism clouds the issue.

In the second half of life, Red/Blue Extroverts continue to seek new challenges, but will slow down and reflect more between activities.

---

case study one

## Chief Executive Officer, Investment Consulting Firm, and Author

Peter Tanous is not your typical CEO and has the sense of humor to prove it. He likes to joke that "an economist is someone who didn't have the personality to become an accountant." He can say things like that because his books *Investment Gurus* and *Wealth Equation* have both been successful enough to be Money Book Club main selections and receive wide critical acclaim.

He started his business, Lynx Investment Advisory, LLC, a Washington, DC-based investment consulting firm, relatively late in life at age 54. The advantage was he brought wisdom, experience, and contacts to the table, making him able to cope with the old business school rule about starting a business: "Double the expense and halve the revenue of your plan and see if you still make it, because that's what's most likely to happen," he says. "As someone I know put it, I never met a business projection I didn't like. That's because they all look good!"

He set about drumming up business, but found the conventional wisdom of making tons of business calls was not the most effective way. "I found you are better off concentrating on the ones where you have a high chance of success . . . that includes people you know or institutions to which you have privileged access," he says. "Anything else is an uphill battle." Red/Blue Extroverts are strong motivators of people, and this was critical to his success. Today, Peter's firm advises on over $1 billion of client assets.

"I understand markets," he adds. "I am a very good sales-person and highly optimistic, which is essential." His Red side enjoys the changeable nature of the financial markets and the diverse needs of his clients, particularly his international ones. "I like dealing with their investment needs based on the political environment that they live and function in," he says.

His biggest energizer? "I enjoy making clients happy," he says. "I enjoy getting new clients by convincing them of the value of what we do for them." The duties he leaves to others include "most administrative, regulatory, and legal tasks. Pure research, as well."

Peter's top three strengths are typical of his Red/Blue Color. He lists them as enthusiasm, understanding what people really mean (as opposed to what they say), and being "not brilliant, but wise."

He serves on the investment committee of his alma mater, Georgetown University, and is on the Board of Advisors to its University Library. He also serves on the corporate boards of MPS Group, Inc. and Worldcare, Limited. "I very much enjoy serving in that capacity and helping management achieve the goals we set for them," he says.

# You on the Job

## As a Leader

"Straightforward, fair, and decisive" describes you. Collegial and persuasive, you back it up with a "down in the trenches" management style. Breaking tension with humor keeps your staff productive.

You are realistic about problems and outcomes. To keep a negotiating process moving, you'll compromise. Projects move forward fast under your take-charge style, while you focus on bottom line results.

## As a Team Player

Having realistic expectations of people and challenges is how you operate. You make things happen, and are skilled at convincing others to participate. While you appear fun-loving, you are quietly adept at obtaining necessary resources to get things accomplished.

You may irritate others by being tardy and/or ill-prepared for meetings.

Look at Figure 11–1 on page 82 for a list of your natural work-related strengths.

## Figure 11-1    Natural Work-Related Strengths

Approximately 80 percent of these attributes will apply to you. Check off those that do and use them in your resume and interviews. This will set you apart from the canned responses of others. You:

☐ Have common sense.
☐ Bring energy and enthusiasm to projects.
☐ Can work through a broad range of people.
☐ Are easy-going and accepting.
☐ Are self-reliant.
☐ Are highly effective in negotiations and sales.
☐ Observe and recall factual information.
☐ Analyze situations quickly and find the most logical course of action.
☐ React fast in crisis or under time pressure.

### case study two

## Employee Benefits/Financial Services Attorney

Attorney Marla Kreindler is one of those rare individuals who doesn't mind working on Sundays. "With some very energetic business owners it is often the best time to catch up," she says. "It works better than having the discussion during business hours. I've got their full attention, and I have focus. Off hours are fine for me."

Marla started her career as an employee benefits lawyer. She now is a partner at Chicago-based law firm Winston & Strawn LLP, working with large corporations, assisting them in their fiduciary duties and handling the legalities of their pension investments.

She also helps firms create financial products for the retirement industry. "It's a very complicated area," she says. "To figure out new products you have to consider a wide range of legal issues, which is what I love doing. The complexity is always challenging."

As a Red, change is an important energizer for her. "Law is very fast-moving, never stagnant. There are new developments every year. You always have to be ready to deal with change. I like that about law," she says.

These characteristics also give her the ability to handle crises well. "I tend to get calmer and just do my best," she says.

She actually gets energized reading complex 90-page legal documents "when there are new and different things in them," she says.

Typical of her Color style, Marla does not feel that she is best utilizing her strengths when asked to attend routine meetings or handle matters in a rote fashion. She is happiest when producing tangible results for her clients and bringing them to the point where they trust her. "I like the fact that I have built up a vibrant practice where clients come to me with lots of interesting issues to work on and trust me with their hardest decisions."

The Red traits also come through in her private life. "I'm not one of those people who says, 'When I retire, I'll go do this.' If I want to do something, I do it now." They also explain her appreciation for life's finer things. "I always felt, if I didn't do this, I could be an art dealer. It would be fun for me to travel, find interesting pieces, and sell them."

## Ideal Work Environment

Freedom and fun define your ideal work space. Get as much of the following in Figure 11–2 as possible.

The WORST type of work culture for an Red/Blue Extrovert is one that emphasizes long-term projects. The daily tone is overly serious; humor and play are frowned upon. You will find it nearly impossible to accomplish anything in hierarchical environments full of meetings and memos.

When Extroverted Red/Blues work in nonideal corporate cultures, productivity is stunted and career achievements become an uphill climb.

## The Red/Blue Extrovert's Ideal Boss

Even a great job can be frustrating under the wrong boss; a mediocre job under a wonderful boss is pretty hard to leave. Red/Blues get along especially well with other Reds. But bosses of other Color types who possess the traits in Figure 11–3 on page 85 also can be good mentors.

**Figure 11–2   The Ideal Red/Blue
                Extrovert Work Environment**

Compare your current work environment to the description below.
Don't be deceived if these descriptions seem "obvious." It confirms you've tested your individual color correctly. Other Colors,
especially Golds, would find this environment uncomfortable and
unproductive. The optimal Red/Blue Extrovert work environment:

☐ Is relaxed, tolerant, and informal. You function best with a minimum of rules, paperwork, and supervision. You need freedom
   to move around.

☐ Provides variety, excitement, and preferably a crisis or two.
   Repetitive, expectable work brings out the worst in you. You'll
   butt heads with bureaucracy.

☐ Rewards entrepreneurial risk-taking and a direct approach.
   You are valued for your directness and ability to handle the
   unexpected. If you can work in multiple locations, you are
   happy and stimulated.

☐ Focuses on short-term problems. You need results NOW to
   feel good about what you're doing; you dislike being forced to
   think or operate long term.

☐ Permits working on tangible products with factual information.
   If you can't see it, touch it, taste it, hear it, smell it, or prove it,
   you are not interested. Spending a day brainstorming is frustrating, except for the camaraderie.

☐ Has associates who are high-energy, fun, and value practical
   experience. You are an enterprising individual who doesn't
   want to be held back.

☐ Provides public recognition. Recognition fuels you to greater
   heights of achievement.

A corporate culture integrating the above elements is fertile soil
for your career advancement.

## Careers That Attract Red/Blue Extroverts

Like Peter Tanous and Marla Kreindler, you are most attracted to careers
that provide freedom, action and the ability to be a troubleshooter.

*Please note that not all* the following careers will appeal to you, but recognize that each, in some way, draws on the strengths of your style and appeals to a significant number of your Color group. This is not a

**Figure 11-3   The Red/Blue Extrovert's Ideal Boss**

Check off if your boss:
- ☐ Is action-oriented, outgoing, and focused on end results rather than schedules and timetables.
- ☐ Gives you the goal, and then leaves you alone.
- ☐ Creates rapport through a sense of humor.
- ☐ Encourages fun in the workplace and post-work activities.

comprehensive list but will show underlying patterns of preference. If unlisted careers offer similar patterns, your chances of success increase. Copy in parentheses highlights the Color style characteristics that create success.

In addition, two codes indicate those jobs that are currently predicted to have an above-average salary and growth potential. This information is based on the continuously revised data provided by the U.S. Department of Labor and Bureau of Labor Statistics available on the O*NET website, *http://online.onetcenter.org/*.

**Bold** indicates that the career is considered to be among the top **100 best-paying jobs** based on the average or median salary paid to individuals *with five years of experience.* Excluded are jobs where salary statistics are not available, such as "business owner," or not indicative such as "actor."

*Italics* identifies the jobs that are predicted to benefit from an above average growth rate over the next several years.

***Bold and italics*** indicates jobs that will benefit from both **higher pay** and *high growth potential.*

Note there are successful people of all Color styles in all occupations. In nonideal jobs you can still shine by creating your own niche.

## Business/Finance/Management/Manufacturing

*business owners of all types* ◆ **financial securities trader** [stocks, bonds, commodities, foreign currency options] ◆ ***advertising promotion manager/sales agent*** ◆ **executive recruiter** ◆ ***financial advisor*** ◆ health/safety specialist ◆ insurance adjuster/broker/claim examiner/investigator ◆ ***investment banker*** ◆ ***marketing manager*** ◆ **industrial production manager** ◆ **risk manager** ◆ **purchasing manager**/agent ◆ sales representative ◆ ***sales manager*** ◆ **stockbroker** ◆ wholesale and retail buyer (autonomy, making fast decisions, variety, and attractive money-making potential).

## Computer/Information Technology

*programmers* ◆ *software engineer/applications* ◆ **hardware engineer** ◆ *support specialist* ◆ *information systems analyst* ◆ *security specialist* (apply technical expertise to immediate and practical problems).

## Entertainment/Media

actor/performer/dancer ◆ *business manager* ◆ *performer and artist* ◆ film/TV camera operator ◆ director stage/motion picture/TV ◆ media specialist ◆ photographer ◆ film/TV/talk show host/producer ◆ special effects technician ◆ talent director (use of creative talents in team settings).

## Health Science

clinical lab technologist ◆ paramedic ◆ *respiratory therapist* ◆ *sports medicine specialist* ◆ *surgeon* ◆ *obstetrician* ◆ *gynecologist* (focus on observing concrete details of the body and practical methods for getting well).

## Hospitality/Recreation

chef ◆ cruise director ◆ **casino/club manager** ◆ tour agent (frequent small crises requiring pragmatic response, motivation of others especially through humor).

## Investigative Work

detective/investigator ◆ insurance fraud investigator ◆ intelligence specialist, (detailed visual memory, ability to size up problems).

## Law/Elected Politics

*lawyer* [especially in criminal, election, entertainment, financial services, litigation, trial, product liability] ◆ **lobbyist** ◆ mediator ◆ negotiator ◆ politicians at all levels (flexibility, ability to persuade, adaptability to the needs of voters).

## Law Enforcement/Government

ballistics expert ◆ corrections officer ◆ FBI agent ◆ firefighter ◆ forensic science technician ◆ military officer ◆ police officer ◆ tax revenue agent (acute visual memory, need for variety).

## Real Estate

land developer ◆ property manager ◆ real estate broker (interaction with people in a fast-moving business).

## Scientific Research/Engineering/Land Related

**civil/electronic/industrial/petroleum engineer** ◆ forester ◆ landscape architect ◆ **industrial safety and health engineer** ◆ marine biologist ◆ **mining engineer** ◆ park naturalist/ranger ◆ **product safety engineer** ◆ farmer and rancher ◆ soil conservationist ◆ technical trainer (for those with technical aptitudes, the opportunity to work close to nature or with other people in a generally collegial environment).

## Sports-Related

athletes of all types ◆ *athletic coach* ◆ sports news reporter ◆ **sports promoter/agent** (generally attracted to physical activity; Red/Blues with special athletic abilities are ideally suited to making this a profession)

## Transportation

**air traffic controller** ◆ aircraft mechanic ◆ flight instructor ◆ **pilot/copilot/flight engineer** ◆ ship/boat captain (appeal to your love of excitement, variety and risk)

## Trades

carpenter ◆ general contractor (variety, eye for detail, ability to coordinate resources)

### case study three

## When a Career Isn't Working

Rick Jackson was the first child in his family to attend college. His family had high hopes that he would become a doctor, but the theoretical nature of his science classes simply didn't appeal to him. Nor did being stuck in a lab all day; Rick loved all sports and counted the minutes each day until he could get outside.

Rick compromised and became one of the first African Americans in biomedical engineering. He loved the concrete, practical nature of the field, working on real-world problems, often with immediate solutions. He still hated the theory part of his classes, but graduated near the top of his class.

He was recruited in his senior year to well-known, fast-growing firm in California. He relished the idea of adding several new sports to his repertoire.

In his first year, he found himself constantly fatigued. Long hours allowed for fewer sports to manage stress. He made his mark for handling crises well, but he had to do constant theoretical research and talk theory with other researchers. It drained him dry.

He was about to float a resume when a job opening for a biomedical community outreach person appeared on the cafeteria bulletin board. It featured lots of variety, outdoor events, people contact, and NO research. Rick went straight to Human Resources and got the job. Today, Rick not only explains his company's products but brings back ideas he then designs for new ones as well. Some of these have become major profit centers for the firm.

## Your Personality's Challenges

Red/Blue Extroverts have a unique set of potential work-related blind spots. We emphasize "potential" because no Red has all of them. Tone down a blind spot by deciding to see it, then choose more productive actions. (Suggestions for doing so are in parentheses below.) You:

- Tend to be casual about rules, procedures, and authority. (This is your number one career-derailing attribute. What makes your job easier may make someone else's much harder, and humor rarely solves that. Think about your salary review time when tempted to skip a mundane procedure.)
- Sometimes do not follow through on commitments. (If a commitment bogs you down, you may skip it. In the professional world, however, instead of appearing focused on important things, you actually look like you don't have your act together at times. Write appointments down; review them each morning; call to cancel well ahead of time.)
- Hate having tight deadlines, repetitive work, and having to work alone. (Avoid or change jobs where these are the norm. This makes you pessimistic and joyless. If unavoidable, approach your tasks as if they were all ridiculous; this will lighten your mood. So will setting yourself up in a conference room near others.)
- Don't think much beyond today. (You are present-centered; often an advantage, but sometimes not. Set long-term goals as a mental discipline.)

- Often do not prepare for a meeting or project. (The ability to "wing it" is vital in some circumstances. But being ill-prepared for meetings and projects damages credibility. Schedule at least twenty minutes for prep beforehand.)

## Your Job Search—the Good, the Bad, and the Ugly

You'd rather be out there taking action than reading this. But here are some quick, practical points to keep in mind.

Your natural strengths easily allow you to:

- Have an extensive network for job information and referrals and be adept at using it.
- Get facts on different careers/companies.
- Sell yourself well, impressing interviewers with energy and responsiveness.
- Be specific and detailed about past work and achievements.
- Respond to unforeseen opportunities without trepidation.
- Logically weigh pros and cons of job offers.

In order to tone down your blind spots, you need to:

- Force yourself to set long-term career objectives; enlist the help of friends or family, particularly Greens or Blues (to identify, read Chapter 25, Adjusting to the Styles of Others).
- Talk less, listen, and ask questions more.
- Be patient with multiple interviews and slow decision making.
- Follow through consistently with the details of a job search, such as phone calls, thank-you notes, company research; get a willing Gold to help you if possible.
- Talk over and decide what's good for you and your family.

## The Red/Blue Extrovert's Interviewing Style

With an interviewer whose Color is close to your own, you will feel immediate rapport. However, if your interviewer seems to have a significantly different style, use the suggestions in parentheses. Mercilessly exploit your natural traits, and you'll get more job offers!

In following your natural style:

- You speak with energy, excitement, charm, and humor. (You may be so energetic that you intimidate some interviewers. If yours seems to get defensive, sit back and answer the next few questions seriously to see if that puts him or her at ease.)

- ◆ You often give personal stories to make a point. (Watch to see if this is well received. If the interviewer gets antsy or breaks eye contact, cut it short.)
- ◆ You focus on the current situation and not on future or strategic issues. (Your ability to focus on the present is a valuable asset, but you may be too short when handling future-oriented questions. Answer slowly and thoughtfully. Then emphasize your talent for turning on a dime if things change.)
- ◆ You get to the point; you prefer to act rather than talk. (Ask for the job at the end of the interview, but don't rush things. Impatience will hurt you here. If your interviewer seems indecisive, take action! Offer to work a trial project or trial period.)
- ◆ You reply quickly and think on your feet. (Normally a plus; but some interviewers may want more thoughtful replies. Periodically sit back, look up at the ceiling, and pause a moment before speaking further.)
- ◆ You convince others with a sense of urgency and excitement. (Don't let your interviewer mistake your excited urgency for desperation. Try not to sit farther forward in your chair than the interviewer is sitting.)
- ◆ You make frequent jokes. (Gauge interviewer receptivity; stick with neutral subjects.)

Okay, go do something active and energizing. Later, check out Chapter 15, Blues Overall, if we've actually hooked you a little on this stuff. You can jot notes if you want to impress someone with your attention and interest in the Roadmap in Chapter 28. The Roadmap is also a great tool to aid a job search.

# CHAPTER 12

# Red/Blue Introverts

**YOU'RE NOT ONLY A RED,** you also have strong secondary characteristics of the Blue personality. And you have tested as a Color Q Introvert, which means you recharge your batteries by being alone, rather than being with others. It's likely you have little patience for this book and are just reading this to please someone. Unless we appeal to you logically and realistically, we know you'll dismiss all this material.

## You Overall

Reflective, down-to-earth, and expedient, Red/Blue Introverts are convinced only by logical reasoning. Self-starting is as natural to you as breathing.

Sharing your thoughts only happens if someone asks. Often absorbed in your own world, you prefer working independently without interruption. Being part of a small collegial team where hierarchy is secondary to getting the job done brings out your best.

You are unusually effective in times of crisis and change. Realistic and pragmatic, you trust only what you have personally observed. With your particularly acute visual memory you excel at observing details. Oriented to the concrete, here-and-now world, you have no use for long-term projects or abstract visions.

Your communication style is succinct and informal. You may appear detached to others. Networking and socializing are low on your list of enjoyable activities. Others enjoy your deadpan humor, but otherwise find you hard to read. Unorthodox approaches to problems intrigue you, which, coupled with the low visibility you prefer, may leave co-workers puzzled. It's likely you couldn't care less; you view the process of getting involved with others as a waste of time (although this characteristic mellows somewhat in the second half of your life). Other Colors are intimidated by how quickly you lose interest and stop listening when topics don't interest you. You just want the facts and respond best to practical solutions.

Though very attentive in the moment, you have a short attention span. You resist making decisions under pressure. You quickly size up problems, but like to keep all options open as long as possible, and this makes you a formidable negotiator. When ready, however, you decide with the speed of light.

You are most irritated by emotional and pompous people who moralize or get caught up in a single way of doing something. Living on the edge, seeking action and variety, is what appeals to you.

In business, you tend to avoid opportunities leading to management positions in large organizations. You'll opt to sell or purchase a franchise while turning your attention to ever-new interests. For you, rising to a position of high responsibility is most likely under crisis conditions; here your flexibility and ability to see the core of a problem make you a most effective leader.

If we've been fairly accurate so far (and we should be since this system has been tested on millions of people worldwide for six decades), give us a little more time. Read the rest of this chapter to see if it might change your life for the better.

## case study one

## Modeling School Owner

Young Charles Nemes knew early on that he was destined to work in a people-oriented industry. At age 16 he had the opportunity to work at the famous Four Seasons Restaurant in New York, "and that's where I began to learn." Reds prefer to learn from real life. He thought he was destined to open multiple restaurants and set about learning how to manage behind the scenes, even attending a hotel/restaurant school in San Francisco.

But Charles had more to offer, and today, the only restaurants he's involved with are the ones he patronizes. He found he had an unusually keen eye for acting talent and modeling-potential beauty; Reds are drawn to, and appreciate, life's finer things. Today he and his wife run a chain of Barbizon Modeling Schools in the Midwest. He is a well-respected scout for top modeling and acting agents in New York, Los Angeles, Milan, and Tokyo, plucking the freshest faces and brightest talents from among his students in nine Midwestern states. Says Charles, "It's fun to discover a young girl between 8 and 17 years old who's going to be the next superstar in terms of acting or fashion."

First, his students have to complete the curriculum, which Charles says, "in essence, is an old-fashioned finishing school where children get social graces and self-confidence. We try to make them into leaders rather than followers; into young people who can say no to drugs and other peer pressures. We are saving the lives of some of these kids; that's when I really feel best." It is typical of a Red to respond to those in crisis.

Charles's strength is being involved in all the many areas that are required to run the school from start to finish. He supports and motivates the staff, directs public relations, identifies new territories, and defines the big picture—definitely a Blue ability. "I am a multitask person," says Charles. "The most important thing for the company is for me to be involved in many areas. Then I can give a very fast and productive perspective of what's wrong in any area."

Twice a year, Charles brings about 150 of his top protégés to modeling conventions on each coast. "We set up special interviews for these high-powered agents in the modeling and acting business," he says. "It's a very stressful week, but my staff is terrific, and they prepare all these kids to be camera-ready. They would have spent tens of thousands of dollars to meet the people I'm able to introduce them to at a fraction of the cost."

Tuition at Barbizon runs about $2000. Charles is frustrated when parents automatically expect their children to be discovered and become stars. "They send their children to baseball camp or piano lessons and don't expect them to become professional athletes or concert pianists, even though they've spent five or ten thousand dollars," he says. "It's a problem we face in our industry."

# You on the Job
## As a Leader

You lead your staff through action, by example. When assessing problems, you are logical and realistic about the easiest way to complete the task. Your communication style is precise, and you engage the skills of your staff efficiently.

When others need information, you are a factual warehouse. Those facts produce creative solutions and allow you to take well-calculated risks.

## Figure 12–1    Natural Work-Related Strengths

Approximately 80 percent of these attributes will apply to you. Check off those that do and use them in your resume and interviews. This will set you apart from the canned responses of others. You:

- ☐ Bring people and tasks together in a way that inspires action.
- ☐ Are highly observant.
- ☐ Pay attention to factual information.
- ☐ Excel in assignments that are action-oriented, practical, and nonrepetitious.
- ☐ Value and promote efficiency.
- ☐ Love to overcome obstacles using a logical approach.
- ☐ Combine a no-nonsense need for facts and figures with openness to new strategies.
- ☐ Can be productive for hours when left on your own.

## As a Team Player

You find working on a team draining and inefficient. Teammates get confused and threatened when you go off and return with your own solutions and ideas.

Your natural reserve is counterbalanced by your love of action. If your team is charged with handling a crisis, you may wind up being its leader, because moving others to action is a natural skill.

Brief meetings are the only ones you tolerate. You may irritate others by not completing tasks you have deemed low priority. They may mistake your detachment for disorganization.

Look at Figure 12–1 for a list of your natural work-related strengths.

Here are some Red/Blue Introverts in action in very different fields.

case study two

## Manufacturing Executive

Stan Waring has worked in manufacturing for over four decades, and for the last two he has been Vice President of Manufacturing for his family's company, which manufactures gaskets. Currently, he oversees 700 people as Executive Advisor to the President and enjoys the ability to select his own projects. "The president says the best thing I do is crisis management," Stan says. "When it comes to day-to-day mundane tasks, I'm not real good at those." Reds typically excel at crises and hate details.

Stan finds his 24/7 manufacturing operation full of variety, which is attractive. In addition to the technical challenges, he is astute at handling the people issues, especially those involving negotiations like labor contracts. Reds are some of the most skilled negotiators of all the Colors.

Despite these accomplishments, Stan admits to having the typical Red/Blue Introvert's impatience. "One of my former accountants told me I have the attention span of a 2-year-old. There's always something happening that I'm not interested in." A classic Introvert, Stan likes to be left alone for stretches of time between crises.

## Ideal Work Environment

Your ideal work environment offers routine crises and a private office to go reflect. Use all the leverage you can when a job offer is made to get as much of the following in Figure 12–2 on page 96 as possible.

The WORST type of work culture for an Introverted Red/Blue is a strongly hierarchical one that runs on meetings and memos. It requires too much collaboration with others, especially if those others need constant reassurance.

When Introverted Red/Blues work in nonideal corporate cultures, productivity is stunted and career achievements become an uphill climb.

## The Red/Blue Introvert's Ideal Boss

Even a great job can be frustrating under the wrong boss; a mediocre job under a great boss is pretty hard to leave. Red/Blues get along especially well with other Reds. But bosses of other Color types who possess the traits in Figure 12–3 on page 97 also can be good mentors.

## Careers That Attract Red/Blue Introverts

Like Stan Waring, you are most attracted to careers that provide freedom, action, and variety. You'll often gravitate to positions where your negotiation skills are appreciated. Look for jobs that reward your key strengths—jumping in, acting immediately, and negotiating whatever it takes to get the job done.

*Please note that not all* the following careers will appeal to you, but recognize that each, in some way, draws on the strengths of your style and appeals to a significant number of your Color group. This is not a

## Figure 12–2    The Ideal Red/Blue Introvert Work Environment

Compare your current work environment to the description below. Don't be deceived if these descriptions seem "obvious." It confirms you've tested your individual color correctly. Other Colors, especially Golds, would find this environment uncomfortable and unproductive. The optimal Red/Blue Introvert work environment:

☐ Is easygoing. You function best with a minimum of rules, paperwork, and supervision.

☐ Focuses on immediate results. You need results NOW to feel good about what you're doing.

☐ Permits working on real things and tangible products. If you can't see it, touch it, taste it, hear it, or smell it, you are not interested. Spending a day brainstorming is a frustrating waste of time for you.

☐ Encourages a blunt, direct approach. Small talk and beating around the bush make you impatient. Subtlety, nuance, and emotion are for other Colors, not you.

☐ Offers opportunities to experiment.

☐ Contains variety, excitement, and openness to high-stakes gambles. A crisis or two to share with action-oriented associates is your definition of a perfect day.

☐ Allows for autonomy and private space. As an Introvert, your batteries get drained when dealing with others, even if your people skills are superb. You recharge your batteries by being alone. If you have to share your work space, you will feel a lot more fatigue at the end of the day. You think and perform better in a private space; insist on one as a condition of employment if at all possible.

A corporate culture integrating the above elements is fertile soil for your career advancement.

comprehensive list but it will show underlying patterns of preference. If unlisted careers offer similar patterns, your chances of success increase. Copy in parentheses highlights the Color style characteristics that create success.

In addition, two codes indicate those jobs that are currently predicted to have an above-average salary and growth potential. This information is based on the continuously revised data provided by the U.S. Department of

Figure 12–3    The Red/Blue Introvert's Ideal Boss

Check off if your boss:

☐ Points you in the right direction, and then leaves you alone.
☐ Shares your sense of humor.
☐ Rewards logic and is not threatened by your independent ways.
☐ Is willing to take risks.

Labor and Bureau of Labor Statistics available on the O*NET website, *http://online.onetcenter.org/*.

**Bold** indicates that the career is considered to be among the top **100 best-paying jobs** based on the average or median salary paid to individuals *with five years of experience.* Excluded are jobs where salary statistics are not available, such as "business owner," or not indicative such as "actor."

*Italics* identifies the jobs that are predicted to benefit from an above-average growth rate over the next several years.

***Bold and italics*** indicates jobs that will benefit from both **higher pay** and *high growth potential.*

Note there are successful people of all Color styles in all occupations. In nonideal jobs you can still shine by creating your own niche.

## Business/Finance/Manufacturing/Management

*entrepreneur/franchise owner* ◆ **financial securities trader** [stocks, bonds, options, commodities, foreign currency, etc.] ◆ ***financial advisor*** ◆ insurance adjuster/claim examiner ◆ negotiator ◆ **production safety engineer** ◆ purchasing agent (operate independently or with few people at a time, logical approaches and fast decision making rewarded, crises provide stimulation).

## Computer/Information Technology

**computer hardware engineer** ◆ *network systems administrator* ◆ *security specialist* ◆ ***software designer/developer*** ◆ ***software engineer*** ◆ ***systems analyst*** ◆ *support specialist* ◆ *technical trainer* (for those with technical aptitudes, the opportunity to work with factual material coupled with spurts of action).

## Entertainment/Media

*audiovisual specialist* ◆ ***agent/business manager of performers and special events*** ◆ film/TV camera operator ◆ photographer ◆ special effects technician ◆ *sound engineering technician* ◆ stage manager (appeal to your need for excitement, freedom, use of technical expertise, and unorthodox approaches).

## Health Science

*anesthesiologist* ◆ *cardiovascular technologist* ◆ *clinical laboratory technologist* ◆ *dental hygienist* ◆ **emergency room physician**/technician ◆ *paramedic* ◆ *radiologic technician* ◆ sports medicine specialist ◆ *surgical technologist* (hands-on activities with sensitive equipment, observing concrete details of the body, and using technical expertise, quick-response situations).

## Hospitality/Recreation

**bar/club owner/manager** ◆ chef ◆ restaurant owner/manager (frequent crises and pressure, need to jump in and act immediately).

## Investigative Work

detective ◆ forensic technician ◆ insurance fraud investigator/adjuster ◆ intelligence agent/specialist (allows independent operation, working alone for long periods).

## Law/Law Enforcement/Government

*ballistics expert* ◆ corrections officer ◆ *criminal investigator* ◆ firefighter ◆ fire inspector ◆ fire prevention specialist ◆ *lawyer* [criminal, energy, litigation, real estate, transportation] ◆ mediator ◆ military officer/special forces ◆ police officer (acute visual memory for details, logical approach to problems, action, and variety).

## Nature-Related

agricultural inspector ◆ farmer ◆ forester ◆ landscape architect ◆ marine biologist ◆ park naturalist ◆ rancher ◆ soil conservationist ◆ surveyor (love of the outdoors and physical activity, ability to work for long periods alone productively, dealing with problems flexibly and expediently).

## Scientific Research/Engineering

**engineer** [civil, electrical, environmental, industrial, health, product safety] (for those with technical aptitudes, the opportunity for hands-on applications).

## Sports Related

athletes of all types ◆ *athletic coach* ◆ **business manager of athletes** (keen awareness of physical nuances, quick ability to respond and negotiate).

## Transportation

**air traffic controller** ◆ aircraft mechanic ◆ flight instructor ◆ **pilot/flight engineer** ◆ racecar driver ◆ ship captain (appeal to your love of excitement and risk).

## Other

carpenter ◆ electrician ◆ general contractor ◆ plumber (need for flexibility, cool under crisis, getting things done expediently).

<hr>

*case study three*

## When a Career Isn't Working

Hector Torres always knew he would one day manage his family's upscale Spanish restaurant. He really enjoyed working there as a teenager, sampling the fine foods on the menu. Reds appreciate good food and fine wine more than most other Colors. Hector enjoyed the pressure and crises, and his social life came to him—an excellent situation for an Introvert who is drained by parties. "Any job where I can move around as much as I do here—that's for me," he always said.

Hector attended the Culinary Institute of America after high school, paying particular attention to restaurant management. He was surprised to find some of it quite boring—inventory control and nightly account balancing in particular. But Hector's mind was set, and upon graduating, his parents retired and he took over the restaurant, eager to implement some new ideas.

He found he had less skill at dealing with employee schedules and temperaments than his parents, causing Hector constant irritation. Several long-time waiters quit, and the small crises Hector enjoyed became big ones he did not. Inventory and account balancing became daily realities. His relationship with his fiancée became strained when he asked to postpone the wedding until he got the restaurant under control.

It all came to a head the day the restaurant was robbed. The police came, but all they could determine was that it was an inside job. Impatient with their progress, Hector undertook his own internal investigation. Within 48 hours he'd identified the culprit and gotten a fair amount of money back. Hector hadn't been this energized since he took over the restaurant.

He went back to school and became a private detective. Today, he is married and has his own investigative agency specializing in restaurant incidents. One of his siblings took over the restaurant, the old waiters returned, and it is thriving.

## Your Personality's Challenges

Red/Blue Introverts have a unique set of potential work-related blind spots. We emphasize "potential" because no Red/Blue has them all. Tone down a blind spot by deciding to see it, then choose more productive actions. (Suggestions for doing so are in parentheses below.) You:

◆ Tend to be casual with rules and procedures valued by others, including meeting deadlines. (This is your number one career-derailing attribute. What makes your job easier may make someone else's much harder, and deadpan humor rarely solves that. Think about salary review time when tempted to push a deadline.)

◆ Sometimes step on the feelings of associates. (Getting involved with people is not a priority for you; being expedient is. Hurt feelings hinder results. It is expedient to pay attention to the feelings of other Colors.)

◆ Hate not having control of your own schedule and being under tight deadlines. (This makes you cynical and frivolous. Give serious consideration to leaving any job in which these are a frequent occurrence.)

◆ May wing things that require preparation. (This undermines your credibility. People will dismiss your special qualities and contributions if they are inconvenienced by your loose approach to areas that are important to them.)

## Your Job Search—the Good, the Bad, and the Ugly

You'd rather be out there hitting the pavement than reading this. But hang in there; you're almost done. You'll benefit from these concrete job search tips:
Your natural strengths easily allow you to:

◆ Respond quickly and decisively to unforeseen opportunities.
◆ Be specific and precise in your interview about past positions and achievements.
◆ Make good career contacts through your love of adventurous hobbies.
◆ Negotiate the terms of a new job well.

In order to tone down your blind spots, you need to:

◆ Force yourself to set long-term goals; enlist the help of friends or family, particularly Golds or Blues (to identify, read Chapter 25, Adjusting to the Styles of Others).

◆ Prepare ahead for emotional, rapport-building questions; practice role-playing with a Green.

◆ Follow through on commitments, deadlines, and the nitty-gritty tasks of a job search such as keeping lists of contacts and sending thank you notes. Enlist the aid of a willing Gold to help.

- ◆ Discipline yourself to think about how a job offer will affect you and your family in the future, not just this month or this year.
- ◆ Be aggressive about soliciting referrals and leads from acquaintances and strangers. Your preferred circle of friends is small.

## The Red/Blue Introvert's Interviewing Style

With an interviewer whose Color is close to your own, you will feel immediate rapport. However, if your interviewer seems to have a significantly different style, use the suggestions in parentheses. Exploit mercilessly these natural traits of yours, and you'll get more job offers!

In following your natural style you:

- ◆ Are concrete and realistic about past responsibilities and accomplishments. (Some interviewers will dig for feelings: "Did you like your previous boss? How did you get along with your co-workers?" Ask a Green to help role play such questions ahead of time.)
- ◆ Avoid sharing personal information. (Keeping your distance will make you look as if you have something to hide. Take a moment if needed, then be honest.)
- ◆ Answer questions succinctly and informally. (Some interviewers look for more formal responses. If there's a pause and the interviewer seems to be waiting for something more, expand your answer with more facts. Your quick thinking should make this easy.)
- ◆ Listen only when your interest is engaged. (Grit your teeth and listen to EVERYTHING your interviewer says, no matter how irrelevant. Patience is a virtue in a job interview.)
- ◆ Use deadpan humor. (This works with people who know you well, but for those who don't know you, it can create social awkwardness. If a joke falls flat in an interview, quickly smile and say, "Just kidding.")
- ◆ Focus on the company's current situation and not on future or strategic issues. (Your ability to focus on the present is a valuable asset, but you may be too short when handling future-oriented questions. Answer slowly and thoughtfully. Then emphasize your talent for turning on a dime if things change.)

Congratulations for making it all the way through this chapter! Most Reds won't. Reward yourself by doing something active now. Later, check out Chapter 15, Blues Overall, if we've actually hooked you a little on this stuff. You can jot notes if you want to impress someone with your attention and interest in the Roadmap in Chapter 28. This is also a good place to record the information you pick up when networking during a job search.

# CHAPTER 13

# Red/Green Extroverts

**YOU'RE NOT ONLY A RED,** you also have strong secondary characteristics of the Green personality. And you have tested as a Color Q Extrovert, which means you recharge your batteries by being with people, rather than being alone. It's likely you have little patience for this book and are just reading this to please someone. So we'll make this realistic and fun, or we know you're out of here!

## You Overall

Warm and energetic, Red/Green Extroverts have wide interests and many friends. You are active, sociable, and adaptable. In entrepreneurial startups or corporate crises, you shine.

Realistic and pragmatic, you trust only what you have personally observed. With a particularly acute visual memory you excel at observing details. Yet you are easy-going, fun-loving, and enjoy the unexpected.

Of all the Colors, you are most in touch with the present moment. Because you are driven to achieve results NOW, you have low tolerance for procedure and routine. Bossy people who insist on having things done "the right way" annoy you mightily. Otherwise, you have an accepting, "live and let live" attitude.

Others see you as exuberant, entertaining, and generous; they feel positive and enthused when you are around. Networking comes naturally to you.

Straightforward communication is your style. You want the facts, but enjoy an anecdote or two (particularly a humorous one). Though very attentive in the moment, your attention span is short. Making decisions under pressure is not for you; instead, you keep all options open as long as possible. When ready, however, you decide with the speed of light.

## case study one

## Entrepreneur, Restaurant, and Mail Order Businesses

Gregory B. Bidou didn't think racing motorcycles as a teenager would ever lead to a career. So he went to college and became an environmental engineer and industrial hygienist. But for thirty years this Red/Green Extrovert was dissatisfied because, "Even if I did my job perfectly—in terms of lives saved and illnesses prevented—it wouldn't be recognized statistically for decades."

So in his spare time, Greg sold parts for vintage British motorcycles. He enjoyed the immediate rewards of refurbishing rusty parts and diagnosing mechanical problems with customers.

Within two years this side business outgrew his garage. Greg had to rent expensive warehouse space, some not secure from theft, for his rapidly growing inventory.

Greg enjoyed meeting these concrete challenges. One Sunday, deep in the countryside, he found a vacant, neglected coffee shop with an apartment above and two barns on the property. By Monday evening, he had purchased it, not even sure what he was going to do with the storefront, but encouraged by the positive response of town hall authorities.

He sold his house for a good price, allowing him to pay cash for his new property and have funds left over to renovate. Members of his new community kept asking him, "Are you going to reopen the coffee shop?" Despite having no restaurant experience, he jumped in. It took a year for him to rebuild the little café essentially by himself.

His business plan became to sell motorcycle parts one-half of the week and operate a biker-friendly café the other half; both businesses helping to build each other.

His previous industrial hygiene career allowed him to deal with stimulating crisis situations. But Greg says, "What drove me nuts was babysitting programs once I had implemented them." Red/Green Extroverts like startups, but find ongoing administration repetitive and stifling.

He was frustrated that he couldn't see results of his work; present-centered Red/Green Extroverts need immediate results. "In the café, I make a dish. Right away customers can tell me if they like it." However, Greg does get frustrated by making the same dishes time and again.

The motorcycle parts business offers constant change and challenge. "No two customers are alike, and no two bikes are alike," Greg says with satisfaction. "I really like diagnosing motorcycle problems over the phone and providing the parts to solve them."

He even likes coping with the heart-stopping cash flow problems new business owners can face. "I see it all as risk management. I've had to sacrifice compared to my old corporate income days, but so far no creditors have come knocking on my door."

Today, Greg's café has been very successful—enough for mention in the *New York Times*. His motorcycle parts business picks up the slack in the winter when café traffic declines, and he lives a modest but much happier life.

## You on the Job

### As a Leader

"Quick"—that's you. You have a fast "down in the trenches" management style, breaking pressured moments with humor. Collegiality is preferred over power plays.

Risk and change do not worry you, because you are realistic about problems and outcomes. Creative solutions that lack a track record intrigue, rather than frighten, you.

### As a Team Player

Realistic and grounded, you make things happen—your enthusiasm inspires everyone to participate. Your image is fun-loving, although you are adept at finding the necessary resources to get things accomplished.

You may irritate others by placing too much focus on fun or the adrenalin rush.

Look at Figure 13–1 for a list of your natural work-related strengths.

Now see how another Red/Green Extrovert uses her strengths in a very different field.

## Figure 13-1   Natural Work-Related Strengths

Approximately 80 percent of these attributes will apply to you. Check off those that do and use them in your resume and interviews. This will set you apart from the canned responses of others. You:

☐ Are realistic about what needs to be done.
☐ Notice and remember factual information.
☐ Can keep several balls in the air at once.
☐ React quickly in crisis or under time pressure.
☐ Bring energy and optimism to projects.
☐ Enjoy collaborating with others.
☐ Are highly effective in negotiations and sales.

case study two

# Veterinarian

Lilliana Goldberg is a veterinarian who owns her own practice in rural Connecticut. At her offices, she oversees three other animal doctors and a support staff of six. In this, she is departing from her Color; typically, Red/Greens prefer flying solo over managing others. But her staff is largely independent and know their jobs well enough not to need much supervision.

Lilliana sees many dogs and cats each week, but she particularly loves her large animal practice. She looks forward to the days when she climbs into her mobile veterinary clinic and makes the rounds of local farms. She loves the freedom and movement of the mobile clinic, as well as working out in the open with cows, horses, pigs, and sheep. The problem-solving challenges she faces at the nearby farms keep her energized and stimulated.

Lilliana often answers emergency calls in the wee hours of the morning from farmers whose animals are having difficulty delivering their colts or calves. During the winter, she has been known to navigate over unplowed back roads in blizzards to help farmers save the animals that support their livelihoods. This is her Red crisis-loving side, and her Green side is happy to help the people who are her neighbors. As an Extrovert, she enjoys the recognition she receives in her small, but appreciative, community.

Reds are very grounded in their own bodies and in the concrete realities of medical care fields. Reds have a special affinity with animals, and their empathy makes them natural veterinarians. Reds also need crises to stay stimulated and involved, and vet work provides these on a daily basis. Reds require physical freedom, and while many vets work only in their offices, Lilliana has the advantage of working in a community where her mobile veterinary clinic is needed and makes economic sense.

## Ideal Work Environment

Greg Bidou's motorcycle business and café both permit working on tangible products that focus on short-term problems—perfect for a Red/Green Extrovert. Red/Green Extroverts also like to operate by their own rules and need very flexible environments, like Lilliana Goldberg.

When a job offer is made, leverage as much as you can from the list in Figure 13–2.

The WORST type of work culture for an Extroverted Red/Green is one that emphasizes long-term projects. Humor and play are frowned upon, and the daily tone is serious. You will find it near impossible to accomplish anything in environments that are hierarchical with many meetings and memos.

When Red/Green Extroverts work in nonideal corporate cultures, productivity is stunted and career achievements become an uphill climb.

## The Red/Green Extrovert's Ideal Boss

Even a great job can be frustrating under the wrong boss; a mediocre job under a wonderful boss is pretty hard to leave. Red/Greens get along especially well with other Reds. But bosses of other Color types who possess the characteristics in Figure 13–3 on page 108 can also be good mentors.

## Careers That Attract Red/Green Extroverts

Like Greg Bidou and Lilliana Goldberg, you are most attracted to careers that provide freedom, action, and the ability to be a troubleshooter.

*Please note that not all* the following careers will appeal to you, but recognize that each, in some way, draws on the strengths of your style and ap-

## Figure 13-2   The Ideal Red/Green Extrovert Work Environment

Compare your current work environment to the descriptions below. Don't be deceived if these seem "obvious." It confirms you've tested your individual color correctly. Other Colors, especially Golds, would find this environment uncomfortable and unproductive. The optimal Red/Green Extrovert work environment:

☐ Is relaxed, tolerant, and informal. You function best with a minimum of rules, paperwork, and supervision.

☐ Provides variety, excitement, and preferably a crisis or two. Repetitive, routine work brings out the worst in you.

☐ Rewards those who move at a fast pace and solve problems. You enjoy the adrenaline rushes that drive other Colors crazy.

☐ Gives opportunities to use troubleshooting skills. Your ability to work fast under pressure makes you the one for projects or departments in chaos.

☐ Focuses on short-term problems. You need results NOW to feel good about what you're doing.

☐ Permits working on real things and tangible products. If you can't see it, touch it, taste it, hear it, or smell it, you are not interested. A day of brainstorming feels like a waste to you, except for the camaraderie.

☐ Is aesthetically appealing and colorful. More than most Colors, unattractive surroundings will distract and irritate you, detracting from productivity. You appreciate the world's finer things, and they inspire you at work.

☐ Has associates who are lively and action-oriented. Energetic people stimulate your productivity.

☐ Factors in needs of both customers and staff. You'll burn out in workplaces that disregard human needs, squeezing every nickel out of each transaction and worker.

A corporate culture integrating the above elements is fertile soil for your career advancement.

**Figure 13-3    The Red/Green Extrovert's Ideal Boss**

Check off if your boss:
☐ Is pragmatic.
☐ Points you in the right direction, and then leaves you alone.
☐ Creates rapport through a sense of humor.
☐ Encourages fun in the workplace.

peals to a significant number of your Color group. This is not a comprehensive list, but it will show underlying patterns of preference. If unlisted careers offer similar patterns, your chances of success increase. Copy in parentheses highlights the Color style characteristics that create success.

In addition, two codes indicate those jobs that are currently predicted to have an above-average salary and growth potential. This information is based on the continuously revised data provided by the U.S. Department of Labor and Bureau of Labor Statistics available on the O*NET website, *http://online.onetcenter.org/.*

**Bold** indicates that the career is considered to be among the top **100 best-paying jobs** based on the average or median salary paid to individuals *with five years of experience.* Excluded are jobs where salary statistics are not available, such as "business owner," or not indicative such as "actor."

*Italics* identifies the jobs that are predicted to benefit from an above-average growth rate over the next several years.

***Bold and italics*** indicates jobs that will benefit from both **higher pay** and *high growth potential.*

Note there are successful people of all Color styles in all occupations. In nonideal jobs you can still shine by creating your own niche.

## Arts/Design/Entertainment/Media

artist [painter, sculptor, illustrator] ◆ art director ◆ actor/performer ◆ *audiovisual specialist* ◆ broadcaster ◆ *costume/wardrobe/set design* ◆ craftsperson/artisan ◆ dancer ◆ *entertainment agent* [actor/performer] ◆ camera operator ◆ fashion designer ◆ photographer ◆ film/TV/stage producer ◆ radio/TV talk show host ◆ special effects technician ◆ stage manager ◆ talent director ◆ tour guide/organizer (allow the use of artistic talents to produce concrete and usable products).

## Animal Care

animal breeder/groomer/trainer ◆ pet store owner ◆ *veterinarian* ◆ *veterinary technician* ◆ **zoologist** (tap into sensitivity to animals and their physical and emotional needs).

## Business/Finance/Law

small business owner ◆ corporate trainer ◆ diversity manager ◆ *financial advisor* ◆ *financial securities trader* [stocks, bonds, commodities] ◆ insurance agent/broker/claim investigator ◆ *lawyer* [real estate, litigation, poverty] ◆ manufacturer's representative ◆ *marketing specialist* ◆ mediator ◆ special event planner ◆ merchandise planner ◆ *public relations specialist* ◆ retail merchandiser ◆ salesperson ◆ *sales manager* (draw on strong communications and selling skills).

## Computer/Information Technology

*computer game programmer* ◆ *software engineer* ◆ *support specialist* (ability to combine design and technical skills with other people in a generally collegial environment).

## Education/Human Services

child care worker ◆ *community service manager* ◆ *child/family counselor* ◆ fundraiser ◆ *instructional coordinator* ◆ *public health instructor* ◆ teacher [lower grades, special education, music, drama, and art] (enjoy counseling or teaching and have rapport-building skills).

## Emergency Services/Government

crisis center worker ◆ firefighter ◆ paramedic ◆ police officer (variety, change, and need for quick response in high-stress situations).

## Health Science

*chiropractor* ◆ **dentist** ◆ *dental assistant/hygienist* ◆ dietitian ◆ *elderly home care* ◆ *hospice nurse* ◆ massage therapist ◆ lab technician ◆ *nurse* [especially emergency room] ◆ *obstetrician/gynecologist* ◆ *pediatrician* ◆ personal fitness trainer ◆ *physical* [*occupational*/recreational therapist] ◆ *primary care physician* ◆ *radiologic technician* ◆ *respiratory therapist* ◆ *speech pathologist substance abuse counselor* (observing concrete details of the body and practical methods for getting well; helping the sick deal with uncomfortable and frightening situations).

## Hospitality/Recreation/Hotel

chef/food service manager ◆ **casino manager** ◆ cruise director ◆ lodging owner/manager ◆ restaurant host/hostess ◆ tour agent (frequent small crises requiring pragmatic response, motivation of others especially through humor).

## Politics, Elected

politicians at all levels (requires flexibility, ability to persuade, adaptability to the needs of voters).

## Real Estate

land developer ◆ property manager ◆ real estate broker ◆ real estate lawyer (allows interaction with people in a fast-moving business).

## Sports-Related

athletes of all types ◆ *athletic coach* (attracted to physical activity; those with special athletic abilities are ideally suited to making sports a profession).

## Transportation

**air traffic controller** ◆ flight attendant/instructor ◆ **pilot/copilot** (appeal to your love of excitement, movement, variety, and risk).

## Other

cosmetologist ◆ farmer ◆ rancher ◆ hairdresser ◆ landscape gardener.

---

### case study three

# When a Career Isn't Working

Bill Lloyd was a born salesman. In his freshman year at university, he saw how much money college textbooks cost and was more excited by that than the engineering major his dad wanted him to pursue. Why go to college, Bill figured, when he could read all the texts and get paid for it? His parents disowned him when he quit to work at a major college textbook publisher.

Starting at the bottom selling the most esoteric titles, Bill quickly became a star salesman. Within three years he was the firm's number one sales producer. That's when the trouble began.

Bill was promoted to sales manager, overseeing twenty-five people selling nationwide. He had to read not just his titles, but all of them, and he hated it. His shoot-from-the-hip style was no longer needed. Instead, he had to think strategically about what professors wanted, a task foreign to here-and-now Red/Green Extroverts. He had much less interaction with people, which made him restless. He started to daydream about the days when he was flying solo around the country, attending conventions and scoring huge sales coups.

At a meeting of top managers at the end of a stellar year, Bill's boss half-kiddingly bemoaned the lack of Porsche franchises in their area. The other managers laughed; Bill started thinking. He contacted Porsche and convinced them to sell him an area franchise, citing his track record with the firm.

Today, Bill owns a Porsche franchise, belongs to the local country club, and has reconciled with his parents. His Red personality gets a kick every morning he walks into his upscale showroom. He oversees only two salespeople and handles a number of clients himself. He finds customers at the country club before they find him. He gets all the business he can handle with the line, "When you're ready for your Porsche, here's my card." He loves his work.

## Your Personality's Challenges

Red/Green Extroverts have a unique set of potential work-related blind spots. Some you have, others you won't. Tone down a blind spot by focusing on it, then choose more productive actions and make them habits. (Suggestions for doing so are in parentheses below.) You:

- Tend to be casual about rules, procedures, and authority. (This is your number one career-derailing attribute. Your superiors may need rules and procedures to control their own job anxieties. Would that make you respond with more respect and compassion? Try it and see how your boss reacts.)
- Have difficulty planning ahead and sometimes do not follow through on commitments. (If a commitment bogs you down, you may skip it. You hate red tape, including making phone calls to cancel appointments. In the professional world, it can look like you don't have your act together at times. Write down commitments, call ahead of time to cancel.)
- Hate having tight deadlines, repetitive work, and working alone. (Reject or change jobs like this; they make you pessimistic and joy-

less. When deadlines or repetitive tasks cannot be avoided, pretend they are all ridiculous; this will lighten your mood. If possible, set yourself up in a conference room to be near others.)

◆ Get frustrated in overly serious environments where humor is not respected. (You withdraw and become moody. If exposed to such environments for too long and put under extreme stress, you may have violent, even abusive, outbursts.)

## Your Job Search—the Good, the Bad, and the Ugly

You Red/Green Extroverts would rather be out there taking action than reading this. But hang in there; we're almost done. You'll benefit from these job search tricks.

Your natural strengths easily allow you to:

◆ Have an extensive network for job information and referrals.
◆ Establish a warm relationship with interviewers who allow it.
◆ Sell yourself well.

In order to tone down your blind spots, you need to:

◆ Force yourself to set long-term career objectives; enlist the help of friends or family, particularly Golds (to identify, read Chapter 4, A Tour of the Prism Company).
◆ Consider the long-term potential of a job, for you AND your family, before accepting.
◆ Take a hard look at the possible downside before jumping into a job.
◆ Develop a thicker skin and don't take rejections personally.
◆ Consistently follow through with details like phone calls, thank you notes, company research; get a willing Gold to help if possible.

## The Red/Green Extrovert's Interviewing Style

With an interviewer whose Color is close to your own, you will feel immediate rapport. However, if your interviewer seems to have a significantly different style, use the suggestions in parentheses. Mercilessly exploit these natural abilities of yours, and get more job offers!

In following your natural style, you:

◆ Speak with tact, excitement, charm, and humor. (You may be so immediately charming that you will intimidate some interviewers. If yours does not warm up, answer a few questions in a serious tone; see if that puts him or her more at ease.)

◆ Develop a rapport with people. (With an interviewer who seems distant, stick to the facts. Let him or her set the tone for any personal exchanges.)

◆ Are concrete and realistic about past responsibilities and accomplishments. (Some interviewers will dig for feelings: "Did you like your previous boss? How did you get along with your co-workers?" Ask a Green to help role play such questions ahead of time.)

◆ Focus on the current situation and not on future or strategic issues. (Your ability to focus on the present is a valuable asset, but your answer may be too short when handling future-oriented questions. Answer slowly and thoughtfully. Then emphasize your talent for turning on a dime if things change.)

◆ Get to the point; you prefer to act rather than talk. (Ask for the job at the end of the interview, but don't rush things. Impatience will hurt you here. If your interviewer seems indecisive, take action! Offer to work a trial project or period.)

◆ Reply quickly and think on your feet. (Normally a plus, but some interviewers may want more thoughtful replies. If so, sit back, look at the ceiling, and pause, even if you know what you want to say.)

Okay, go do something exciting now. Later, skim Chapter 5, Greens Overall, if we've actually gotten you a little hooked on this stuff. You can jot notes if you want to impress someone with your diligence in the Roadmap in Chapter 28. The Roadmap is an excellent place to keep networking notes during a job search.

# CHAPTER 14

# Red/Green Introverts

**YOU'RE NOT ONLY A RED,** you also have strong secondary characteristics of the Green personality. And you have tested as a Color Q Introvert, which means you recharge your batteries by being alone, rather than being with others. It's likely you have little patience for this book and are just reading this to please someone. So we'll keep it pragmatic.

## You Overall

Warm and attentive, Red/Green Introverts have an unusual sensitivity to both people and animals. A low need to lead or control, but a great desire to encourage others, is your style. Small collegial teams where hierarchy is secondary to getting the job done efficiently bring out the best in you. Where possible, you like to operate outside norms and rules followed by others.

Realistic and pragmatic, you trust only what you have personally observed. You have a particularly acute visual memory.

Your communication style is straightforward. You want the facts, but enjoy an anecdote or two (particularly a humorous one). You are easygoing, fun-loving, and enjoy the unexpected. Though very attentive in the moment, you have a short attention span.

You resist making decisions under pressure, keeping all options open as long as possible. When ready, however, you decide with the speed of light.

Others see you as speaking clearly without hidden agendas. They experience you as calm, modest, and cheerful. Although you are very tolerant of most folks, you get annoyed by bossy people who insist on having things done "the right way."

## case study one

# Internal Coach, Financial Services

Ever wonder why people think working at a huge Wall Street firm is the pinnacle of their careers? It's because they have someone like Joyce Jenkins behind the scenes coaching them on how to make all the right behavioral moves. Joyce is a First Vice President at New York-based Citigroup Corporate and Investment Banking CIB. It's her job to coach many of their internal managers on an individual basis in the leadership programs that she facilitates. She also runs a number of leadership programs a year for Citigroup CIB employees (vice president level and above) and manages the hiring and use of outside consultants.

It's a very visible job for an Introvert, but Joyce loves it. Her most energizing days are spent in one-on-one coaching "because I can make the biggest difference, and I can get into the person," she says. This is a high priority for Red/Green Introverts. What drags her down is also typical of her Color—back office reporting, negotiating with outside consultants, and navigating the landmines of office politics.

Delivering keynote addresses both inside and outside her organization may not seem attractive to an Introvert, but Joyce has made it a comfort zone. "I am in charge on the platform; I can control the situation, which makes me feel secure," she says. "Also, I am passionate about my subject matter."

She presents on how to optimize your career, doing things like partnering with your boss. One tip: "Ask your boss, 'What keeps you up at night?' and then offer to help with that." Her definition of success? "For me, it is when others succeed because of something I said."

Her top strengths are classic Red/Green—compassion, hearing what is not being said, and doing realistic assessments of situations. She is a skilled and active listener. "People wind up saying things they never intended to," she says. She knows how to pay attention to what she calls "the funniest of details," such as a quick wrinkle on someone's face or a new hairstyle.

From these she gauges honest concerns, not just what others want her to see.

As to her future, two things intrigue her right now and both involve greater participation in religious activities. "I'd like to go back to school to get a master's in clinical psychology to counsel within the framework of my church," she says, "or I may want to study to be a minister." Both would be fulfilling Red/Green choices.

# You on the Job

## As a Leader

You lead your staff by example. Hierarchical power structures and ruling others with an iron fist are not your way.

Realistic about problems and outcomes, you prefer collegiality to conquest. Your first impulse is to break tension with humor. You'll find other Colors require more structure than you do.

## As a Team Player

You have common sense and a knack for getting others to focus. They trust you—you really do want to accomplish the task at hand without playing political games. You provide a role model for your teammates.

### Figure 14–1    Natural Work-Related Strengths

Approximately 80 percent of these attributes will apply to you. Check off those that do and use them in your resume and interviews. This will set you apart from the canned responses of others. You:

☐ Like to initiate and implement change.

☐ Bring people and tasks together in a cooperative style.

☐ Provide supportive feedback to others.

☐ Excel in assignments that are action-oriented, practical, and nonrepetitious.

☐ Love to overcome obstacles using a tactical approach.

☐ Bring creativity and well-developed aesthetics to your work.

☐ Have a strong customer service attitude, no matter what level of job you have.

☐ Are most productive when left on your own.

All ideas floated by team members get a hearing before you begin drilling down to the final decision. You are most likely to irritate other teammates by being overly sensitive to people who disagree with you.

Look at Figure 14–1 for a list of your natural work-related strengths.

## case study two

## Upper Management, Utility Field

Christopher L. Dutton has been President and Chief Executive Officer of Green Mountain Power Corporation in Colchester, Vermont, since 1997. Previously, he had been its General Counsel, Chief Financial Officer, Treasurer, and Vice President.

Chris, now 56, started his career as a trial lawyer. He liked the work, he says, "because each case was different." Red/Green Introverts crave challenge and nonrepetitious work, especially if they can be involved on a personal level. Thus well-suited to trial law, Chris spent the first decade of his career trying cases.

Today, he says, "I spend 45 percent of my time focusing on the policy issues that confront us because we are a regulated utility company. I have to be externally oriented; every decision we make affects the kind of power we buy or the generating facilities that we build."

He is constantly dealing with politics. Five months after taking the helm, a public service commission made a decision "that put us in extreme financial peril," Chris recounts. While Red/Green Introverts enjoy surprises and challenges, this stretched Chris to his professional limits. His solution? "We figured out how to convince the regulators to change their minds in a face-saving way without admitting they made a mistake." Red/Green Introverts are keen observers of human nature; this talent kept Chris's organization viable.

Another 40 percent of Chris's time "I spend on Board relations, as well as dealing with the financial community, investors, and ratings agencies." The Red/Green Introvert's tendency to listen to all sides before making a decision helps Chris here.

He offloads the detail work (an irritant to Red/Green Introverts) to his Chief Operating Officer (COO) Mary Powell. "I recognize she has strengths I don't."

How does Chris create the egalitarian workplace he prefers? During their early crisis days, Chris led the decision to sell their lavish offices and move into their service center, where their line and bucket trucks were. "We wanted everybody on the same floor; we wanted no private offices, just low partitions where necessary. We wanted all employees to have the same amount of office space so there could be no hidden agendas."

Today, Chris and COO Mary Powell are physically visible to 90 of their 195 employees.  "If I get a call about a sensitive matter, I'll call back later," Chris says.

Answering to so many entities, Chris knows obstacles are a recurring part of the job. But these are stimulating rather than stifling to him. Red/Green Introverts are tactical, practical, and enjoy solving concrete problems.

They also value and welcome change, which gives Chris an edge in his role as CEO. So does his Red/Green flexibility and customer service orientation.

Their open floor plan is ideal for helping Chris keep his finger on the pulse of his organization. Red/Green Introverts thrive when they can focus on the human side of things. As an Introvert, however, he expends extra energy coping with the resulting lack of privacy.

Chris's job makes ample use of his inborn Red/Green preferences. He doesn't have to try to be a success in this position; instead his natural instincts provide the right response.

case study three

## Innkeeper

Bud Murdock owns a cozy, 20-room inn called Ocean House in Port Clyde, Maine (population 200). He is the kind of innkeeper who takes a personal interest in his guests and remembers them over the years. The rugged coast of Maine and the remoteness of Port Clyde appeal to Bud, his core of regulars, and celebrities alike. On any given night artists may share a common wall with Supreme Court justices.

Bud has a quiet smile and is an intent listener. He has run Ocean House for twenty-two years and loves it. But it was never his life's ambition.

"I had no intention of buying an inn," Bud recalls. "After my divorce I had lost both my job and my house. A guy called and offered it to me, knowing it was a way to be closer to my kids who live on an island nearby. So I looked at it, said, 'Whoa! This is a pretty good deal. It would give me a place to live, and it would give me a job.' I had enough money to buy the place mortgage free. So I did." Red/Greens respond well to unexpected opportunities.

True to his Color, Bud loves the flexibility of owning an inn. He enjoys the variety of people he meets. (As an Introvert it gives him the advantage of having his social life come to him.) He posts no guest rules. "You don't make policy because one person does something upsetting," he says. Reds dislike policy in any case.

"The stressful part of running an inn is the things you have no control over, like electric power," Bud says. He is twenty miles from any major center of services; Port Clyde has an antiquated water system and no police department. But a true Red, Bud takes crises as they come. "I am the chairman of the water department here because I am the biggest user," he says.

Bud's top work-related strength is delegating, which he mainly exercises overseeing his housekeeping staff.

Most people find his life romantic. Bud is quick to dispel the myth in down-to-earth, practical Red fashion. "The main reason people fail as innkeepers is they are not realistic. They overromanticize it. There is nothing romantic about being an innkeeper. But I do like coastal life; I like looking at the ocean. It's a different scene every day."

## Ideal Work Environment

Beautiful, private and relaxed . . . who wouldn't want to work in a place like Bud Murdock's? Actually, some Colors are uncomfortable in relaxed, informal settings. Extroverts opt for bullpens or open cubicles. But for you, it's the most productive way to go.

Use all the leverage you can when a job offer is made to get as much from Figure 14–2 as possible.

The WORST type of work culture for an Red/Green Introvert is one where you are micromanaged on tight deadline projects that emphasize long-term strategic thinking. The daily tone is overly serious, and humor is

## Figure 14–2    The Ideal Red/Green Introvert Work Environment

Compare your current work environment to the description below. Don't be deceived if these descriptions seem "obvious." It confirms you've tested your individual Color correctly. Other Colors, especially Golds, would find this environment uncomfortable and unproductive. The optimal Red/Green Introvert work environment:

☐ Is relaxed and informal. You function best with a minimum of rules, paperwork, and supervision.

☐ Is supportive and harmonious. Backstabbing, confrontation, and malicious gossip really irritate and distract you from the task at hand.

☐ Permits making an immediate contribution. You need real results with tangible products NOW, and chafe doing grunt work in your early career years. Brainstorming feels like a waste of time to you.

☐ Is aesthetically appealing. More than most Colors, unattractive surroundings will distract and irritate you, detracting from productivity. While declining a job on the basis of ugly offices might sound frivolous, for you it is a genuine matter of mental health.

☐ Allows for private space. As an Introvert, your batteries get drained when dealing with people, even if your people skills are superb. You recharge your batteries by being alone. If you have to share your work space with others, you will feel a lot more fatigue at the end of the day. You think and perform better in a private space; insist on one as a condition of employment if at all possible.

A corporate culture integrating the above elements is fertile soil for your career advancement.

frowned upon. You will find it draining to work in noisy environments that do not respect your real need for privacy.

When Red/Green Introverts work in nonideal corporate cultures, productivity is stunted and career achievements become an uphill climb.

## The Red/Green Introvert's Ideal Boss

Even a great job can be frustrating under the wrong boss; a mediocre job under a wonderful boss is pretty hard to leave. Red/Greens get along es-

**Figure 14–3   The Red/Green Introvert's Ideal Boss**

Check off if your boss:

☐ Points you in the right direction, and then leaves you alone.
☐ Encourages rapport through a sense of humor.
☐ Rewards ingenuity and is not threatened by your free-wheeling ways.
☐ Offers a high degree of trust.
☐ Is appropriately interested in your personal life.

pecially well with other Reds. But bosses of other Color types who possess the characteristics in Figure 14–3 also can be good mentors.

## Careers That Attract Red/Green Introverts

You are most attracted to careers that provide freedom, action, and the ability to be of service, like Chris Dutton.

*Please note that not all* the following careers will appeal to you, but recognize that each, in some way, draws on the strengths of your style and appeals to a significant number of your Color group. This is not a comprehensive list, but it will show underlying patterns of preference. If unlisted careers offer similar patterns, your chances of success increase. Copy in parentheses highlights the Color style characteristics that create success.

In addition, two codes indicate those jobs that are currently predicted to have an above-average salary and growth potential. This information is based on the continuously revised data provided by the U.S. Department of Labor and Bureau of Labor Statistics available on the O*NET website, *http://online.onetcenter.org/*.

**Bold** indicates that the career is considered to be among the top **100 best-paying jobs** based on the average or median salary paid to individuals *with five years of experience*. Excluded are jobs where salary statistics are not available, such as "business owner," or not indicative such as "actor."

*Italics* identifies the jobs that are predicted to benefit from an above-average growth rate over the next several years.

***Bold and italics*** indicates jobs that will benefit from both **higher pay** and *high growth potential.*

Note there are successful people of all Color styles in all occupations. In nonideal jobs you can still shine by creating your own niche.

## Arts/Design/Entertainment/Media

artist [painter, sculptor, illustrator, animator] ◆ actor/performer ◆ *audiovisual specialist* ◆ broadcaster ◆ *costume/wardrobe/set designer* ◆ craftsperson ◆ dancer ◆ *entertainment agent* [actor/performer] ◆ fashion designer ◆ *graphic designer* ◆ jeweler ◆ *film/DVD editor* ◆ photographer ◆ talent director ◆ *web designer/**art director*** (allow the use of artistic talents to produce concrete and usable products).

## Animal Care

animal breeder/groomer/trainer ◆ pet store owner ◆ ***veterinarian*** ◆ *veterinary technician* ◆ **zoologist** (draw on sensitivity to animals and their physical and emotional needs).

## Business/Finance/Law

*business owner* ◆ *business coach/diversity manager* ◆ insurance appraiser/claim investigator ◆ ***lawyer*** [not highly represented but found mostly in children, entertainment, real estate, poverty, and trial specialties] ◆ mediator ◆ retail merchandise buyer ◆ **product designer** ◆ *public relations specialist* (draw on need to provide people with practical service and products).

## Computer/Information Technology

*computer game programmer* ◆ ***software engineer*** ◆ ***support specialist*** (ability to combine design and technical skills).

## Education/Human Services

child care worker ◆ *community service* ◆ *health educator* ◆ *social worker* ◆ *counselor* ◆ *rehabilitation counselor* ◆ *substance abuse counselor* ◆ religious leader ◆ teacher [lower grades, special education, music, drama, art] (enjoy counseling or teaching and have rapport-building skills).

## Emergency Services/Government

crisis center worker ◆ firefighter ◆ paramedic ◆ police officer (variety, change, and need for quick response in high-stress situations).

## Health Science

*anesthesiologist* ◆ *chiropractor* ◆ *dental assistant/hygienist* ◆ *diagnostic sonographer* ◆ dietitian ◆ *elderly home care* ◆ *gynecologist* ◆ lab technician ◆ massage therapist ◆ *nurse* [especially emergency room] ◆ **optometrist** ◆ *pediatrician* ◆ *personal fitness trainer* ◆ *pharmacist* ◆ *therapist* [physical, occupational, recreational, respiratory] ◆ *primary care physician* ◆ *radiologic technician* ◆ *speech pathologist* (observing concrete details of the body and practical methods for getting well, helping the sick deal with uncomfortable and frightening situations).

## Hospitality/Recreation/Sports

athletes of all types ◆ chef/food service manager ◆ innkeeper owner/manager ◆ restaurant host/hostess ◆ tour agent (provide variety and frequent small crises requiring pragmatic response).

## Real Estate

land developer ◆ property manager (fast-moving business).

## Other

antique dealer ◆ cosmetologist ◆ flight attendant ◆ florist ◆ gardener/landscape designer ◆ hairdresser ◆ interior decorator ◆ museum curator (focus on beauty, nature, and personal service).

---

### case study four

## When a Career Isn't Working

Mallory, a Red/Green Introvert, was a real estate salesperson and a good one. She enjoyed the sales process and the people with whom she dealt. She even had that marvelous Red ability to enjoy a crisis every now and then.

But Mallory was feeling a seven-year itch. She was burning out on the unrelenting aggressiveness of making cold calls and drumming up business. She was a good negotiator, but pushing to close deals the way her boss taught her never felt natural. While she enjoyed people, her Introverted nature was feeling overwhelmed by sheer numbers, and the intrusions on her quiet time made her edgy.

One of the properties Mallory listed was a kennel with several beautiful surrounding acres. She found herself pointing out all its flaws to potential customers and steering them away. Finally, she realized she wanted to buy it herself.

Mallory pooled all her resources and purchased the property. She moved into its small caretaker's cottage and started a doggie daycare sideline business. Red/Green Introverts adore animals and are very sensitive to their needs. Within the year, she had quit her real estate job to run her business full time. Local celebrities loved her unique doggie pampering services; Mallory is now able to command top dollar and has a long waiting list.

## Your Personality's Challenges

Red/Green Introverts have a unique set of potential work-related blind spots. We emphasize "potential" because you won't have all of them. Tone down a blind spot by deciding to see it, then choose more productive actions. (Suggestions for doing so are in parentheses below.) You:

◆ Tend to be casual with rules and procedures valued by others, including meeting deadlines. (This is your number one career-derailing attribute. Your superiors may need rules and procedures to control their own job anxieties. Would that make you respond with more respect and compassion? Try it and see how your boss reacts.)

◆ Either avoid conflict or become defensive when confronted. (You've got two great tools—humor and practicality. Get control over the tone of the interaction.  Start with, or interject, humor. Then get practical about how to resolve the issue.)

◆ Hate not having control of your own schedule and having tight deadlines. (This makes you hyperactive, blunt, pessimistic, and joyless. For you, it is critical to avoid or change jobs where tight deadlines are the norm. When deadlines cannot be avoided, approach your tasks as if they were all ridiculous; this will lighten your mood.)

## Your Job Search—the Good, the Bad, and the Ugly

You'd rather be out there hitting the pavement than reading this. But hang in there; you're almost done. You'll benefit from these concrete job search tips:

Your natural strengths easily allow you to:

- Get the facts on careers and companies. You are particularly adept at Internet research.
- Respond quickly and decisively to new opportunities.
- Weigh whether a job meets your personal values.
- Be detailed in your interview about past positions and achievements.
- Appreciate and appropriately thank others for their help and introductions.
- Assemble a small but loyal group of acquaintances who will provide referrals and leads.

In order to tone down your blind spots, you need to:

- Force yourself to set long-term goals; enlist the help of friends or family, particularly Golds (to identify, read Chapter 4, A Tour of the Prism Company).
- Prepare ahead for hypothetical questions; practice role-playing rather than "winging it."
- Speak up in interviews, rather than just listening, to avoid appearing "too quiet."
- Sell, don't just state, your accomplishments—role-play to reduce discomfort.
- Follow through on commitments, deadlines, and the nitty-gritty tasks of a job search. Enlist the aid of a willing Gold to help (to identify, read Chapter 25, Adjusting to the Styles of Others)
- Hang in there when the hiring process drags on through multiple interviews; avoid snap decisions to drop out of the race.
- Be aggressive about soliciting referrals and leads from acquaintances and strangers. Your preferred circle of friends is intimate but small.

# The Red/Green Introvert's Interviewing Style

With an interviewer whose Color is close to your own, you will feel immediate rapport. However, if your interviewer seems to have a significantly different style, use the suggestions in parentheses.

In following your natural style, you:

- Are a calm, quiet listener. (With an interviewer who asks short questions and expects long answers, take more of a lead. Practice selling your accomplishments. Communicate a sense of pride. Rather than egotistical, you will appear self-confident.)
- Develop a rapport with people. (With an interviewer who seems distant, stick to the facts. Let them set the tone for any personal exchanges.)

- Are concrete and realistic about past responsibilities and accomplishments.
- Avoid sharing personal information until trust is established. (Keeping your distance or answering vaguely will make you look as if you have something to hide. Use humor to gain space, if needed, then be honest.)
- Focus on the current situation and not on future or strategic issues. (Your ability to focus on the present is a valuable asset, but you to may be too brief when handling future-oriented questions. Answer slowly and thoughtfully. (Then emphasize your talent for turning on a dime if things change.)
- You prefer to act rather than talk. (Ask for the job at the end of the interview, but don't rush things. Impatience will hurt you here. If your interviewer seems indecisive, take action! Offer to work a trial project or period.)
- Speak up when your values are threatened. (While this may lose you a job, NEVER hide this valuable instinct of yours. You will save yourself wasted years working for firms you don't respect.)

Okay, go do something new now. Later, check out Chapter 5, Greens Overall, if we've actually hooked you a little on this stuff. You can jot notes if you want to impress someone with your diligence in the Roadmap in Chapter 28. It's also a great place to keep notes during a job interview that will help with follow-through.

# PART 4

# BLUES
## *"Let's Change It"*

Blues enjoy complex problems and work tirelessly to improve ideas and systems until they are just right.

# CHAPTER 15

# Blues Overall

**BLUES REPRESENT 10 PERCENT** of the overall world population. If you are not a Blue, but want to read about how to identify or improve communications with one, go to Figure 15–1.

## Senator Hillary Rodham Clinton, D-New York

Senator Hillary Rodham Clinton of New York is one of the most interesting women in the United States, and one of the best-known Blues (who are the rarest of the four Color types).

Growing up in Park Ridge, Illinois, Hillary was seen even as a child to be assertive, purposeful, and determined, all in-born Blue characteristics. A tireless worker and consistent overachiever, she was a National Merit Scholar in high school. Her teachers noted her exceptional ability to take in information, argue a point thoroughly, but change her mind when new input demanded it (core Blue abilities).

In her senior year, she was voted most likely to succeed. She went on to become a high achiever in both college (Wellesley student body president) and at Yale law school.

Her Blue abilities served her well early in her career. Assigned as part of the impeachment inquiry staff investigating Richard Nixon, she worked dawn to midnight seven days a week. Hillary is remembered as "determined and dutiful, grinding away in a mildewed office overlooking an alleyway."[8] This typifies the Blue ability to work relentlessly on a problem of interest, functioning without significant stress in solemn and tense environments.

[8]Evan Thomas, "Bill and Hillary's Long, Hot Summer," *Newsweek* (October, 19, 1998), p. 38

## Figure 15–1   How to Recognize a Blue

☐ Prefer talking about ideas or the future.
☐ Speak in compound sentences.
☐ Use precise vocabulary with lots of abstract words.
☐ Express clear and direct ideas.
☐ Read voraciously.
☐ Are insatiably curious.
☐ Have jousting wit.
☐ Are competitive.
☐ Often have advanced degree(s).
☐ Disregard opposition and what others think of them.

HOW TO COMMUNICATE WITH A BLUE

✔ Keep relationship professional, limit chit-chat, be brief and concise.
✔ Acknowledge intellectual skills.
✔ Emphasize your own competence; use sophisticated vocabulary.
✔ Present the "big picture."
✔ Outline the theoretical framework.
✔ Bring up comparative studies.
✔ Limit facts and details; reduce to essentials in executive summary.
✔ Show long-term potential of your new idea or solution.
✔ Use ingenuity and logic.
✔ Allow the Blue to challenge and question.
✔ Don't take critiques and challenges personally; these actually are signs of interest in the topic under discussion.
✔ Joust back with their jousting wit.
✔ Avoid emotional approach and words like "feel" or "believe."
✔ Compose a strategy WITH the Blue, not FOR the Blue; use his or her input.

That summer she worked on Bill Clinton's campaign for an Arkansas congressional seat, already emotionally involved with the young up-and-comer. Campaign manager Paul Fray struggled with the hard-nosed young woman over the strategies he deemed his turf, but later admitted, "She was an organizational genius."[9]

During her time in the White House as First Lady, Hillary helped President Clinton draw and clarify battle lines. Her personal goals (healthcare reform, legal rights of children) were typical of a Blue – long-term, strategic, and abstract. Hillary was and is not concerned about stepping on toes while pursuing the ability to set her own agenda.[10]

When her two-decade marriage to Bill Clinton was tested by the Monica Lewinsky scandal in the glare of international media, it endured, and many wondered why. Put in Color Q terms, the answer was simple.

Hillary is a Blue/Gold. Bill is a Red/Green. (NOTE: Neither has reported taking the Myers-Briggs Type Indicator questionnaire or the derivative Color Q Self-Assessment, but these personalities have been extrapolated by Dr. David Keirsey, noted temperament specialist in the Myers-Briggs community,[11] and author Shoya Zichy from a personal meeting with Hillary. These results are supported by extensive research, candid conversations with journalists, and Hillary's personal friends.) He loves politics; she prefers making policy. He is a quick study; she, like most Blues, has depth and focus. He looks for ways to compromise; she, in typical Blue fashion, weighs alternative strategies. He forgives and forgets; she remembers and keeps score. He dives into a crowd with the abandon of an Red/Green Extrovert; Hillary reaches out but remains at the Blue/Gold's cool distance. He works from the gut; she is guided by logical analysis—again, another Blue tendency. He thrives on risk; Blue Hillary circles it cautiously.[12] It's a case of opposites attracting . . . and complementing each other in deeply important (and binding) ways for the challenges they have faced together.

After her role as First Lady of the United States ended, Hillary did what comes naturally to all Blues: She took charge. She chose to run for a seat in the U. S. Senate and made it happen, tactically using her political contacts and name recognition. As of this writing she continues to place herself strategically in the spotlight on carefully chosen issues, fueling the possibility that she herself eventually will run for President of the United States.

---

[9]*Ibid.*, p. 41.
[10]Lucinda Franks, "The Intimate Hillary," *Talk* (September, 1999), p. 174.
[11]David Keirsey and Ray Choiniere, *Presidential Temperament* (Del Mar, CA: Prometheus Nemesis, 1999), appendix.
[12]James Bennett, "The Next Clinton," *New York Times* (May 30, 1999), p. 26.

Other famous Blues in politics are Madeleine Albright, Vice President Dick Cheney, Al Gore, Thomas Jefferson, Abraham Lincoln, Condoleezza Rice, and Lady Margaret Thatcher. Microsoft founder Bill Gates and IBM's Lou Gerstener represent Blues in the corporate world. Walt Disney illustrates the Blue style in entertainment, Citibank chairman John Reed and mega-investor George Soros in finance, and Albert Einstein in academia.

Use this chapter to determine if you've tested your primary and backup personality color correctly. It also will help identify Blues among people you know, as will Chapter 4, A Tour of the Prism Company/The Blue Department, and Chapter 25, Adjusting to the Styles of Others. We added Figure 15–1 for other Colors to have a list of ways to identify and communicate with Blues.

As a Blue, you are the rarest of the four Colors. You are the most strategic of all personality types, thriving when grappling with complex theoretical challenges. Your talent for new system designs brings you recognition and appreciation.

A Blue who grew rich on these natural talents is Charles R. ("Chuck") Schwab, founder, chairman and Chief Executive Officer of The Charles Schwab Corporation. The Corporation is a leading provider of financial services with more than 325 offices, 7.1 million client accounts and $1.2 trillion in client assets. When Schwab started his business in the 1970s, he was $100,000 in debt and going through a divorce. But he saw the baby-boomer demographics and their meaning—28 percent of the U.S. population would be in the pre-retirement age range of 45 to 64 by the year 2010.[13] And he invested big in pre-Internet technology in the late 1970s—"a bet-the-company decision"—that gave Schwab a crucial headstart into Internet trading and investing. These two things together—demand and technology—grew into a trillion-dollar business . . . and made Chuck Schwab a billionaire twice over.

Described by *Fortune Magazine* in 2005 as "private and aloof,"[14] Schwab's demeanor is typical of Blues who focus on systems and their improvement. After retiring, Schwab reclaimed the CEO position of his firm when his designated successor was deemed as being "not really inclined toward the visionary, blue-sky stuff,"[15] and the company floundered in the early 2000s. Blues are the visionaries of the world, just what the company

[13]Terence P. Pare, *Fortune Magazine* (June 1, 1992). Accessed February 20, 2006 from www.highbeam.com
[14]Betsy Morris, "Charles Schwab's Big Challenge," *Fortune Magazine* (May 2005). Accessed February 20, 2006, from www.highbeam.com
[15]*Ibid.*

needed at that time. He plans to remain at the helm until January 2007,[16] keeping the company focused on its strengths and improving internal processes so it "skates to where the puck is going to be,"[17] as he likes to say.

You as a Blue will critique every point made in a book like this, preferring instead to deal with things more intellectual and less emotional. However, if you are interested in learning how to work more effectively and efficiently with other personality types, this book will be the key that unlocks those secrets. Color Q shows you how to handle even the most emotional and disorganized people in your life. It describes what to do when all your best efforts have failed.

The most logical way to proceed with this book is to read about your own Color first, and then learn how you interact with others by reading their profiles as needed. You especially want to learn about Reds, with whom you are most likely to clash because they are relentlessly present-centered and view deadlines and commitments merely as loose guidelines in both personal and professional life. Reds, however, will help you achieve more than you could on your own. Harness their strengths to handle crises in troubled teams, departments, or companies. Turn to their present-moment thinking when strategic, future-oriented logic breaks down.

You'll get along better with Greens and Golds. They, too, have strengths with which you should become familiar. Successful Blue entrepreneurs and leaders know how to engage the strengths of each Color and hire accordingly.

---

[16] *Ibid.*
[17] Rebecca McReynolds, "Doing It the Schwab Way," *U.S. Banker* (July 1, 1998). Accessed February 20, 2006 from www.highbeam.com

# CHAPTER 16

# Blue/Gold Extroverts

**YOU'RE NOT ONLY A BLUE,** you also have strong secondary characteristics of the Gold personality. And you have tested as a Color Q Extrovert, which means you recharge your batteries by being with people, rather than being alone. Your Color group makes things happen in decisive and take charge ways. A lifelong learner, you typically are quite well-informed. It is likely you already are challenging and critiquing this profile, if you're at all interested in the material. Please note the underlying components of this profile have been researched for nearly six decades worldwide and verified across age, sex, ethnic, and socioeconomic boundaries.

## You Overall

Dynamic and capable, your talents dominate at every step of a project from creating the vision to making it happen. Along the way, your abilities to devise strategies, establish plans (and contingencies), and take charge are all quite strong. Blue/Gold Extroverts do well in a broader range of careers than other Colors, due to your love of lifelong learning, sharp logic, and executive abilities.

Two core strengths combine in you to create a fast rise to the top—a high need for control and strong leadership skills. Combined with your frank, direct, intuitive, and focused communication style, you are an executive dynamo . . . but at times overly challenging and alienating to those around you. Most other Colors cannot keep up with your drive, which can make your entire staff uncomfortable and rebellious.

The world of theories, future possibilities, and bold new designs are your territory. Existing systems and assumptions are just jumping-off points. You create long-range plans that incorporate ideas others do not yet see. If such plans create complex problems to be solved, so much the better! Not only will you marshal all necessary resources, you will gleefully solve them all.

Your greatest challenge is managing and controlling how others respond to you. On the plus side, you often come across as articulate, vivid, and confident. You persuade others through clear logic and thoughtful debate. On the down side, you are impatient with people who focus on what you consider irrelevant, redundant, and obvious issues. Those who are intimidated by you instantly lose your respect; you can't imagine why anyone would personalize competition or debate.

To be an effective leader or team player, you will need to learn which other Colors do personalize such things, and adopt alternate strategies for interacting with them. Such reactions are deep in their core, offer a different (and usable) strength than yours and cannot be changed by choice or willpower.

## case study one

## Chief Financial Officer, Investments and Wealth Management

Rehana Farrell of Merrill Lynch loves that her calendar is booked with meetings from first thing in the morning to 7 PM at night. "I like to brainstorm, to build new functions, to effectively leverage people, and to construct a more diverse organization."

Rehana and her two-dozen-member team are responsible for product finance for over $7 billion of Global Private Client revenue. This includes pricing and business strategy in addition to financial reporting, forecasting, and budgeting, and controls. What Rehana most enjoys is transforming her department into what she calls "a strategic finance function." "We would like finance to be viewed as a strategic business partner for all of our business heads," she says, "and not just being the people who give you data and prevent you from doing anything wrong."

Like most Blue/Gold Extroverts, Rehana is most energized by strategies and processes. She describes a process she is trying to institute that will encourage people to look up from their routine tasks and capture more innovative thinking. "This process could end up producing some game-changing ideas for Merrill Lynch. That is the kind of stuff I really enjoy."

In Blue fashion, Rehana focuses on the big picture and avoids positions where she cannot understand the overall firm strategy or help influence and achieve it. She loves being in the center of the action, working on the core priorities of the business. "I am interested in understanding the broader perspective about the firm as a whole. Finance is a really great way to start, advance, or evolve your career," she says. Blue/Golds are happiest when managing big projects and avoiding political turf struggles.

Rehana is a doer as well as a thinker. "If I, or someone else, have a great idea, I tend to be the person who makes sure it gets done," she says. Dealing with people who aren't smart, aren't hard-working, and who are political or who don't see the big picture stresses her out.

Right now, Rehana has one of the best jobs a Blue/Gold Extrovert can have, and enjoys going to work. "I love being part of a large organization and helping to move it forward," she says.

## You on the Job

### As a Leader

"I don't take no for an answer" is a phrase that must first have been uttered by a Blue/Gold Extrovert. Once you create a vision, you spring into action, mobilizing the talents of others, eliminating confusion and inefficiencies, making the tough decisions. Understanding the inner workings of any organization is your special talent; you can manipulate most bureaucracies to achieve your ends.

You often are the first one who sees connections between unrelated facts and ideas, which gives you an edge at handling global issues. You recognize the potential of new ideas before others do, and your company profits accordingly.

### As a Team Player

Your natural leadership comes to the fore even in teams. Your ability to see the big picture and energize the group to achieve shows itself, whether you are the team leader or not. Cutting to the core of issues saves your team time. In order to meet deadlines you will encourage (and work to) high standards, avoid wasting resources, and even consider untried solutions rather than fail.

You can irritate your teammates by being overly controlling and at times pushing too hard to get the job done.

## Figure 16–1    Natural Work-Related Strengths

Approximately 80 percent of these attributes will apply to you. Check off those that do and use them in your resume and interviews. This will set you apart from the canned responses of others. You:

☐ Are outgoing and energetic.
☐ Can see the big picture, create compelling visions, and make it happen.
☐ Enjoy finding new and more creative solutions by connecting unrelated variables.
☐ Use a new perspective when analyzing problems and developing new systems.
☐ Are willing, and eager, to take charge of challenging, complex problems.
☐ Are task oriented and organized.
☐ Constantly seek improvements.
☐ Make tough, logical decisions.
☐ See the long-term consequences of your decisions.
☐ Will push your team to achieve goals, whether you are the leader or not.

Look at Figure 16–1 for a list of your natural work-related strengths.
Now see how some Blue/Gold Extroverts use these strengths in very different fields.

### case study two

## Chief Executive Officer

Nobody is going to burst Michael Isaacs's balloon, at least not any time soon. He is the Chief Executive Officer of U.S. Balloon Company, the largest wholesale distributor of balloons and related accessories in the United States. The company, which Michael started with a $750 investment, now annually grosses $30 million. It has a hundred employees and a catalog of products that is 592 pages long.

Michael sees his function as being answerable to all the company's constituencies—the employees, suppliers, customers, and bankers. "I set the direction of the company," he says. "I determine the targeted market and profitability goals."

Although he views himself more as an entrepreneur than a manager, he works very hard at building his managerial skills. "Most of all," he says, "I try to get the job done by hiring the right team."

Originally a junior high science teacher, Michael had always run side businesses to augment his family's income. He started selling balloons in a shopping mall. The business got bigger, and he left to pursue it full time. Michael attributes his success to his natural "persistence and persuasiveness; the ability to translate my vision into an action plan and be very serious about measuring results."

He is most energized when his team makes an outstanding effort. He prefers to deal with others in groups rather than individually, very typical of a Blue/Gold Extrovert. Also true to his Color, he likes finance and accounting and finds very few things boring about his business. "I try to improve every process, even if mundane," he says "There is always a factor, cheaper, and better way of doing it."

Michael has achieved success by his own definition. "What I do must have economic benefit for my family, employees, and other stakeholders," he says. Beyond that, success to Michael is being recognized by industry peers and customers, as well as being viewed as a knowledge resource.

There is still some teacher in him. "I do believe people can and do learn and grow," he says. "I create a teaching environment, and I never stop learning."

## Ideal Work Environment

If, like Rehana Farrell, you are surrounded at work by highly competent and independent people who meet their deadlines, you are in the right place. Your superiors must also be highly competent and professional and respect you enough to let you work autonomously.

When a job offer is made, leverage as much as you can from the list in Figure 16–2 on page 138.

The WORST type of work culture for a Blue/Gold Extrovert is overly bureaucratic and/or full of sensitive people who need exorbitant amounts

## Figure 16–2    The Ideal Blue/Gold Extrovert Work Environment

Compare your current work environment to the description below. Check all that ring true for you. Don't be deceived if these descriptions seem "obvious." It confirms you've tested your individual color correctly. Other Colors, especially Greens and Reds, would find this environment uncomfortable and unproductive. The optimal Blue/Gold Extrovert work environment:

☐ Provides a demanding and competitive atmosphere.
☐ Has high standards.
☐ Has highly competent bosses and co-workers.
☐ Encourages creative approaches to long-range problems.
☐ Rewards innovation and drive rather than playing by the rules.
☐ Funnels you into a leadership role.
☐ Assists you in dealing with the emotional reactions of others.
☐ Is a well-respected institution in need of change.

of handholding. Too much emphasis is put on detail work, not enough on long-range thinking and strategizing.

When Blue/Gold Extroverts work in nonideal corporate cultures, productivity is stunted and career achievements become an uphill climb.

## The Blue/Gold Extrovert's Ideal Boss

Even a great job can be frustrating under the wrong boss; a mediocre job under a wonderful boss is pretty hard to leave. Blue/Golds get along especially well with other Blues. But bosses of other Color types who possess the characteristics in Figure 16–3 also can be good mentors.

## Careers That Attract Blue/Gold Extroverts

Blue/Gold Extroverts cluster in fields that provide intellectual challenge, complex and theoretical problems, and mastering new technologies. Routine, repetitive tasks are minimized; risk-taking and original projects predominate. Autonomy, competition, and people you respect characterize jobs that provide your highest degree of satisfaction.

*Please note that not all* the following careers will appeal to you, but recognize that each, in some way, draws on the strengths of your style and ap-

## Figure 16-3 The Blue/Gold Extrovert's Ideal Boss

Check off if your boss:

☐ Is someone you respect.

☐ Enjoys a hearty exchange of views and does not react to debate as a personal challenge.

☐ Values your independence and energy.

☐ Grants you sufficient autonomy.

☐ Helps you deal with the emotional outbursts of others.

☐ Shelters you from bureaucracy and detail work as much as possible.

peals to a significant number of your Color group. This is not a comprehensive list, but it will show underlying patterns of preference. If unlisted careers offer similar patterns, your chances of success increase. Copy in parentheses highlights the Color style characteristics that create success.

In addition, two codes indicate those jobs that are currently predicted to have an above-average salary and growth potential. This information is based on the continuously revised data provided by the U.S. Department of Labor and Bureau of Labor Statistics available on the O*NET website, *http://online.onetcenter.org/*.

**Bold** indicates that the career is considered to be among the top **100 best-paying jobs** based on the average or median salary paid to individuals *with five years of experience.* Excluded are jobs where salary statistics are not available, such as "business owner," or not indicative such as "actor."

*Italics* identifies the jobs that are predicted to benefit from an above-average growth rate over the next several years.

***Bold and italics*** indicates jobs that will benefit from both **higher pay** and *high growth potential.*

Note there are successful people of all Color styles in all occupations. In nonideal jobs you can still shine by creating your own niche.

## Architecture/Law

architect ◆ *lawyer* [especially corporate, employment, project finance, securities, mergers and acquisitions, product liability] (intellectual challenge, high need for control, complex problem solving, high standards).

## Business/Management

**chief financial officer** ◆ **executive** [private sector/government service/arts and entertainment] ◆ insurance agent/examiner/underwriter ◆ *managers of all types* [marketing, financial operations, human resources, sales, training and development] ◆ *new business developer* ◆ real estate manager ◆ strategic planner ◆ *training and development manager* ◆ *venture capitalist* (decisive, focused, take-charge, high standards, solving complex problems, long-range strategic thinking, natural leadership skills).

## Business/Finance

banker ◆ credit investigator ◆ **economist** ◆ *financial planner* ◆ *investment banker* ◆ *investment/securities broker* ◆ mortgage broker ◆ security analyst (intellectual challenge, intuition, strategic thinking, complex problem solving, high need for control, competition, insatiable curiosity, well-informed, logical thinking, make tough decisions).

## Computer/Information Technology

*computer analyst* ◆ *database manager* ◆ *executive computer firm* ◆ *programmer* ◆ *computer security specialist* ◆ *software/hardware engineer* (mastering new technologies, solving complex and/or theoretical problems, autonomy, long-range planning, future possibilities, bold new designs, contingency planning, need for control).

## Consulting

**management consultant** ◆ **industrial psychologist/organizational development specialist** (autonomy, solve complex problems, work with theories and future possibilities, long-range planning).

## Education

*educational administrator* ◆ *higher education teacher/professor* [especially law, political science, science, or social studies] ◆ **university president** (desire to deal with competent people, establish long-range visions, strategic planning, few routine tasks, autonomy, debate skill).

## Government/Public Administration

government service executive ◆ judge ◆ **policy maker** ◆ **urban and regional planner** ◆ *community services manager* (ability to tackle complex issues, long-range planning, respect of community).

## Health Science/Human Services

*anesthesiologist* ◆ *internist* ◆ *psychiatrist* ◆ *neurologist* ◆ *surgeon* ◆ *medical health services manager* ◆ **philanthropic**/*community service executive* (intellectual challenge, opportunity to lead, respect of community).

## Scientific Research, Engineering, Mathematics

chemical/environmental engineer ◆ engineering manager ◆ geologist (insatiable curiosity, need for control, deal with confusion and inefficiencies, tackle complex problems, interact with people you respect)

### case study three

### Fixing a Broken Career

In order to escape her violent marriage, 18-year-old Kathlene Burke needed a job. But the only things on her resume were her stints in group homes, living on the streets, hitchhiking across the country, and waitressing.

Waitressing would leave her vulnerable both economically and to the threats of her violent husband. She needed a safe place to stay, a chance to continue her education, and help in getting her life back on track.

There was one option, and Kathlene took it. She enlisted in the U. S. Army, with the single focus of getting an education. This was her path away from poverty and violence, and she embraced it with a vengeance.

In the military, she learned pride, duty, honor, leadership, service to the community, and how to rebuild her self-esteem. She reclaimed these natural Blue/Gold strengths.

After the military, Kathlene enrolled at Baruch College in New York City to get a Bachelor of Business Administration. There she was elected to the student government and become President of the PreLaw Society. Now she is in law school. Why did this ambitious Blue/Gold Extrovert chose law? "People in the field are smart and driven," she explains. She hopes to find kindred spirits.

## Your Personality's Challenges

Blue/Gold Extroverts have a unique set of potential work-related blind spots. Some you have, others you don't. No one has them all. Tone down a blind spot by focusing on it, then choose more productive actions and make them habits. (Suggestions for doing so are in parentheses below.) You:

◆ May decide too quickly and overlook practical considerations. (High intellectual capability is no substitute for street smarts. You are more than capable of determining practicalities if you decide to focus. Especially early in your career, doing things too fast may create inefficiencies.)

◆ May be too abrupt, harsh, or dogmatic. (Everyone needs allies at some point. Alienating others is a strategic error, even if they seem less competent or less intellectual. Patience is a [long-range] virtue.)

◆ May pay insufficient attention to human needs and concerns. (Learn the wisdom that lies in emotions. They underpin every successful product and team, equally with all your best strategic thinking. Once a day, require yourself to have empathy for someone.)

◆ May manipulate others to achieve goals. (It is tempting, when navigating bureaucracy, to cut to the chase. But when those people realize you've manipulated them, there can be hell to pay . . . and no second chances.)

## Your Job Search—the Good, the Bad, and the Ugly

Blue/Gold Extroverts create accurate and well-presented resumes that elicit positive responses. With some interviewers, particularly Blues and Golds, you will feel a comfortable rapport. But with those of other Colors, you need to prepare and rehearse responses outside your comfort zone. Many human resource people are Greens; make a study of how to communicate effectively with this Color group before your first interviews by reading Chapter 5, Greens Overall.

Your natural strengths easily allow you to:

◆ Have an unusually creative job search plan that you implement in an orderly way.
◆ Perform good research on prospective companies.
◆ Have a wide network from which to draw job leads.
◆ Impress new contacts with your energy, insight, and competence.
◆ Predict future needs and trends, possibly creating new jobs for yourself.
◆ Create time lines, daily status reports, and budgets to lessen stress on you and your family.
◆ Handle obstacles with creativity and strategy.

In order to tone down your blind spots, you need to:

◆ Think of what you can do in return for those who help you; your networking sometimes comes off as too self-serving.
◆ Cushion your tendency to be abrupt by extending answers beyond a few words and listening longer.
◆ Learn to control your tendency to come across as arrogant; role play with a willing Green.
◆ Pay attention to the personal aspects of job hunting, i.e., creating rapport with the interviewer and sending thank-you notes.

◆ Get help with the nitty-gritty of the job search to temper your natural impatience with administrative tasks; ask a willing Gold for assistance.

◆ Employ your creativity and strategic thinking to address unexpected delays and obstacles.

◆ Postpone any job decision until effects on family and personal life are reviewed.

## The Blue/Gold Extrovert's Interviewing Style

With an interviewer whose Color is close to your own, you will feel immediate rapport. However, if your interviewer seems to have a significantly different style (and it's statistically likely that many will have a Green component), use the suggestions in parentheses. Exploit these natural abilities of yours, and get more job offers!

In following your natural style, you:

◆ Focus on future strategies. (Be ready to handle more mundane questions with equal dynamism. Don't continually pull the conversation back to the future.)

◆ Will have multiple and well-defined long-term goals. (Also practice talking about how you plan to "hit the ground running.")

◆ Tend to talk too much and not ask enough questions about the job. (If it has been a while since the interviewer said anything, PAUSE. Let him or her ask a few questions. Prepare a list of questions about the job ahead of time and refer to it.)

◆ May not pick up on critical dynamics of corporate culture that will impact you. (You have an above-the-surface, rather than below-the-surface, focus. Yet ignoring corporate culture can make a move disastrous. Rehash interviews with willing Greens who will help you spot such intangibles.)

◆ Logically consider the pros and cons of a job opportunity. (NEVER accept a job offer on the spot. Go home and thoroughly consider how it will impact your family and personal life.)

Once you've critiqued this profile and decided we've gotten enough things right to make it worthwhile, go on and read Chapter 20, Golds Overall, then carefully read Chapter 4, A Tour of the Prism Company, to learn about the strengths of other Colors. Read up on the Greens in Chapter 5 to prepare for job interviews (a large number of human resource people are Greens) and the Reds in Chapter 10 if you have to interact with any at work or at home.

If you are actively engaging in a job search, keep notes in the Roadmap in Chapter 28. Recording your strengths and strategies is a concrete and results-oriented way to navigate the minefields of a job search and promote creative thinking.

# CHAPTER 17

# Blue/Gold Introverts

**YOU'RE NOT ONLY A BLUE,** you also have strong secondary characteristics of the Gold personality. And you have tested as a Color Q Introvert, which means you recharge your batteries by being alone, rather than being with people. People in your Color group rise to the top of any profession that requires strategic thinking, because you work tirelessly to very high standards. You excel at creating new systems and ideas.

You already have begun challenging and critiquing the last few claims, especially if you have any interest in this material. Please note the underlying components of the following profile have been researched for nearly six decades worldwide and verified across age, sex, ethnic, and socioeconomic boundaries.

## You Overall

Creative, focused, and quite independent, you are superior at establishing links between seemingly unrelated ideas and facts. From such mental intricacies you construct models of anything from the cities of tomorrow to the conspiracy theories of yesterday.

Like your cousins the Blue/Gold Extroverts, you, too, have strengths to apply at all phases of a project. You can create the vision, devise the strategy, establish plans and contingencies, and make it all happen.

Unlike them, you come across as more calm, self-reliant, and enigmatic. Your deep powers of concentration make it seem as if you are in another world at times; but that's just you working with tireless focus on your latest project.

Opposition does not intimidate you or shake your utter faith in your own insights. Your impressive scope of knowledge usually overcomes any challenges.

The world of theories, future possibilities, and bold new designs is your territory. Existing systems and assumptions to you are just jumping-off points. Departments or companies that need new direction will flourish using your long-range plans that incorporate ideas others do not yet see. If such plans create complex problems to be solved, so much the better! Not only will you marshal all the necessary resources, you will gleefully solve all the problems.

Your greatest challenge is managing and controlling how others see and respond to you. On the plus side, you come across as clear thinking, thoughtful, and insatiably curious. You persuade others through clear logic and convincing debate. On the down side, you are impatient with people who focus on what you consider irrelevant, redundant, and obvious issues. To avoid these irritants, you prefer written communications over face-to-face.

To be an effective leader or team player, however, you will need to adopt alternate strategies for working with Colors who do personalize things. Such reactions are deep in their core, offer a different (and usable) strength than yours and cannot be changed by choice or willpower.

## case study one

### Coach for Small and Medium-Sized Businesses

Jeannette Hobson's high-powered New York career has made her a visible force in the financial and small business communities. It all started with a young woman who lacked courage.

"I considered a career in international business," says Jeannette. "But I didn't have the courage actually to go alone, find a job, and live on my own in a different land." Instead, she found a training program for female college graduates at AT&T, moving eventually into a twenty-year career as a vice president of investment management at The Bank of New York. There, Jeannette sold economic and investment strategy services to corporations—a natural fit for a Blue. "I enjoy blue-sky thinking," she says. She progressed to managing investment portfolios for high-net-worth individuals and small pension funds, ultimately managing a team of eight.

But Jeannette envisioned a broader future. Today, she runs chief executive officer (CEO) peer advisory groups for Vistage International, the world's largest CEO membership organization. She also coaches, on a monthly basis, fifty CFOs of small to medium-sized companies. "Coaching and facilitating meetings draws on my natural strengths," says Jeannette. "I ask probing questions."

At one of her sessions, for example, those probing questions helped a leading provider of commercial coin-operated laundry equipment realize that technology would be the company's single greatest competitive advantage. Subsequent strategizing around this theme doubled the company's growth rate and helped attract more national-level attention.

As an Introvert, Jeannette finds it stressful to network in groups of complete strangers and to make cold prospecting calls to form new CEO groups. She admits to overpreparing for presentations: "Impromptu is very stressful for me." Her top three strengths, typical for her Color group, are thinking/analyzing, listening, and planning future strategies.

Today she would not hesitate, if given the opportunity, to live and work in a foreign land. But her family and the job of her passion will likely keep her in New York.

# You on the Job

## As a Leader

"I don't take no for an answer" is a phrase that must first have been uttered by a Blue/Gold. Once you create a vision you spring into action, mobilizing the talents of others, addressing confusion and inefficiencies, making the tough decisions. Understanding the inner workings of any organization is one of your unique talents, and you can manipulate most bureaucracies to achieve your ends.

You often are the first one who sees connections between unrelated facts and ideas, which gives you an edge at handling global issues. You recognize the potential of new ideas before others do, and your company profits accordingly.

## As a Team Player

While not keen on the rapport-building aspects of working on a team, your contributions nevertheless are substantial. You bypass small talk, going straight to the big picture. After a few precise and penetrating questions, you've cut to the core of even the most complex problems and begun synthesizing a strategy. Often you leave your teammates in the dust. If they

## Figure 17-1   Natural Work-Related Strengths

Approximately 80 percent of these attributes will apply to you. Check off those that do and use them in your resume and interviews. This will set you apart from the canned responses of others. You:

- ☐ Are often the first to see the big picture.
- ☐ Are highly focused and goal oriented.
- ☐ Deal well with complex problems.
- ☐ Develop sophisticated new systems using the latest technology.
- ☐ Strategize final outcomes accurately.
- ☐ Work well with other competent people.

have to ask what you consider to be obvious or incompetent questions, your impatience flairs. Often you tap your foot waiting for others to catch up and see what's been obvious to you from the start.

To amuse yourself you'll formulate unusual insights and run through untried and unique solutions. When your teammates finally understand the problem, you're there ready with (one or more) solutions. You make fast decisions once you have reviewed all known data.

This may make team members feel rushed or pressured; it also can excite and galvanize them to action. Often you find yourself in the role of catalyst, moving the group to timely completion of deadlines using minimal time and resources, yet working to highest standards.

Look at Figure 17-1 for a list of your natural work-related strengths.

Now see how some Blue/Gold Introverts use these strengths in very different fields.

### case study two

## Producer/Director, Multimedia Production, Operation Training/Human Resources, MTA New York City Transit

Glenn Frontera was going to be a doctor until he broke his ankle. Then, two things happened. First, he missed just enough classes to eliminate his chances of being accepted into a U.S.

medical school. And second, after long and deep pondering about his career direction, he had a dream: to study the art and craft of film production and become a filmmaker.

Glenn had never even held a camera before. But he switched his college major. "The study of film came naturally to me, and I excelled at it," he says. He received highest marks in his class, produced an award-winning film in his senior year and was selected by Brooklyn College faculty as Outstanding Film Production Student. Such recognition comes naturally to motivated Blue/Golds.

Upon graduation he worked freelance in the film industry, but ran up against what seemed like another broken ankle. His father, exasperated by his son's pipe dreams of Hollywood film production, gave him an ultimatum—either accept an offered job as Railroad Clerk for New York City Transit, or move out and support himself. Lacking resources, Glenn reluctantly accepted the job.

For a while, he led two lives—one as a producer of five low-budget independent films, and another as a successful transit employee. One day, he discovered a computer instructor's position in the Training Division of the Human Resources Department. At that point, all of Glenn's abilities began to converge.

"When an opportunity to produce a training film presented itself, I seized upon it and created an outstanding example of what such a film should be," he says.

Shortly thereafter, he was put in charge of New York City Transit's whole production unit. He now produces all their training films with a staff of seven, plus three to five interns. This involves script writing, electronic cinematography, nonlinear editing, animation production, graphic art production, sound production and editing, web page production and e-learning programs. The broad range of activities satisfies the Blue need for variety and constant learning.

He describes his greatest strength as seeing how all the pieces fit into the final product, a natural ability for strategic Blue/Golds. Organization, vision, and persistence are the characteristics to which he attributes his success. Like most Blues, administrative tasks are his least favorite, but he is energized by every other aspect of his creative job.

case study three

## Music Composer, Television and Motion Pictures

Joshua Stone can take still pictures and make a piano describe what's in them. He can sit at a keyboard, ask you to name an emotion, and create it through his fingertips. He can play the same 15-second music bridge over and over for seven days, improving it with each pass, and never get bored. And yet this Emmy Award winner describes his achievements writing music for movies and television with great modesty: "As a child, I didn't think, 'I am going to grow up and write music that nobody notices.' That is essentially what I do."

Music is a very direct conduit to Josh's emotions. He is highly disciplined about codifying those emotions to enhance movies and TV programs. He has written for *CBS News,* A&E Network, the Smithsonian Institute, and *Nickelodeon,* and scored films about fine artists among other projects.

"I have to understand the period of the time these people lived in to adequately compose music about them," Josh says. Like most Blues, he enjoys the research phase of his work. He has composed in many musical styles, from 1930s swing music to various African styles. "I now actually feel there's no style I couldn't compose in," Josh says. "I found that if I subjugated my personality in service of the project at hand, it broadened the boundaries of what I had previously thought was possible."

He can talk about music endlessly, attributing his continuing fascination to his typical Blue curiosity and insatiable desire to keep learning. "There's no amount that's too much to learn to be good at what I do. Generally speaking, I'm not good at marketing, but people can see my curiosity and the passion I have," he says.

Like most Blues, Josh is very into using technology in his work. "I have a bank of 45 sound modules, samplers, and computers in my studio that all interact in a constant wrestling match!" he says. "Within my software programs are many things I didn't know could be done. When I discover them, I can't wait to tweak with the results in my studio."

Fortunately for Josh, the business and bookkeeping side that Blues hate is minimal for him. "It's not too much fun," he says, "but with the advent of computers, the billing isn't bad."

He works alone for hours and often works for clients he's never met. That suits his Introverted sidejust fine. "When clients have musical knowledge, it can be even worse than when they don't," he says.

Josh's top three strengths would sound surprising to anyone but another Blue. "I can take criticism," he says. "My biggest strength is my curiosity. And I always had great self-discipline."

## Ideal Work Environment

Key to your job satisfaction are four conditions: smart, competent, competitive, and independent co-workers like Glen Frontera has; control over your own projects like Josh Stone has; intellectual stimulation from complex problems and continuous learning like Jeanette Hobson has; and privacy to think things through in great depth. If all these conditions are present within your workplace as they are at Jeannette Hobson's and Glenn Frontera's, your success (barring politics) is inevitable.

When a job offer is made, leverage as much as you can from the list in Figure 17–2.

The WORST type of work culture for an Blue/Gold Introvert is overly bureaucratic. It is full of sensitive people who need exorbitant amounts of handholding. Too much emphasis is put on detail work, not enough on long-range thinking and strategizing. You need private space and unbridled creativity and competition in order to feel comfortable at work.

When Blue/Gold Introverts work in nonideal corporate cultures, productivity is stunted and career achievements become an uphill climb.

## The Blue/Gold Introvert's Ideal Boss

Even a great job can be frustrating under the wrong boss; a mediocre job under a wonderful boss is pretty hard to leave. Blue/Golds get along especially well with other Blues. But bosses of other Color types who possess the characteristics in Figure 17–3 also can be good mentors.

## Careers That Attract Blue/Gold Introverts

Autonomy is critical to you. Environments that reward original thinking, solving complex problems, and mastering new technology provide fertile soil for a stellar career like Josh Stone's.

## Figure 17-2    The Ideal Blue/Gold Introvert Work Environment

Compare your current work environment to the description below. Check all that ring true for you. Don't be deceived if these descriptions seem "obvious." It confirms you've tested your individual color correctly. Other Colors, especially Greens and Reds, would find this environment uncomfortable and unproductive. The optimal Blue/Gold Introvert work environment:

☐ Must provide privacy for uninterrupted thought.
☐ Affords ability to work independently.
☐ Permits control of your own projects.
☐ Must be intellectually challenging with high standards.
☐ Values creativity.
☐ Rewards your strategic skills.
☐ Contains competent and competitive people.
☐ Compensates you for meeting your goals.

*Please note that not all* the following careers will appeal to you, but recognize that each, in some way, draws on the strengths of your style and appeals to a significant number of your Color group. This is not a comprehensive list, but it will show underlying patterns of preference. If unlisted careers offer similar patterns, your chances of success increase. Copy in parentheses highlights the Color style characteristics that create success.

In addition, two codes indicate those jobs that are currently predicted to have an above-average salary and growth potential. This information is

## Figure 17-3    The Blue/Gold Introvert's Ideal Boss

Check off if your boss:

☐ Is a well-respected expert in the field.
☐ Can make the tough decisions.
☐ Sets high standards for you and him- or herself.
☐ Encourages creative problem solving.
☐ Gives you a high degree of autonomy.
☐ Trusts and respects your competence.

based on the continuously revised data provided by the U.S. Department of Labor and Bureau of Labor Statistics available on the O*NET website, *http://online.onetcenter.org/*.

> **Bold** indicates that the career is considered to be among the top **100 best-paying jobs** based on the average or median salary paid to individuals *with five years of experience.* Excluded are jobs where salary statistics are not available, such as "business owner," or not indicative such as "actor."
>
> *Italics* identifies the jobs that are predicted to benefit from an above-average growth rate over the next several years.
>
> ***Bold and italics*** indicates jobs that will benefit from both **higher pay** and *high growth potential.*
>
> Note there are successful people of all Color styles in all occupations. In nonideal jobs you can still shine by creating your own niche.

## Arts/Architecture/Communication/Media

**architect** ◆ composer ◆ art/movie/theatre critic ◆ *book publishing professional* ◆ *literary agent* ◆ *film producer/director* ◆ *multimedia training specialist* ◆ news analyst/reporter ◆ ***web designer*** (see complex interconnections, insatiably curious, have many facts at your fingertips, gifted strategic thinker, autonomy, deep concentration powers, faith in own insights, high standards).

## Business/Management/Finance

**actuary** ◆ bankers of all types ◆ **budget analyst** ◆ credit analyst ◆ **chief financial officer/controller** ◆ *compensation and benefits manager* ◆ **economist** ◆ **executive coach** ◆ **executive** [private sector, government] ◆ **financial analyst** ◆ *financial planner* ◆ *franchise/small business owner* ◆ *investment analyst* ◆ *investment banker* ◆ *investment/securities broker* ◆ **manager-financial branch/department** ◆ *marketing manager* ◆ *market research analyst* ◆ **operation research analyst** ◆ **venture capitalist** (decisive, focused, take-charge, high standards, need for control, solving complex problems, long-range strategic thinking, natural leadership skills).

## Computer/Information Technology

*database administrator* ◆ *hardware/software engineer* ◆ *information systems manager* ◆ *network systems and data communication analyst* ◆ **programmer** ◆ **security specialist** ◆ **systems analyst** ◆ *support specialist* ◆

*internet marketer* (mastering new technologies, solving complex and/or theoretical problems, autonomy, clear and direct communications, long-range planning, future possibilities, bold new designs, contingency planning, high need for control).

## Consulting

*management consultant* ◆ **organizational development specialist** ◆ political consultant ◆ *telecommunications security consultant* (see the big picture in unrelated facts and concepts, solve complex problems, at ease with theories and future possibilities, long-range planning, contingency planning).

## Education

*higher education teacher/university professor* [especially economics, science, or social studies] ◆ **university president** (need to deal with competent people, establish long-range visions, strategic planning, few routine tasks, autonomy, debate skill).

## Government/Public Administration

government service executives ◆ financial examiner ◆ judge ◆ **urban and regional planners** (ability to tackle complex issues, long-range planning, respect of community).

## Health Science

*anesthesiologist* ◆ *cardiologist* ◆ *geneticist* ◆ *internist* ◆ *neurologist* ◆ nuclear medicine technologist ◆ *pathologist* ◆ *surgeon* ◆ *psychiatrist* (intellectual challenge, need for control, tackle complex problems).

## Law

*lawyer* [administrative, aeronautic, corporate, employment, entertainment, product liability, project finance, among others] ◆ *paralegal* (solving complex problems, intellectual stimulation, high compensation).

## Scientific Research, Engineering, Mathematics

**aerospace engineer** ◆ **astronomer** ◆ *biochemist* ◆ *biomedical engineer* ◆ *biophysicist* ◆ **chemical/environmental/nuclear engineer** ◆ **economist** ◆ *environmental scientist* ◆ **industrial psychologist** ◆ inventor ◆ *medical scientist* ◆ **political scientist** ◆ **space scientist** (strategic thinking, long-range planning, intellectual challenges, little routine or repetitive work, insatiable curiosity, need for control, tackle complex problems, opportunity to interact with people you respect).

## When a Career Isn't Working

Web designer Rory MacAfee was having a bad day. The design he knew from research and testing would work best for his firm's biggest client had just been shot down. Even Rory's boss was shocked. But ultimately Rory knew it would come back to haunt him.

The client had insisted on "something more artistic and less logical-sounding; something more today and less futuristic." All the appreciation Rory had been anticipating for his long hours and deep strategic thought had evaporated. In its place came a nightmare of requests he had no clue how to fulfill. He wished he owned the brilliant design and its vast potential. But all his work was copyrighted by his employer. Rory had no alternative but to struggle with the client's requests.

After college, he had been so enthused about web design. He saw it as a way to spend the day doing what he loved—programming and being around other techies. This had happened; but Rory never anticipated the amount of artistic demands he would have to handle, for which he frankly had little aptitude. Today's dressing down was the worst yet; he could feel his temples start to throb with yet another of the excruciating tension headaches he'd started having since he took this job.

Rory knew that day he had to make a change. He started talking to Tetiran, his cubicle neighbor, about the idea of starting a firm of their own. Tetiran was enthusiastic. So were Tetiran's rich relatives, who bankrolled the two young programmers to start their own company designing security software for financial corporations.

Rory's role in the new firm was strategic planning and implementation. He took to it like a fish to water. Today he loves his job and deals with matters of future rather than artistic direction. He and Tetiran own all the programs they've created and are well on their way to making their first million.

## Your Personality's Challenges

Blue/Gold Introverts have a unique set of potential work-related blind spots. Some you have, others you don't. No one has them all. Tone down a blind spot by focusing on it, then choose more productive actions and make them habits. (Suggestions for doing so are in parentheses below.) You:

◆ May be too abrupt, harsh, or dogmatic. (Everyone needs allies at some point. Alienating others is a strategic error, even if they seem less competent or less intellectual. Patience is a [long-range] virtue. Emotions underpin every successful product and team, equally with all your best strategic thinking. Once daily, require yourself to show empathy to someone and note the results.)

◆ Can be unwilling to open your complex thought processes to review or challenge. (You may find it difficult even to get people to understand your deep and brilliant insights, much less agree with or sign off on them. But refusing to discuss them until the end of a project, then being unwilling to change them at that point, is a bad strategy. "You against the world" is pretty poor odds. Break your plan down into steps, and then share it from the beginning to prevent opposition.)

◆ Believe you must do things yourself because no one else is capable. (This comes off as arrogance, which co-workers and bosses resent. They may not do things your way, but each Color brings strengths that you may or may not recognize to the table. There are many paths to the same destination, some even better than yours, believe it or not! Don't you at least want to know what they are?)

◆ May irritate others by being overly skeptical when information is presented. (Many Colors take this as a personal challenge, thinking you don't trust or respect their work. Ask all the questions you want, but soften them with the lead-in phrase, "This seems like good work that you've spent considerable time on. I have some questions, if you don't mind.")

## Your Job Search—the Good, the Bad, and the Ugly

Blue/Gold Introverts are direct and to the point, creating resumes that follow a systematic process of presenting career achievements. With some interviewers, particularly Blues and Golds, you will feel a comfortable rapport. But with those of other Colors, you need to prepare and rehearse responses outside your comfort zone. Many human resource people are Greens; make a study of how to communicate effectively with this Color group before your first interviews.

Your natural strengths easily allow you to:

◆ Create measurable and long-term goals for your career.
◆ Research and integrate new trends into your job search plan.
◆ Get jobs created for you by presenting enough innovative ideas.
◆ Are disciplined about following through on leads.
◆ Create time lines, daily status reports, and realistic budgets for your job search that reduce stress on you and your family.

In order to tone down your blind spots, you need to:

◆ Think outside your select but limited network of associates; overcome your reluctance to ask for job leads from those you don't know.
◆ Pay attention to the personal aspects of job hunting, i.e., establishing rapport with the interviewer, sending thank-you notes, overtly appreciating the efforts of secretaries and support staff you encounter.
◆ Cushion your tendency to be abrupt by extending answers and listening without interrupting.
◆ Realize when you're sounding arrogant so you can control it at will; role play with a willing Green.
◆ Request support from friends and family to stay on track when setbacks and obstacles upset you.

## The Blue/Gold Introvert's Interviewing Style

With an interviewer whose Color is close to your own, you will feel immediate rapport. However, if your interviewer seems to have a significantly different style (and it's statistically likely that they will have a Green component), use the suggestions in parentheses.

In following your natural style, you:

◆ Will impress interviewers as competent and insightful. (A Green interviewer will ask emotion-based questions like "Did you enjoy those duties?" Be prepared with answers more extended than "Yes." A Red interviewer will want to establish some kind of rapport.)
◆ May come across as arrogant or too abstract. (It is not necessary to humble yourself, but don't attempt to build up your accomplishments at anyone's expense. Show respect for previous colleagues so future ones know they can expect it, too. You'll gain no points by overwhelming your interviewer with highly technical jargon. Keep in it plain English; let your resume communicate your abilities.)
◆ Might not convey enough enthusiasm during the interview. (You are passionate about ideas, but don't express it freely. Role-play sharing

just a little of that passion; ask a willing Green or Red. You'll come across as really wanting the job. This also will overcome your tendency to appear enigmatic.)

◆ May need to be more flexible when considering a job offer. ("My way or the highway" is not a good strategy for negotiating duties and compensation. Listen, counter-offer, take a day to think through what's right for you and your family, and counter-offer again. Establish in advance realistic boundaries for what is acceptable; don't make it a competitive fight to the death.)

Once you've critiqued this profile and decided we've gotten enough things right to make it worthwhile, go on and read Chapter 20, Golds Overall, first, then carefully read Chapter 25, Adjusting to the Styles of Others, to learn about the strengths of other Colors. Read up on the Greens to prepare for job interviews (a large number of human resource people are Greens) and the Reds if you have to interact with any at work or at home.

If you are actively engaging in a job search, keep notes in the Roadmap in Chapter 28. Recording your strengths and strategies is a concrete and results-oriented way to navigate the minefields of a job search. You also can keep track of contacts for follow-up.

# CHAPTER 18

# Blue/Red Extroverts

YOU'RE NOT ONLY A BLUE, you also have strong secondary characteristics of the adventurous Red personality. And you have tested as a Color Q Extrovert, which means you recharge your batteries by being with people, rather than being alone. Your Color group prides itself on finding innovative ways to do things. You take initiative and surmount all limitations with a "can do" attitude. Please note the underlying components of the following profile have been researched for nearly six decades worldwide and verified across age, sex, ethnic, and socioeconomic boundaries. So if we don't get you right, nobody will!

## You Overall

Blue/Red Extroverts radiate a contagious enthusiasm for anything that captures their interest. You constantly scan the universe for those new and unusual ideas that fire your vivid imagination. Creative, insightful, and mentally stimulating, you love the challenge and excitement of pursuing your latest goal . . . until it ceases to interest you. But until then, you are tireless, energizing others as you charge ahead.

Whether you've got advanced degrees or not, you are blessed with high intellectual energy, constantly on the alert for the latest and greatest opportunities. When you see them, you pounce. Inquisitive and clever, you need a great deal of freedom to use your many talents. A flexible environment is key. Unconventional approaches are fun for you, and you will bend or break rules as needed to make things happen. Following through to the bitter end once the project has been launched, however, is of little interest.

You are used to people disagreeing with your perceptions. Whether others agree with you is not important. Since childhood you've enjoyed an inborn ability to debate from either side of an issue, confounding opponents at times by jumping back and forth. You are naturally quick on your feet. Ultimately, your enthusiasm and the compelling power of your ideas persuade all.

You are unique among the Colors for your ability to be both serious and humorous, speaking with passion and wit. However, you prefer logic to emotion and are irritated by others who require too much handholding. People who refuse to consider new ways of doing things really annoy you.

case study one

## Chief Executive Officer, Chairman, Board Member, Financial Services

If Blue/Red Extroverts are overachievers, then Alger B. ("Duke") Chapman is their poster boy. Starting his law career in the late 1950s at the Securities and Exchange Commission (SEC), he rapidly moved on to the New York Stock Exchange as its Vice President for civic, legal, and government affairs.

Six years later he joined Shearson and Hamill Company, one of the pre-eminent wirehouses of the day, as Vice President. Within four years he became their President at age 39, and subsequently their Chief Executive Officer. Later he became co-chair (with the famous Sanford "Sandy" Weill) of Shearson Hayden Stone (which became Shearson Loeb Rhodes, and finally Shearson American Express). It is not unusual for Blue/Reds to rise to such ranks at young ages.

Duke's upward climb was just beginning. In 1981 he became Vice Chairman of American Express International Bank. Five years later he moved into the CEO/Chairman role at the Chicago Board Options Exchange, where he stayed longer than anywhere else—eleven years.

He then joined ABN AMRO Financial Services, Inc. as Chairman and CEO before retiring. To stay plugged in, Duke now serves as senior advisor to the consulting firm The Cambridge Group and serves on numerous boards.

Duke defines his experiences in terms of the fun he had with people or the challenges he faced. At the SEC, he recalls, "We all had opportunities we never would have had in private law practice. It was fast-moving, dealing with exciting people and big issues." Blue/Reds revel in grappling with the issues of today that shape tomorrow. At Shearson and Hamill, "It was great fun. There were terrific guys to work with, and we all had a great time; it was a great run." These experiences appealed to Duke's Red and Extroverted sides.

His Blue ability to analyze and solve problems propelled him to the attention of senior management at Shearson and Hamill. His bosses would ask him to identify "the next biggest problem we have." "So I would tell them what I thought," says Duke, "and then I'd be told, 'Go do something about it.'" This grooming led to his role as President and CEO, right in time for the economic downturn of the early 1970s.

Duke then found himself pressured to find a partner company in order to keep Shearson economically viable. He met American Express chairman Sandy Weill, and they decided to merge. The press had a field day. "The only difference between this merger and the Titanic is that on the Titanic they had a piano," wrote the *Wall Street Journal*. Duke's Red side, even with its natural crisis management strengths, took it on the chin. But he emerged victorious: "I think I function well under a lot of pressure," Duke says. His Blue strategic ability led him to acquire several other firms. Seven years later, the newly combined entity was sold directly to American Express for almost $1 billion in American Express stock. Duke stayed on as co-chair, but later moved to the American Express International Banking Corporation as Vice Chairman to build an offshore banking business. Onerous world travel commitments finally led to accepting the CEO position at the Chicago Board Options Exchange.

He assesses his top three strengths as the ability to manage people and create relationships, strategically analyze and move a company in the best direction, and put the business and its customers first. He prefers to delegate the nitty-gritty of back office processing and implementation details.

I personally had the privilege of working with Duke Chapman at American Express. Here's my favorite story about him: One morning we sat in Singapore's airport, noting with horror that the travel office had forgotten to get him the required business visa for Indonesia. The plane was taking off in 60 minutes. A dozen high-level appointments awaited us in Jakarta. Duke thought for a minute. Then, with a grin, he dove into the nearest clothing store, emerging shortly in a garish floral shirt and camera, looking very much the tourist. (Tourists, according to regulations, didn't need this visa.) The trip went off without a hitch. Several hours later he emerged in formal business attire to meet his clients, a natural Blue/Red problem-solver chalking up another great story.

# You on the Job

## As a Leader

"Let's exceed goals!" will be the theme of any pep talk given by a Blue/Red Extrovert. You lead and motivate with energy, taking initiative, making the tough decisions, comfortable with risk. Your well-developed problem-solving skills and tendency to challenge conventional wisdom move everyone forward.

You set the bar high for your people, and you don't hire the marginally competent. Your people exceed limitations and quickly adapt to changing conditions because you respect their independence. This is especially critical since you often gravitate to global issues.

## As a Team Player

A "can do" approach is how you begin each project. You are apt to suggest high standards and encourage everyone to go the extra mile. Contributing best at the first half of a project, you ask imaginative questions and provide clear analysis. Your ability to think strategically long-term always helps set team direction. When coping with fatigue and tension, humor is your tool of choice.

Finding unique ways of solving problems is another strength, and you will generate many options for consideration. While it is unusual for teammates to dislike you, you occasionally may irritate them by proposing too many possibilities.

Look at Figure 18–1 on page 162 for a list of your natural work-related strengths.

Now see how some Blue/Red Extroverts use these strengths in very different fields.

### Figure 18-1    Natural Work-Related Strengths

Approximately 80 percent of these attributes will apply to you. Check off those that do and use them in your resume and interviews. This will set you apart from the canned responses of others. You:

☐ Are particularly good at startups or the initial stage of a project.
☐ See the big picture.
☐ Inspire others through energy, enthusiasm, and colorful communication.
☐ Take an interest in complex problems.
☐ Are energized when seeking new and more creative solutions.
☐ Enjoy brainstorming and are one of the most effective Colors at it.
☐ Can work with a broad range of people.
☐ Analyze situations objectively.
☐ Reduce tension with humor.
☐ Are willing to take risks.

case study two
_____

## Surgeon

Dr. Charles "Chuck" Sheaff is a classic Blue/Red Extrovert. He got his undergraduate degree in engineering and intended to become a biomedical engineer. "In medical school, I got sidetracked," he says. "I ended up getting a Ph.D. in biochemistry instead. Then I became more interested in surgery, because there's a lot of immediate gratification in it. At the end of an operation, the problem is fixed and the person usually gets well and goes home."

With his Red backup, Chuck was drawn to emergency surgery, which he taught for two years. "When I am faced with a patient who is bleeding to death and a lot of things have to be done in a short period of time, that tends to make me more focused and organized," he says. "I tend to be almost easier to get along with then than I am in some other situations."

One thing Chuck's Red side enjoys is flying. "I like instrument flying," he says, "and solving the navigational problems." This is an excellent combination of his Blue and Red characteristics.

Chuck has served in leadership positions at his hospital for the last ten years. "I like politics," he says. "It's rewarding to solve problems in a political arena." Blue/Red Extroverts make excellent politicians and are drawn to the politics of any field in which they work.

In classic Blue/Red Extrovert fashion, Chuck uses his engineering skills to create innovative solutions wherever he is. "I saw a Christmas tree hanging upside down in a shop, and it made more sense that the ornaments could hang so they were easily seen," he recalls. "I devised a way to keep the tree better watered upside down, and the project worked out well. The tree stayed alive until Easter."

A true Blue innovator, Chuck fantasizes about establishing a small think tank organization. "It would be fun," he says, "to have some people working for me to solve problems, invent new things, and take them to market."

case study three

## Managing Director, Executive Recruiting

Some people's resumes are too big for ordinary jobs, and such is the case with Chuck Wardell. If you don't know his name, you are not high enough up in the corporate food chain. Chuck is the Managing Director for the Northeast Region of Korn/Ferry International, the world's largest recruiting firm. He got the job because his own background brought him into contact with many high-level people. Today he knows who to call for almost any executive placement need.

After a distinguished career in the military and graduation from Harvard, Chuck worked for Henry Kissinger as Deputy Assistant Secretary of State. He served in the White House under two Presidents. He was the Chief Operating Officer of American Express's private bank and ran its Middle East Credit Card Division. He also managed The Business Diversification Group, a large division of Traveller's Insurance. "Search requires years of judging and leading people," he says, "dealing with their successes and failures, formulating the building blocks of what they need to get ahead."

Chuck likes meeting the demands of today's changing workforce, dealing with baby boomers whose experience now suddenly is back in vogue after the dotcom implosion. "Firms are beginning to realize they have to invest and keep good people," he notes. "Companies are demanding experience over academic credentials. Now we want senior people with experience who get compensated for performance."

Chuck most enjoys the variety his work affords him, something important to his Color style. He especially likes working with those at senior levels on important issues, where the people he places have real world impact. "What I do influences how the capitalist system works," he says. But Chuck has three priorities for himself—maximizing his income, keeping his independence, and enjoying what he does—all hallmarks of his Color style.

Blues enjoy complex challenges more than many Colors, and that's a good thing because Chuck gets some esoteric requests. "The other day someone wanted a manager for a steel mill north of Beijing. The workforce speaks Mandarin. The company manual is in German. The financing is Canadian, and the current manager is English. How do you find an executive who can step into this and do all the pieces?"

## Ideal Work Environment

The opportunity to meet stimulating, powerful, and influential people often is the key that gets you to accept a job. (This motivated Duke Chapman to join the SEC.) Working on cutting-edge ideas is right where you want to be.

When a job offer is made, leverage as much as you can from the list in Figure 18–2.

The WORST type of work culture for an Blue/Red Extrovert is one in which you are micromanaged and surrounded by co-workers who lack initiative. It emphasizes detailed work with predictable results.

When Blue/Red Extrovert work in nonideal corporate cultures, productivity is stunted, and career achievements become an uphill climb.

**Figure 18-2   The Ideal Blue/Red Extrovert Work Environment**

Compare your current work environment to the description below. Don't be deceived if these descriptions seem "obvious." It confirms you've tested your individual Color correctly. Other Colors, especially Golds, would find this environment uncomfortable and unproductive. The optimal Blue/Red Extrovert work environment:

☐ Provides a variety of tasks and projects.
☐ Is creative, entrepreneurial, and nonstructured.
☐ Rewards expertise and quick thinking.
☐ Creates new products and solutions.
☐ Is a continuous opportunity for new learning.
☐ Lets you assemble a competent staff of people who do not need to be micromanaged.
☐ Offers the opportunity to interact with powerful or influential people.

## The Extroverted Blue/Red's Ideal Boss

Even a great job can be frustrating under the wrong boss; a mediocre job under a wonderful boss is pretty hard to leave. Blue/Reds get along especially well with other Blues. But bosses of other Color types who possess the characteristics in Figure 18–3 also can be good mentors.

**Figure 18-3   The Blue/Red Extrovert's Ideal Boss**

Check off if your boss:

☐ Can make tough decisions.
☐ Is competent and respected.
☐ Keeps bureaucracy at bay.
☐ Has a sense of humor.
☐ Does not micromanage you.
☐ Sets high standards.
☐ Values and rewards innovation.
☐ Provides all necessary resources to ensure tasks are accomplished.

## Careers That Attract Blue/Red Extroverts

Blue/Red Extroverts are most productive in environments that reward their intellectual energy, original ideas, and risk-taking. You especially enjoy original projects dealing with global issues.

*Please note that not all* the following careers will appeal to you, but recognize that each, in some way, draws on the strengths of your style and appeals to a significant number of your Color group. This is not a comprehensive list but it will show underlying patterns of preference. If unlisted careers offer similar patterns, your chances of success increase. Copy in parentheses highlights the Color style characteristics that create success.

In addition, two codes indicate those jobs that are currently predicted to have an above-average salary and growth potential. This information is based on the continuously revised data provided by the U.S. Department of Labor and Bureau of Labor Statistics available on the O*NET website, *http://online.onetcenter.org/*.

---

**Bold** indicates that the career is considered to be among the top **100 best-paying jobs** based on the average or median salary paid to individuals *with five years of experience.* Excluded are jobs where salary statistics are not available, such as "business owner," or not indicative such as "actor."

*Italics* identifies the jobs that are predicted to benefit from an above-average growth rate over the next several years.

***Bold and italics*** indicates jobs that will benefit from both **higher pay** and *high growth potential*.

Note there are successful people of all Color styles in all occupations. In nonideal jobs you can still shine by creating your own niche.

---

### Business/Finance/Administration

*executive* [business, financial services, healthcare, entertainment] ◆ *financial planner* ◆ **hotel manager** ◆ *investment banker* ◆ *broker/securities sales agent* ◆ *management consultant* ◆ *new business development specialist* ◆ property manager ◆ **financial analyst** ◆ *sales manager* ◆ *training and development specialist* ◆ **venture capitalist** (inquisitive, take initiative, compelling interest in everything around you, insightful, open to new and unusual opportunities, quick on your feet).

### Communications/Creative/Marketing

*advertising director* ◆ *business manager* [artists, entertainers, athletes] ◆ writer ◆ editor ◆ *journalist* ◆ *literary agent* ◆ ***public relations director***/publicist ◆ talk show host ◆ stage/film producer ◆ *web developer/designer* (high intellectual energy, love of excitement and challenge, responsive to new opportunities, clever, enjoy company of influential people).

## Computer/Information Technology

*computer analyst/engineer/programmer* ◆ *computer security specialist/ information and systems manager* ◆ *Internet strategic partnerships specialist* ◆ *network integration specialist* ◆ *systems analyst* (provides variety of projects, creation of new products and solutions, autonomy, opportunity to brainstorm, problem solving, flexible environment, need for unconventional methods).

## Education

*athletic coach* ◆ professor/*teacher* [upper levels] (high intellectual energy, flexible environments, see both sides of issues, quick on your feet, prefer logic).

## Entrepreneurship/Hospitality

inventor ◆ restaurant/bar owner ◆ *small business owner* (make tough decisions, flexible entrepreneurial atmosphere, turn innovative ideas into reality, responsive to new opportunities and unusual ideas, contagious enthusiasm, freedom, quick on your feet).

## Health Science/Psychology

*emergency room doctor/surgeon* ◆ *family practitioner* ◆ *internist* ◆ *psychiatrist* (variety, autonomy, flexible environment, quick on your feet, high intellectual energy, problem solving).

## Politics/Government

politician/political manager ◆ regional/urban planner (quickly see possibilities of new situations, provide clear analysis to issues, generate many options, strategic and long-range thinking, enjoy company of powerful and influential people)

## Law

*lawyer* [especially bankruptcy, immigration, litigation, mergers and acquisitions, intellectual property, among others] (analytical ability, insightful, see both sides of issues, quick on your feet, enjoy company of influential people)

## Professions

**architect** ◆ detective ◆ **industrial engineer** ◆ **industrial psychologist** (high standards, clear analytical ability, love excitement and challenge, insightful, always looking to increase competence, ability to debate from both sides of an issue, autonomy, responsibility for own projects, quick on your feet)

## case study four

# When a Career Isn't Working

Brad Kittering's great-grandfather had founded the First National Bank in the town where he grew up, and Brad determined to go into banking to follow family tradition.

From the day Brad started at First National as a bank teller, it looked to the world like another young Kittering was on his way up the ladder to the bank president's office. Brad was great with the customers and rapidly developed a loyal group of depositors who never complained if he made a mistake. Behind the scenes, he was a disaster. Try as he might, Brad miscounted money, was terrible at following the bank's many arcane rules, and was bored out of his skull dealing with the details of his drawer. He was warned several times to shape up and would have been fired but for his last name.

Brad was intrigued by the internal bank newsletter, and on a whim contributed an article on how to deal with difficult customers. It was very well received, and a highly regarded banking trade journal asked to run it nationwide. Blue/Red Extroverts make excellent journalists because they are interested in people to the point of nosiness and often are good writers.

Brad continued submitting articles and was asked to be a regular columnist to the trade journal. Today he writes and lectures on banking customer service through his own consulting company.

## Your Personality's Challenges

Blue/Red Extroverts have a unique set of potential work-related blind spots. Some you have, others you don't. No one has them all. Tone down a blind spot by focusing on it, then choose more productive actions and make them habits. (Suggestions for doing so are in parentheses below.) You:

- ◆ Initiate too many projects, some of which don't get completed. (You can get swept away by your own enthusiasm. A good rule for you: Don't start something until you've finished the last project.)

- Can be too casual about deadlines and commitments. (Work is fun, but it's still work. If you're getting paid to meet deadlines, then meet them. Your work ethic will incorporate this value more as you mature and get yelled at by your bosses.)
- Intimidate those less quick-witted. (You have little use for those less competent than yourself. Particularly when you're young, it's a sport to run them around verbally. But, one of them could end up as your boss. Diplomacy can be your friend.)
- Sometimes change plans and strategies too frequently. (If you're working on your own, you will lose focus; within a company, you will upset all those whose talents you need to make things happen. But lost focus often equals lost money.)
- Want too much of the limelight. (Put yourself out to be noticed when someone else deserves the attention, and you create bad blood. Be sure to share the limelight once you have it with those who deserve applause, or else watch your back!)

## Your Job Search—the Good, the Bad, and the Ugly

Blue/Red Extroverts create succinct, objective resumes but prefer talking in person. With some interviewers, particularly Blues and Reds, you will feel a comfortable rapport. But with those of other Colors, you need to prepare and rehearse responses outside your comfort zone. Many human resource people are Greens; make a study of how to communicate effectively with this Color group before your first interviews.

Your natural strengths easily allow you to:

- Find multiple paths to explore during job searches.
- Have an extensive network to tap for referrals and job leads.
- Rebound quickly from obstacles and rejections.

In order to tone down your blind spots, you need to:

- Write down long-term goals and your plans for getting there; include priorities and checkpoints.
- Limit your time off to play during the job search.
- Remember your goals while networking and don't get lost in the fun of it.
- Make a budget for your job search based on a realistic timeframe.
- Follow through on all administrative details of the job search; ask assistance from a willing Gold.
- Temper initial excitement about a prospective job; review impact on your family and personal life before accepting.

## The Blue/Red Extrovert's Interviewing Style

With an interviewer whose Color is close to your own, you will feel immediate rapport. However, if your interviewer seems to have a significantly different style, use the suggestions in parentheses. In following your natural style, you:

◆ Come across as energetic, flexible, adaptable, and creative. (You establish rapport with interviewers easily. With cooler ones, address them by their last names until invited to use first names, then let them set the tone.)

◆ Might talk too much and not ask enough pertinent questions. (Write critical questions down on a list and refer to them. Slip them in between the fun parts of the conversation.)

◆ May overwhelm more concrete types with possibilities and theory. (If your interviewer seems to glaze over when you go into theoretical areas, back away. Let him or her lead the conversation until you can assess his or her areas of interest.)

If you're having fun with this material, go on and read Chapter 10, Reds Overall, to understand your backup. Then carefully read Chapter 4, A Tour of the Prism Company, and Chapter 25, Adjusting to the Styles of Others, to learn about the strengths of other Colors. Read up on the Greens to prepare for job interviews (a large number of human resource people are Greens) and the Golds if you have to interact with any at work or at home.

If you are actively engaging in a job search, keep notes in the Roadmap in Chapter 28. Recording your strengths and strategies is a logical and results-oriented way to navigate the minefields of a job search and brainstorm some unconventional approaches. It also will help keep your networking activities focused.

# CHAPTER 19

# Blue/Red Introverts

**YOU'RE NOT ONLY A BLUE,** you also have strong secondary characteristics of the Red personality. And you have tested as a Color Q Introvert, which means you recharge your batteries by being alone, rather than being with others. Much, but not all, of this material will focus on human and emotional subjects, which your Color finds irritating. You will be more open to this if you are in the second half of your life, but will need it more if you are younger. But since you respond to new ideas, the aim will be to surprise you with our accuracy.

## You Overall

Did the paragraph above surprise you? Okay, let's see what else we can say to rock your highly logical world. After all, you are open-minded. Mental stimulation is as necessary to you as breathing. Color Q is a new derivative of a decades-old, tried-and-true system of personality profiling. It goes back to concepts proposed by Carl Jung. There are a lot of perspectives in here for you to debate, so get a friend to read this chapter with you and go at it from all angles. You're good at that.

Your group of friends is small, but intimate. Few see your real feelings. Emotional stuff is usually last on your list, but many of your friendships are formed over shared projects. Privacy is important, though, because when concentrating on something, you find interruptions irritating. So just view reading this as a new project on which you've decided to risk 20 minutes (or fewer; it's likely you skim or read fast).

New projects draw you like a magnet, often propelling you to the cutting edge of your field. Independent, resourceful, and a skeptic at heart, you are unafraid to take controversial positions.

It's necessary for you to have flexibility to critique, redesign, and improve—whether others understand or agree with your changes is irrelevant. You are confident of your ability to improvise your way through difficult problems that you doubt others even understand. Project follow-through, however, is of low interest.

Your unusual insights make you, at times, almost psychic about future trends, so people count on you for the most innovative systems and solutions. In your interest areas, you communicate with speed and enthusiasm; otherwise, you may not communicate at all.

People see you as clever, critical, challenging, and sometimes disorganized. You are most irritated by people who refuse to consider new ideas, who are overly emotional or who apply faulty logic.

case study one

## Entrepreneur, Small Business Expert

Jack Rubinstein "views the world at 50,000 feet" and aspires to view it at 60,000. He is Chairman of the Board of credit card processing company Pipeline Data and General Partner of DICA Partners, an investment hedge fund. For fifteen years, he has been an advisor to small public entities through his company Capital Market Advisory Network. He employs his ability to see three years out to mold small firms into multibillion dollar entities.

"My function," says Jack, "is to create alternate solutions for people who are too involved in the day-to-day nitty-gritty."

Jack's father owned a small business, and Jack remembers discussing the day's problems with him at the dinner table when he was 8 years old. When Jack began his career, he trained as a research analyst. "It's a curiosity, analyzing businesses of all sorts," Jack says.

Jack helps business owners navigate the capital markets and finds innovative ways to help them expand. "I was an advisor to a $20 million company, showing them how to 'creep the market' making 37 different acquisitions over a 24-month period," Jack recalls. "Then they were sold to GE Capital for over $1 billion.

"I was also an original backer of Sirius Satellite Radio when they had three employees, a driven entrepreneur, and virtually no money. I saw a combination of possibilities that allowed me to get the vision, whereas very few other people could. Now their market capitalization is $10 billion."

Jack has the Blue/Red Introvert's vision for small companies that can become large. He delegates all his detail work and recordkeeping to a Gold family member.

## You on the Job

### As a Leader

"High quality" is the cornerstone of your leadership. Whether it applies to the new ideas you propose, the people you hire to implement them, or the work standards you set, high quality is always the theme. To meet standards, you'll even challenge conventional wisdom or push your people to develop themselves intellectually.

Flexible and quick to adapt to change, you will be the first both to see and solve problems. Understanding global issues is your real talent.

### Figure 19-1   Natural Work-Related Strengths

Approximately 80 percent of these attributes will apply to you. Check off those that do and use them in your resume and interviews. This will set you apart from the canned responses of others. You:

☐ Keep creating and improving ideas.
☐ Evaluate situations logically and analytically.
☐ Provide calm amidst emotional storms.
☐ Solve complex problems creatively.
☐ Are open to new information and will change decisions if necessary.
☐ Demand high-quality and rigorous intellectual application.
☐ Rarely get sidetracked into chitchat.
☐ Focus intensely for long periods.

## As a Team Player

Asking imaginative questions, generating many unique solutions, and accepting the good contributions of others are characteristics for which you are valued.

You may NOT be valued for pointing out every flaw or inconsistency or for indulging in overly intellectual or complicated descriptions.

Look at Figure 19–1 for a list of your natural work-related strengths.

Here are some Blue/Red Introverts in action in very different fields.

case study two

## Medical Research Scientist and University Professor

Bruce I. Terman, Ph.D.'s resume is replete with long lists of medical research experience, grants awarded, and papers published. Behind the credentials is actually a likable guy (not unusual for those with a Red backup), who cares about doing the right thing.

Between the classes he teaches as Associate Professor of the Medicine/Cardiology Division and Associate Professor of Pathology at the Albert Einstein College of Medicine in the Bronx, New York, Dr. Terman strives to be a good citizen at his university. Along with his main work in research, "I try to serve on administrative committees and participate in teaching and research seminars," he says.

As an Introvert, he especially enjoys the activities he performs on his own. Of his three top natural strengths, he does two of them alone. "I'm best at performing experiments and planning the scientific direction of the laboratory," he says. His third strength is teaching. He is energized by successfully obtaining grants, getting his papers published, and having his laboratory experiments produce expected or interesting results.

Another aspect of his job that well suits his Introverted side is obtaining funding to support his research. He applies for numerous grants. He also must keep abreast of his field by constantly reading scientific literature and attending national meetings of his peers (the latter he says is one of his least interesting duties). In the laboratory, he supervises the research activities of five individuals (a task that includes training of students and mentoring of other scientists). Typical of a Blue who chooses a scientific career, he is persistent about achieving his goals.

Dr. Terman's three biggest stressors are "supervising or interacting with noncooperative, nonproductive, or obnoxious individuals; waiting to hear about or having grants and manuscripts rejected; and getting poor experimental results."

That doesn't happen often. In 1994 he was named the Winner of the American Cyanamid Scientific Achievement Award. Dr. Terman is straightforward about his successes. "I am smart and honest," he says, a very typical Blue/Red combination. Then it's back into the lab to continue his life's work.

## case study three

## Hedge Fund Manager, Investment Industry

At age 26, Ari Levy is well on his way to recognizing and developing his unique Blue/Red Introvert strengths. He is the founder, President, and Chief Investment Officer of Chicago-based Lakeview Investment Group. Additionally, he functions as Portfolio Manager of the firm's limited partnership, Lakeview Fund, a long-short equity product focused on long-term investments in small and micro cap value securities.

True to his Blue/Red nature, he prefers the portfolio management and research functions over marketing and governmental compliance demands. "There is nothing more satisfying than doing thorough research on a stock and finding some inefficiency that makes it undervalued before Wall Street discovers it," Ari says.

Ari finds marketing less interesting, especially when "I don't find the person that I'm marketing to particularly interesting, or he or she doesn't understand what we do," he admits. This is typical of Blue/Red Introverts.

He prides himself on his understanding of financial risk and reward and his management skills. Blue/Red Introverts are deeply disciplined in their areas of interest. Ari is very disciplined in the portfolio management process, "although I am not as organized in certain areas of my personal life!"

Ari is a typical Blue/Red Introvert in other ways. He enjoys probability-based activities like gambling, investments, and card playing. His enjoyment of cutting edge activities is indulged every day at his hedge fund, forever trying to perfect investment models. Even at leisure, his interest lies in sports statistics.

## Ideal Work Environment

Jack's ability is to think innovatively about business is supported by a flexible environment. He also has the administrative support he needs to stay focused on what he does best. Ari, too, has created his own firm and sets his own agenda.

### Figure 19–2    The Ideal Blue/Red Introvert Work Environment

Compare your current work environment to the description below. Don't be deceived if these descriptions seem "obvious." It confirms you've tested your individual Color correctly. Other Colors, especially Golds, would find this environment uncomfortable and unproductive. The optimal Blue/Red Introvert work environment:

☐ Is flexible with a minimum of rules, procedures, and meetings. Nothing should impede the intellectual process.

☐ Values independent and creative thinking. You look at a problem as if it were a Rubik's cube—from all sides. Then you rearrange it until a solution becomes evident.

☐ Focuses on start-up phase of projects. Implementation and administration are left to the support staff in place for that purpose.

☐ Allows privacy and ability to work alone without too much time pressure. Two things you really hate—interruptions, and people breathing down your neck. You're much more productive without them.

☐ Is a nonemotional, logical culture that rewards competence and risk-taking. Emotions take time and energy. You'd rather put those resources into the risk-taking, which you analyze thoroughly beforehand to minimize.

☐ Contains an informal network of scholarly, independent, and motivated associates. You need to verbalize all sides of a problem and debate solutions. Hard to do by yourself, or with less competent co-workers.

When a job offer is made, leverage as much as you can from the list in Figure 19–2.

The WORST type of work culture for a Blue/Red Introvert is overly bureaucratic and controlled. Strict time management and required work area tidiness drive you to distraction. When co-workers are emotionally sensitive, or less competent than you, it stresses you to the limits of your patience.

When Blue/Reds Introverts work in nonideal corporate cultures, productivity is stunted and career achievements become an uphill climb.

## The Blue/Red Introvert's Ideal Boss

Even a great job can be frustrating under the wrong boss; a mediocre job under a wonderful boss is pretty hard to leave. Blue/Reds get along especially well with other Blues. But bosses of other Color types who possess the characteristics in Figure 19–3 also can be good mentors.

## Careers That Attract Blue/Red Introverts

You, like Bruce Terman, are most attracted to careers that require intellectual energy, original ideas, and achievement. You prefer involvement with theoretical problems and new technologies. Original projects are a must; routine and repeated tasks are sorely taxing.

*Please note that not all* the following careers will appeal to you, but recognize that each, in some way, draws on the strengths of your style and ap-

**Figure 19–3    The Blue/Red Introvert's Ideal Boss**

Check off if your boss:

☐ Permits complete autonomy.
☐ Treats employees as equals.
☐ Is smart, quick-witted, and stimulating.
☐ Shields you from the organization's bureaucracy.
☐ Does not saddle you with administrative work.
☐ Is open to improving existing systems and procedures.
☐ Asks you to come up with ideas, then has others implement.
☐ Recognizes and respects your expertise.
☐ Lets you have a say in how you are evaluated and compensated.

peals to a significant number of your Color group. This is not a comprehensive list, but it will show underlying patterns of preference. If unlisted careers offer similar patterns, your chances of success increase. Copy in parentheses highlights the Color style characteristics that create success.

In addition, two codes indicate those jobs that are currently predicted to have an above-average salary and growth potential. This information is based on the continuously revised data provided by the U.S. Department of Labor and Bureau of Labor Statistics available on the O*NET website, *http://online.onetcenter.org/*.

---

**Bold** indicates that the career is considered to be among the top **100 best-paying jobs** based on the average or median salary paid to individuals *with five years of experience.* Excluded are jobs where salary statistics are not available, such as "business owner," or not indicative such as "actor."

*Italics* identifies the jobs that are predicted to benefit from an above-average growth rate over the next several years.

***Bold and italics*** indicates jobs that will benefit from both **higher pay** and *high growth potential.*

Note there are successful people of all Color styles in all occupations. In nonideal jobs you can still shine by creating your own niche.

---

## Architecture/Creative/Media

**architect** ◆ artist ◆ creative writer ◆ critic ◆ editor ◆ graphic designer ◆ journalist ◆ musician ◆ news analyst ◆ photographer ◆ *film/stage/motion picture producer* ◆ *web developer/**designer*** (enjoy play and surprises, intense focus on everything around you).

## Business/Finance

**business analyst** ◆ change management consultant ◆ **economist** ◆ *financial planner* ◆ **financial analyst** ◆ **hedge fund manager** ◆ *investment banker* ◆ investment broker ◆ ***management consultant*** ◆ new market/ product designer ◆ *market research/ development specialist* ◆ **security analyst** ◆ *small business owner* ◆ strategic planner ◆ **statistician** ◆ **venture capitalist** (intellectual and insightful about future trends).

## Computer/Information Technology

*database administrator* ◆ *hardware/software engineer* ◆ *information systems manager* ◆ *network systems administrator* ◆ ***network integration specialist*** ◆ *programmer* ◆ *software designer* ◆ *security specialist* ◆ *systems* *analyst* ◆ *web developer/webmaster* (flexible environments where you can create, critique, redesign, and improve).

## Education

researcher ◆ *university professor* (intellectual stimulation, colleagues who enjoy debate).

## Health Science/Psychology

*medical scientist/researcher* ◆ **medical faculty** ◆ **neurologist** ◆ *pharmacist* ◆ *pharmaceutical researcher* ◆ **plastic surgeon** ◆ *psychologist/psychiatrist* (independence and intellectual stimulation, plus need for your ability to concentrate for long periods of time).

## Law

*lawyer* [especially banking, corporate finance, energy, product liability, intellectual property] (enjoy difficult problems, intellectual stimulation, love of debate).

## Scientific Research, Engineering, Mathematics

**aerospace/aeronautical/aircraft engineer** ◆ **astronomer** ◆ *biomedical engineer* ◆ chemist ◆ *biochemist* ◆ *biologist* ◆ *biophysicist* ◆ **chemical/civil engineer** ◆ *environmental scientist* ◆ **geneticist** ◆ **geologist** ◆ inventor ◆ **mathematician** ◆ *microbiologist* ◆ **natural science manager** ◆ **physicist** ◆ **space scientist** (opportunities to apply your love of solving difficult problems, be on cutting edge).

---

### case study four

## When a Career Isn't Working

Gretchen Kinderhook's father was a property manager for a large Midwestern office building. As a teenager, Gretchen used to join her dad after school to help out. She became fascinated anticipating the problems of the tenants and being ready to solve them as they arose. She also enjoyed the charged atmosphere when a tenant crisis arose. She thought her dad had the best job in the world.

When Gretchen was in her junior year at college studying business, her father died unexpectedly. With little life insurance in place, the family's security was threatened. Using all her Red crisis management skill, Gretchen dropped out and took over his job.

It was just as she had remembered it, and most of the tenants knew her by her first name. What Gretchen had not anticipated were the tasks her father had performed. They were so structured and stifling! Her Blue/Red Introvert's ability to see far in the future and strategize got little use as she dealt with getting the trash out, the leases renewed, the vendors contracted, the security staff hired, and the cleaning crew to show up.

Gretchen felt trapped by her obligation to help support her family. Dutifully, she went around to the tenants to renew leases. On the 18th floor was a small think tank with fifteen employees whose job it was to predict market trends for their blue chip clients. Gretchen lingered here, throwing out so many free ideas that the company president joked he would start paying her as well as the rent. Gretchen's heart leapt at the idea, surprising her. But she didn't think he was serious and did not feel she could let her family down.

Two years of valuable free ideas later, Gretchen actually accepted a genuine job offer from the think tank. The salary was substantially higher than what she made managing the property and would allow her to help her family even more. The choice was a no-brainer, and today the new property manager frequently comes up to the 18th floor to take Gretchen to lunch when he has a problem. Her job at the think tank puts her right in her strategic-thinking element, and she has completed her degree online.

## Your Personality's Challenges

Blue/Red Introverts have a unique set of potential work-related blind spots. Some you have; others you don't. No one has them all. Tone down a blind spot by focusing on it, then choose more productive actions and make them habits. (Suggestions for doing so are in parentheses below.) You:

- Can be too casual about deadlines and/or commitments when lost in intellectual projects. (Set aside time in the morning when you focus on such things; then you can concentrate on more important things.)
- May initiate too many projects that cannot be completed. (So much of interest, so little time. Give yourself permission to work on more

than two major projects ONLY if you have adequate staff on projects three and up and your role is to oversee.)

- Intimidate those less quick-witted. (Admit it, you like the power your braininess gives you over your brawny and less-blessed colleagues. Just don't make a habit of humiliating them—one of them could eventually become your boss.)
- Can be overly critical, complex, and competitive. (The competitive drive is necessary in your preferred fields, but know where to draw the line. Same goes for critical and opinionated behavior. PICK YOUR BATTLES.)
- Change plans and strategies too frequently. (Changing course with each new fact can be overwhelming for other Colors and subordinates. Admit that you're not an expert implementer. Show respect for and cooperate with those who are.)
- When fatigued, you become bitingly sarcastic and have uncontrolled emotional outbursts. (Apologize and say, "I think it's time for a break." Don't talk to anyone until you're in a better frame of mind; you'll save allies this way.)

## Your Job Search—the Good, the Bad, and the Ugly

Abundant creative ideas for pursuing your job search come easily to you. You think it unlikely we'll have anything new or useful in such a "generalized" book. But aren't job searches about improvising your way through a series of difficult problems? To improvise, you need background material and strategy. Thus . . .

Your natural strengths easily allow you to:

- See future trends and incorporate them into a career plan.
- Find unusual ways of getting interviews.
- Impress interviewers with your insights and competence.
- Logically evaluate the future of different job opportunities.

In order to tone down your blind spots, you need to:

- Pay attention to details.
- Express more enthusiasm during interviews instead of just trying to wow the interview intellectually (which may backfire).
- Create a job search plan and stay with it as much as possible.
- Reign in your tendency to act smug with an interviewer you judge less intellectually competent than you.
- Express appreciation to those who have helped you– thank you notes, follow-up calls.

# The Blue/Red Introvert's Interviewing Style

With an interviewer whose Color is close to your own, you will feel immediate rapport. However, if your interviewer seems to have a significantly different style, use the suggestions in parentheses.

In following your natural style you:

- ◆ Summarize and identify root causes. (A job interview may be too early for critiquing how an organization works. Preface such remarks with the phrase, "As an outsider looking in . . . " That way, you are excused from knowing the political implications of your opinions.)
- ◆ Avoid personal chitchat. (While you downplay its importance, chitchat is meaningful to other Colors looking to see if you are compatible within the corporate culture. Yes, it's hateful, but smile and do your best. Practice beforehand with a willing Green (to identify, read Chapter 4, A Tour of the Prism Company/Green Department, and Chapter 5, Greens Overall).
- ◆ Talk about insights and unusual approaches. (Your ideas flow like water, but beware the interview that has been scheduled only to pick your brain. This is especially likely if a competitor has "recruited" you out of the blue. He or she wants to know what you know, and there's no job to be had at the end of it. Your ideas often are worth thousands of dollars; allude to them, but get a real paycheck before laying them out in detail.)
- ◆ Frequently debate the pros and cons of various options. (A job offer is on the table. Now's the time to know the difference between debate and negotiation. Role-play negotiation techniques with a willing Red (to identify, read Chapter 4, A Tour of the Prism Company/ Red Department, and Chapter 10, Reds Overall). You'll see the difference and understand debating is impolitic.)

Use this book to learn how to leverage your own strengths with those of other Colors. First, learn more about your own strengths by reading the Chapter 10, Reds Overall. Then select a few colleagues of whose skills you'd like to make better use of. Read Chapter 4, A Tour of the Prism Company, and Chapter 25, Adjusting to the Styles of Other Colors, to recognize their Colors, or ask them to take the Self-Assessment. Study Figure 3 in each Overall Color chapter, and experiment with a few new approaches. Do it scientifically; see if they work.

If you are actively job-hunting, keep notes in the Roadmap in Chapter 28. It will keep your strengths in front of you for encouragement and help you cultivate that elusive rapport-building function.

# PART 5

# GOLDS
## *"Let's Do It Right"*

Golds are precise and organized and admire all those qualities in others.

# CHAPTER 20

# Golds Overall

**GOLDS REPRESENT 46 PERCENT** of the overall world population. If you are not a Gold, but want to learn how to identify or improve communications with one, go to Figure 20–1.

This chapter will help you determine if you've tested your primary or backup personality Color correctly. It also will help you identify other Golds among people you know, as will Chapter 4, A Tour of the Prism Company/The Gold Department.

## A Well-Known Gold: Kay Bailey Hutchison, U.S. Senator, R-Texas

Kay Bailey Hutchison is Texas's first woman Senator and a rising star in the Republican Party. This accomplishment is all the more impressive for the fact that, fresh out of law school in the mid-1960s, Hutchison couldn't even land a job.

One of five women in her law school class of 500, the Texas law establishment simply didn't hire women in the early days of the movement for women's equality. But Kay showed the typical Gold's tenacity in the face of adversity. "Not being able to get a job was my first big failure. I was devastated," Kay recalls. "I had to reach deep into myself and find a new way."

She took a job as a television news reporter. Being a TV personality gave her the visibility to go into politics. It was then that she met Anne Armstrong, co-chair of the Republican National Committee. Kay began as Arm-

## Figure 20–1    How to Recognize a Gold

- ☐ Always on time.
- ☐ Solid-seeming personality.
- ☐ Dress conservatively with quality clothing.
- ☐ Clean desks, maybe one family picture.
- ☐ Think and speak in linear fashion.
- ☐ Like to devise and follow rules and procedures.
- ☐ Frequently found in administrative and managerial roles.
- ☐ Detail-oriented.
- ☐ Logistically skilled.
- ☐ Accountable.
- ☐ No-frills type.
- ☐ Well-organized files.
- ☐ Skeptical and cautious.
- ☐ Thrive on recognition and appreciation.

HOW TO COMMUNICATE WITH A GOLD

- ✔ Acknowledge his or her power, position, and achievements.
- ✔ Make your points sequentially or chronologically.
- ✔ Be factual and accurate.
- ✔ Be precise and down-to-earth.
- ✔ Avoid vague information and abstract theories.
- ✔ Be reliable; show up on time and do what you commit to.
- ✔ Have your own act together and presentations running smoothly.
- ✔ Follow procedures; respect the hierarchy.
- ✔ Be socially and materially responsible; do not waste resources.

strong's press secretary, and then ran for office herself. At age 29 Kay became the first Republican woman elected to the Texas House of Representatives.

In 1976, President Gerald R. Ford appointed Kay vice chairman of the National Transportation Safety Board. Her political career was on the ascent until 1982, when she lost her race for Congress. Thinking she would never be in politics again, for the next ten years she turned to business, ultimately becoming the owner of a candy manufacturing company.

Then she was asked to run for State Treasurer. "This was an absolute turning point," she says. "I was qualified for the Treasury post because of my banking and business experience, and it gave me the statewide exposure needed ultimately to run for the U.S. Senate." Her business experience, seemingly a career sidetrack at the time, "helps me deal with economic issues, making me a more effective Senator."

Hutchison considers her greatest strengths to be perseverance, tenacity, going the extra mile, and never taking no for an answer (all core Gold characteristics). Running for the governorship of Texas or President of the United States are possibilities under consideration.

She is able to identify key issues and bring others on board to solve them. These are all hallmarks of the Gold personality. Golds pay attention to details and hold themselves accountable for results. They typically are no-frills types who are loyal, responsible, and logistically oriented. While demanding top productivity from others, they expect no less from themselves.

Golds comprise 46 percent of the world's population, are the largest of the four Color groups, and the most grounded. You are the backbones of corporate and public institutions. Society's administrators, you are naturally talented at protecting others and directing the logistics of people, goods, schedules, and services. You value detail and procedures, are known for your follow-through ability, and can mobilize others to achieve well-defined goals. As leaders like Kay, Golds shine when establishing policy and aim for status, respect, and power. "Let's do it right" is typical of the Gold mentality.

You are the most solid of all personality types, thriving on having many responsibilities for which you are recognized and appreciated. You will be skeptical reading a book like this, preferring instead to deal with things more concrete and less abstract. However, if you are interested in learning how to work more effectively and efficiently with other personality types, this book will be a key that unlocks the secret to motivating even the most unfocused and disorganized people in your life. It will show you what to do when all your best efforts have failed.

## Another Gold: Joan Shapiro Green

Focus and organization were never issues for Joan Shapiro Green. For ten years, she was President and Chief Executive Officer (CEO) of BT Brokerage, a subsidiary of Bankers Trust, trading stocks and bonds for institutional clients. During that decade revenues increased sevenfold. Apart from leading the staff to achieve the company's objectives, what Joan enjoyed most was acquiring new clients and meeting with them to solve their problems.

Today she uses her well-developed Gold managerial abilities to support the Financial Women's Association, The American Red Cross in Greater New York, and The UJA Women's Executive Circle. While colleagues frequently poke fun at her calendar—a sweep of multicolored sticky notes that regulate a complicated life, none dispute her passion or the Gold drive to consistently deliver superior performance. Joan describes her top strength as motivating and inspiring teams to accomplish their goals. Serving on boards enables her to apply her energy and enthusiasm for important and valuable organizations.

Are these your top strengths, too? The best way to proceed with this book is to read about your own primary and secondary Colors first, then learn how you interact with others by reading their profiles as needed.

Famous Golds in politics are President George Bush, Sr. and his wife Barbara, Queen Elizabeth, President Harry Truman, President George Washington, and Queen Victoria. Former chairman of IBM Thomas Watson Jr., Sam Walton, and J.C. Penney represent Golds in the corporate world. Kareem Abdul-Jabbar illustrates the Gold style in sports, Colin Powell in the military, Warren Buffett in finance, Jimmy Stewart and Martha Stewart in entertainment, and Barbara Walters in the field of journalism.

This chapter should help you determine if you've tested your primary and backup personality Color correctly. You now have tools for identifying Golds among the people you know. Chapter 4, A Tour of the Prism Company, and Chapter 25, Adjusting to the Styles of Others, give additional tips for Color-coding others.

# CHAPTER 21

# Gold/Blue Extroverts

**YOU'RE NOT ONLY A GOLD**, you also have strong secondary characteristics of the Blue personality. And you have tested as a Color Q Extrovert, which means you recharge your batteries by being with people, rather than being alone. Your Color group values efficiency, tradition, accuracy, predictability, and structure. Achieving goals on time and under budget is a strong inner drive in you.

## You Overall

In your community, you are a pillar—indispensable, well-respected, and firmly represented in important volunteer positions. You are realistic, grounded, and responsible, getting things done no matter how difficult. This does not make you stodgy, though; the hallmarks of your Color are boldness and drive.

Reinventing the wheel is not your style. Working on real as opposed to intangible things and going with your own experience instead of new theories are your usual choices. You value "the system" and prefer to organize life around procedures and contract agreements.

Your inner need for control makes it virtually inevitable that you will hold responsible positions during your career; administrative skills are second nature to you. Creating security and stability for family and co-workers is a priority.

Once in charge, you relish mapping out what needs to be done. Task assignments make best use of each staff member's strengths. Woe to those who fall short of your expectations! You show little sympathy for the ineffective and inefficient.

With a direct and clear communication style, you are gifted at implementing policies and ensuring things remain orderly and on track. Planning ahead, setting goals, and controlling schedules are activities that come naturally. Highly observant of details, you let little fall between the cracks.

You are not shy about criticizing those who break rules, dress flamboyantly, or behave in unusual ways. What you see as appropriate, right, or wrong comes from a place of deep moral certitude. Traditional and conservative ways keep the universe organized and orderly, and you cannot understand why anyone would ever want to disturb that. People who are disloyal, unreliable, disorganized, or who miss deadlines irritate you.

Rituals, traditions, holidays, birthdays, and religious or cultural events are not just celebrated, but honored, by you. These to you are symbols of continuity to be passed on to the next generation, and require appropriate fanfare. Family is your central focus.

case study one

## Chairman of the Executive Committee, Wall Street

In a world where people job hop and best performers go to the highest bidder, Alan "Ace" Greenberg is unique. He started at Bear Stearns as a clerk making $35 a week and in true Gold fashion stuck to the course. Fifty-seven years later he is Chairman of the Executive Committee, noting with satisfaction that his company, now the fifth largest investment banking firm in the United States, has outlived 95 percent of its competitors.

Like many Golds, people say he is not complex, but smart and disciplined. He prizes brevity, not using two words when one will do. As a result he can do 39 phone calls within an hour because, as he notes with a grin, "I force people to get to the point."

Ace's meetings start on time and end swiftly, and he is not a believer in change for its own sake. "If it is not broken, I am certainly not going to waste my time trying to fix it," he quips.

His management style is unique, but always consistent. Ace is known for his reverence for common sense and obsession about keeping office overhead down, all distinctive Gold characteristics. His published book, *Memos from the Chairman*, offers seventeen years of quirky messages to his staff, exhorting them to recycle paper clips and office envelopes. They also express his pragmatic view of the world of work: "If an MBA applies for a job, we don't hold it against them [sic], but we are really looking for people with PSD degrees (poor, smart, and with a deep desire to become rich)."

On any given day he can be found at his slightly raised desk on the firm's trading floor surrounded by some 400 traders. His large corner office is usually unoccupied. While many consider him one of the shrewdest players on Wall Street, he remains down to earth, adhering to his own counsel, "Thou will do well in commerce, as long as thou does not believe thine own odor is perfume!" And his advice to others? "Pick something you love to do or you won't win. You may be competing with people who are intellectually inferior, but if they like what they do, they will beat you every time!"

Like most Golds, Ace takes his work very seriously. Outside of the office he plays hard as well. He is a champion bridge player, accomplished amateur magician, and a dedicated dog trainer. His numerous philanthropic contributions express the Gold need to take care of the community.

# You on the Job

## As a Leader

"Getting the right things to the right people, in the right amounts, to the right place at the right time" is the crux of your talent. Outstanding logistical skills are the hallmark of Gold/Blue Extroverts in leadership roles. With a clearly defined chain of command and well-defined expectations and duties for the staff, you can achieve anything. Those who play by the rules and perform up to your exacting standards are rewarded in fair measure.

Like Ace Greenberg, you are decisive, providing for your organization's practical needs in a reliable and consistent manner. Getting to the core of a situation quickly, managing fairly, providing consistent feedback, and crafting clear and measurable goals are your tools for getting things done.

## As a Team Player

Your positive attributes as a team member are many. Defining problems quickly; clarifying issues, obstacles, and goals; bringing logic to the table; preventing important details from falling through the cracks; ensuring needed resources are available; acting as a reality check about feasibility and costs . . . no team functions at its peak without a Gold/Blue Extrovert.

## Figure 21–1   Natural Work-Related Strengths

Approximately 80 percent of these attributes will apply to you. Check off those that do and use them in your resume and interviews. This will set you apart from the canned responses of others. You:

☐ Are predictable and stable.
☐ Are decisive.
☐ Expect and have high work standards.
☐ Use resources efficiently.
☐ Respect rules and established procedures.
☐ Get results through good time and task management.
☐ Imbue confidence in your people or co-workers.
☐ Finish projects on time and on budget.

You are able to make the tough decisions when needed. However, you may irritate team members by taking charge without being asked, or being too blunt.

Look at Figure 21–1 for a list of your natural work-related strengths.

Now see how other Gold/Blue Extroverts use these strengths in very different fields.

### case study two

## Senior Executive, Investment Management Firm

Without a doubt, 36-year-old Mellody Hobson is a "golden girl." President of the $21 billion Chicago-based investment firm Ariel Capital Management, she appears regularly on ABC's *Good Morning America*. *Working Woman* and *Vogue* magazines have done features on her. She is a member of such prestigious boards as Chicago's Field Museum, The Chicago Public Library, and Princeton University (where she earned her degree in international relations and public policy). She is the highest ranking African American female in the mutual fund industry. She also is charismatic, personable, and an admitted "fashionista."

Gold/Blue Extroverts are driven to succeed from an early age. Mellody was no exception. At age 5, she set herself the goal of attending an Ivy League university. By fifth grade she would stay up into the early morning hours doing homework. "Slow and steady wins the race" became her mantra, and at Ariel Capital she frequently wears a whimsical little turtle symbol incorporated into her otherwise classic dress style. The firm adopted this theme for its highly recognized ad campaign. "Slow and steady" also was how she rose to become president of Ariel Capital . . . fourteen years after she started there as a college intern.

In typical Gold/Blue Extrovert fashion, Mellody lists her top three strengths as communication, organization, and energy. "I'm very decisive, and I need a lot of work to do. I don't like managing people who need a lot of managing; I'm much better with self-starters," Mellody says. "Waffling and indifference drive me crazy; I am most stressed out by incompetence."

Mellody's family background was not privileged. She grew up with five siblings, none of whom graduated from college. She herself does not know how she came by the drive to achieve all that she has. But Gold/Blue Extroverts have an innate need for control, which impels them to acquire responsible positions. They also value security and stability, things Mellody did not have as a child. "I hated not having money," she says of her formative years. "I hated the insecurity of being evicted. The great thing about money is freedom; you have choice. That's all I ever cared about . . . I'm going to work until I die."

Mellody also says, "You really have to stay diligent about your values and beliefs and not compromise." Some of her deepest values are reflected in her work to educate young black children and their families about the investing process. To this end she has, with the help of her firm, created and funded Ariel Community Academy in Chicago. Here, the first-grade class is given $20,000 to invest; by eighth grade the kids control the whole amount. Upon graduation, they return their initial $20,000 to the incoming first-graders and distribute their profits to charities and academic scholarships.[1] Mellody's stated goal is to make investing into dinner table conversation among black families. A top priority of Golds is to render community service.

[18]Robert Kurson, "Mellody Hobson, thirty-three, is a financier with a big dream: to teach the poor how to be rich, one classroom at a time. (The Benefactor)," *Esquire Magazine*, (December 1, 2001). Accessed, Dec. 21, 2005 from www.Highbeam.com

In December 2004, Senator Bill Bradley told *Time Magazine,* "Mellody has a deep set of values about what's right and what's wrong."[2] She definitely puts this into practice on a daily basis. This is a core Gold/Blue characteristic.

case study three

## Literary Agent

New York City–based literary agent Linda Konner is a woman who knows what she wants and gets it. "For me, it means not having a boss, not working in an office/corporate environment and choosing the people with whom I wish to work," she says.

Linda defines her principal functions as finding suitable publishers for her clients' books (only adult practical nonfiction), negotiating their contracts, editing clients' book proposals and sample chapters, troubleshooting with and providing information to both clients and publishers, helping clients find co-writers and publicists if needed, and brainstorming ideas for future books. These draw on her true-to-form Gold/Blue Extrovert strengths of editing, creating ideas, negotiating, problem-solving, and networking.

She has always gravitated to what most recognize as glamorous careers. Previously, Linda was a successful author of eight books, including *Just the Weigh You Are: How to Be Fit and Healthy Whatever Your Size* (Houghton Mifflin), *The Last Ten Pounds* (Barnes & Noble), and *Your Perfect Weight* (Rodale). She also served as editor-in-chief of *Weight Watchers Magazine* and features editor at *Redbook, Seventeen Magazine,* and *Woman's World.*

Her columns have appeared in *Glamour* and *Fitness* magazines and her articles in *The New York Times, TV Guide, Satur-*

[19]Noah Jackson, "The New Breed," *TIME Magazine* (December 20, 2004). Accessed, Dec. 21, 2005 from www.Highbeam.com

*day Evening Post, Christian Science Monitor,* and *Playboy,* among others. She has been in the publishing field for 29 years.

A natural editor, Linda is precise in her words. When asked for her top three strengths, her Gold desire to answer precisely shows: "Do you mean things like intelligence, creativity, sense of humor? Or writing, editing, and problem solving? Take your pick! They all apply." The most energizing for Linda are brainstorming ideas, editing, and negotiating, true to her Gold/Blue core.

Her Extroverted and Blue sides enjoyed the success and media attention she received as an author. Her Gold side came into play in editorial positions. "I love editing, and I'm good at it," she says simply.

She is a precise, thorough, and assertive negotiator, bringing all aspects of her personality Color to the table in her current job. She recently celebrated her tenth anniversary as a literary agent, no mean feat in an industry that inspires more burnout than longevity. Linda Konner illustrates how working through, instead of against, your Color optimizes career success.

## Ideal Work Environment

A stable and well-respected institution with a predictable future is where Gold/Blue Extroverts like Ace Greenberg and Mellody Hobson feel most at home.

When a job offer is made, leverage as much as you can from the list in Figure 21–2.

The WORST type of work culture for a Gold/Blue Extrovert is loose and disorganized. It does not allow you access to reliable and critical information. Constant change and ambiguity diminish your great administrative and organizational strengths. You need facts, bottom line costs, and rules in order to feel comfortable at work.

When Gold/Blue Extroverts work in less-ideal corporate cultures, productivity is stunted and career achievements become an uphill climb.

## The Extroverted Gold/Blue's Ideal Boss

Even a great job can be frustrating under the wrong boss; a mediocre job under a wonderful boss is pretty hard to leave. Gold/Blues get along especially well with other Golds. But bosses of other Color types who possess the characteristics in Figure 21–3 on page 196 also can be good mentors.

**Figure 21–2   The Ideal Blue/Gold Extrovert Work Environment**

Compare your current work environment to the description below. Don't be deceived if these descriptions seem "obvious." It confirms you've tested your individual color correctly. Other Colors, especially Greens and Reds, would find this environment uncomfortable and unproductive. The optimal Gold/Blue Extrovert work environment:

☐ Is a stable and well-respected institution with a predictable future. You work hard and want to be rewarded with money and respect. Small, growing companies or distressed companies can't offer this. You are the quintessential corporate worker.

☐ Provides job security. Life change is a slow process for you; having it forced upon you is harder on you than other Colors.

☐ Involves concrete and practical projects and products. Intangible services are tough for you to quantify and measure. Stick with the things you can touch and see.

☐ Has clear rules and expectations. Valuable time is wasted making up rules as you go along. You don't want to be bothered by this.

☐ Is organized and efficient. You cannot respect or work effectively within a company that isn't.

☐ Includes hard-working co-workers who pride themselves on doing things right. You see crises and emotionalism as unnecessary weakness, even slacking, on the part of others.

☐ Allows you to work within a group or team. You need people to organize!

☐ Rewards those who are steady, accountable, and focused on results. Others may have time for drama and politics; you're the one who gets things done.

☐ Offers progressively higher levels of responsibility. A clear career path gives you focus and helps you concentrate on the tasks at hand.

A corporate culture integrating the above elements is fertile soil for your career advancement.

**Figure 21–3    The Gold/Blue Extrovert's Ideal Boss**

Check off if your boss:

☐ Always knows and clearly states what needs to be done.
☐ Reliably provides needed resources.
☐ Has clout with superiors.
☐ Will confront workers who don't deliver on commitments.
☐ Gives more responsibility and perks when you've earned them.

## Careers That Attract Gold/Blue Extroverts

Gold/Blue Extroverts like Linda Konner cluster in fields that provide professional respect, require high levels of competence, and contribute in a meaningful way to society. You need the ability to create predictability and stability to be at your best.

*Please note that not all* the following careers will appeal to you, but recognize that each, in some way, draws on the strengths of your style and appeals to a significant number of your Color group. This is not a comprehensive list, but it will show underlying patterns of preference. If unlisted careers offer similar patterns, your chances of success increase. Copy in parentheses highlights the Color style characteristics that create success.

In addition, two codes indicate those jobs that are currently predicted to have an above-average salary and growth potential. This information is based on the continuously revised data provided by the U.S. Department of Labor and Bureau of Labor Statistics available on the O*NET website, *http://online.onetcenter.org/*.

**Bold** indicates that the career is considered to be among the top **100 best-paying jobs** based on the average or median salary paid to individuals *with five years of experience.* Excluded are jobs where salary statistics are not available, such as "business owner," or not indicative such as "actor."

*Italics* identifies the jobs that are predicted to benefit from an above-average growth rate over the next several years.

***Bold and italics*** indicates jobs that will benefit from both **higher pay** and *high growth potential.*

Note there are successful people of all Color styles in all occupations. In nonideal jobs you can still shine by creating your own niche.

## Business/Management/Manufacturing

actuary ◆ *administrative services manager* ◆ *auditor* ◆ *business owner* ◆ *chief information officer* ◆ **chief financial officer** ◆ *compensation and benefits manager* ◆ efficiency expert ◆ **executive** ◆ insurance claim examiner/underwriter ◆ *human resources manager* ◆ *management consultant* ◆ *managers of all types* [construction, database, factory, financial institution, hospital, hotel, office, **industrial production manager**, sales, etc.] ◆ **insurance agent/broker** ◆ project manager ◆ **purchasing manager**/agent ◆ real estate agent ◆ sales/*sales manager* [tangible products] (accurate memory for details, bottom-line and cost-oriented, well-developed administrative skills, need for order, give clear directions).

## Business/Finance

*accountant* ◆ bank officer (all types) ◆ **financial analyst** ◆ *financial advisor* ◆ **financial examiner** ◆ *investment banker* ◆ *stockbroker* ◆ **venture capitalist** (efficiency, observant of details, moral certitude and appropriateness, low tolerance for unconventionality).

## Computer/Information Technology

*computer analyst/security specialist* ◆ *information system manager* ◆ *network administrator* (good memory for details, efficient, solid administrative skills, keep things orderly and on track).

## Education

*athletic coach/trainer* ◆ *business professor* ◆ *school principal/administrator* ◆ **university president** ◆ vocational teacher (administrative skills, respect for "the system," common sense, thoughtfulness, practical experience).

## Health Science

dentist ◆ *medical and health service manager* ◆ *pharmacist* ◆ *optometrist* ◆ *primary care physician* (accuracy, keen observation of details, practical and measurable work, organizational skills).

## Law/Law Enforcement/Government

compliance officer ◆ *corrections officer* ◆ **division manager** ◆ firefighter ◆ *investigator* ◆ IRS agent ◆ **judge** ◆ **lawyer** [particularly administrative, criminal, corporate, employment, energy, real estate, product liability, securities, transportation] ◆ military officer ◆ *police officer* ◆ security consultant/ guard (respect for rules and procedures, good administrative skills, observant of details, fact-oriented, boldness).

## Science Research, Engineering, Mathematics

**civil engineer** ◆ geologist (respect for clear procedures and rules, high standards, respect for contracts, sense of appropriateness, drive, ability to make tough decisions).

## Other

carpenter ◆ **general contractor** ◆ electronic repair ◆ mechanic ◆ **pilot** ◆ plumber ◆ surveyor.

case study four

# When a Career Isn't Working

Three of eight students were crying—loudly—and a fourth was starting. Early childhood development teacher Jeanine Beckwith could see no earthly reason for the outburst, but started to feel like joining in. She had hoped her second year would be easier than her first, but it all seemed to be going downhill.

All Jeanine's female relatives had been teachers, and she was proud when they applauded her on graduation day. Her celebration afterwards had made her feel so important, so much a part of a long family tradition. Now, she was on her own in a sea of slobbering 3-year-olds trying to maintain order.

What she didn't want to admit was that kids drove her nuts. From the time she started babysitting at age 12, she always felt awkward trying to follow their nonlinear thinking, being sensitive to their changing needs. As a teacher, there was no way to maintain order, everyone's learning happened at different levels, and nothing about her day was ever predictable. Jeanine was at wit's end; such an environment will drive any Gold/Blue Extrovert crazy!

Confiding in her aunt, Jeanine explored how to use her education degree to find a job more organized and predictable. Her aunt suggested that Jeanine apply for an assistant principal position in a nearby town. Jeanine was ecstatic when she got the job. Being in charge, in control, and with the ability to manage and organize was very satisfying to her Gold/Blue Extroverted nature. She is in line for the principal's job in a few years, and well-respected by her peers. Life is under control again.

## Your Personality's Challenges

Gold/Blue Extroverts have a unique set of potential work-related blind spots. Some you have, others you don't. No one has them all. Tone down a blind spot by focusing on it, then choose more productive actions and make them habits. (Suggestions for doing so are in parentheses below.) You:

- May prematurely dismiss new ideas. (Dismiss nothing until you investigate the who, what, where, when, why, and cost of a new idea. Profitable ventures start with untested ideas; learn how to allow others to brainstorm and present their conclusions to you.)
- May focus on the flaws in the efforts of others and not give credit where credit is due. (Make a point of affirming the efforts of deserving colleagues after listing flaws.)
- Are fixed in supporting established ways of doing things. (The tried-and-true contribute to efficiency, but they may not keep your company alive when the market is moving or changing. When faced with change, focus on details and costs—your areas of strength.)
- Push through your own ideas by being verbally aggressive. (Getting things done well requires buy-in, not submission. Study the art of persuasion, since you already have a natural talent for the art of ruling. Read about how to persuade other Colors in Figure 3 of each Color's "Overall" chapter.)

## Your Job Search—the Good, the Bad, and the Ugly

Gold/Blue Extroverts create accurate and well-presented resumes that elicit positive responses. With some interviewers, particularly Golds and Blues, you will feel a comfortable rapport. But with those of other Colors, you need to prepare and rehearse responses outside your comfort zone. Many human resource people are Greens; make a study of how to communicate effectively with this Color group before your first interviews.

Your natural strengths easily allow you to:

- Have a wide network of friends for job leads.
- Set measurable, realistic, and well-defined goals.
- Create time lines, daily status reports, and budgets that reduce job search stress on both you and the family.
- Adequately research prospective employers.
- Be well prepared for interviews.
- Come across as hard-working and bottom-line-oriented in an interview.
- Logically consider pros and cons of job offers.

In order to tone down your blind spots, you need to:

- Balance networking with research.
- Do something in return for those who help you; your networking sometimes comes off as too self-serving.
- Cushion your tendency to be abrupt; rehearse some areas of small talk.
- Prepare to talk about yourself on a personal level (ask a willing Green to role play with you).
- Think about a prospective company's future direction (ask a willing Blue to help).
- Be willing to consider career opportunities in other industries.
- Don't allow unexpected delays and obstacles to frustrate you.
- Plan a "think-through day" when tempted to jump on a job offer.

## The Gold/Blue Extrovert's Interviewing Style

With an interviewer whose Color is close to your own, you will feel immediate rapport. However, if your interviewer seems to have a significantly different style (and it's statistically likely that he or she will have a Green component), use the suggestions in parentheses. Mercilessly exploit these natural abilities of yours, and get more job offers!

In following your natural style, you:

- Describe past accomplishments in appropriate detail. (A Green interviewer may draw you out with questions like "Did you enjoy those duties?" Be prepared with answers more thorough than "Yes.")
- Tend to talk too much and not ask enough questions about the job. (If it has been a while since the interviewer said anything, PAUSE. Let him or her lead. Prepare a list of job questions ahead of time and refer to it.)
- Focus on the present. (Especially if interviewing for a senior level position, you will need to prepare for questions on future planning. Take a Blue colleague to lunch and run a few ideas by him or her before an interview. At least read public statements about company direction prior to an interview.)
- May not think outside the box. (Your orderly mind knows what your next career step should be, but tends to close off other possibilities. New fields, or even established ones you haven't considered, may allow you to ascend higher and faster than your planned career path.)

Take a break now to do something administratively important. Later, check out the Chapter 15, Blues Overall, first, then carefully read Chapter 4, A Tour of the Prism Company, and Chapter 25, Adjusting to the Styles of Others, to learn about the strengths of other Colors.

Like all Colors, you need the strengths of others, and you can put them to work for you if you know where to look and how to ask. If you invest time learning how to recognize the Colors who can best assist you (visit Figure 3 in each of the "Overall" Color chapters), it will make everyone more effective and productive.

If you are actively engaging in a job search, jot notes in the Roadmap in Chapter 28. Recording your strengths and strategies is a concrete and results-oriented way to navigate the minefields of a job search.

# CHAPTER 22

# Gold/Blue Introverts

**YOU'RE NOT ONLY A GOLD,** you also have strong secondary characteristics of the Blue personality. And you have tested as a Color Q Introvert, which means you recharge your batteries by being alone, rather than being with people. You are most happy when things are orderly, efficient, and predictable. Because of your innate talent at it, you have a strong drive toward managing.

## You Overall

A pillar of whatever organization or community you join, you are thorough, responsible, and hard-working. Your unusually accurate memory records what others say and do with astonishing precision. While thoughtful, you can overlook such formal niceties as thank-you notes or praise for jobs well done by others.

Realistic and practical, you take your commitments seriously. You value "the system" of whatever organization you are in, trust contracts, and organize your life and work around procedures. Your children and co-workers all feel secure and stable under your watch; that is, if they measure up to your high standards. You can be the classic "Type A" personality, demanding much of others both at home and work. But those demands are never made capriciously; you think things through and always are cautious about changes.

With your highly developed administrative skills, duty-bound work ethic, and great ability to concentrate, you float to top-level positions wherever you invest your efforts. Fierce loyalty to your company cements your status.

When undertaking a task, you bring to it logic, impersonal analysis, common sense, and practical experience. You gravitate to situations where you have to plan ahead, set goals, and control the schedule. You are gifted at implementing well-defined policies and ensuring that things remain orderly and on track. Because doing a good job is your primary focus, you expect to be judged and compensated on your own merits. You are fair and consistent when dealing with others.

Family is your central focus. You honor traditions and rituals, observing holidays, birthdays, and religious and cultural events with appropriate fanfare. For you, these times are important symbols of continuity to be passed on to the next generation. Gold/Blue Introverts often trace their roots and record the family heritage for their progeny.

"Appropriateness" is your watchword. Your strong morals lead you to judge others and speak up if they seem to blur right and wrong. You simply want the world to stay organized, free from the chaos that follows when rules are broken. Even flamboyant dress and unconventional behavior try your tolerance.

## case study one

# College President

Dr. Kathleen Waldron is president of Baruch College in New York City. With 15,500 students, Baruch is the nation's largest accredited business school and one of the most selective public colleges in the northeastern United States. It has been named the most diverse college for six straight years by *U.S. News and World Report.* Dr. Waldron moves effortlessly between her many constituencies—students, faculty, staff, alumni, donors, and public officials. She is a natural and graceful leader with superior management skills.

A Fulbright scholar who received her doctorate in Latin American history in 1977, she had a thirteen-year career at Citibank, capped by her turn as President of Citibank International in Miami from 1991–1996. She then spent six years as Dean of the School of Business at Long Island University before joining Baruch.

She has achieved success by leveraging, rather than working against, her Introverted nature. For instance, others describe her as a great listener. "I am a fairly private person who can read three books a week. Now that is very hard to do with all the evening entertainment and events that take away my private time," she reflects. "But I knew that going in." While quite reserved in her early years, today her people skills are superior. "It's been a long process," she says, "to develop a comfort level for public speaking, of going forward to people with my hand outstretched, taking the initiative to do that. That was hard."

Fundraising is a substantial part of her job, one where her banking background and Gold/Blue strengths are useful. When she sits down to solicit corporate leaders, "they know I am a business person who sets goals, measures accomplishments, and is a serious manager. They feel more comfortable that their donations are going to be properly utilized." Dr. Waldron stresses to them and her staff the importance of "accountability, stewardship, and reporting back to people." She is known for expressing her opinions with tact. All these are prime Gold/Blue values.

She is also very involved with instituting proper instruments for educational evaluation. This typical Gold/Blue interest in results and accountability helps her nearly 1,000 faculty members institute assessment models that work within their particular business disciplines. "Getting a job is such a narrow definition of a successful education," says Kathleen. "I changed the dialog to broaden those evaluation measures to instill in students analytical capabilities, communications skills, and a broader sense of life including art and music."

She also has a typical Gold/Blue approach to organizing her work. "I have all my systems in place; I am very structured in getting to my goals. I keep very careful agendas, cross-checked to be certain things are on schedule. I know exactly where I'm going to be a year from now."

Early in her career, Kathleen was a natural analytical problem solver. Now, her feeling/intuitive side is coming in to play. "I believe that leadership is people developing people. What gets me excited is to watch people do better than they have." Kathleen exhibits most of the key characteristics of her Color style, especially in her aptitude for taking the helm and running a smooth ship.

# You on the Job

## As a Leader

"Getting the right things to the right people, in the right amounts, to the right place at the right time" is the crux of your talent. Outstanding logistical skills are the hallmark of Gold/Blue Introverts in leadership roles. With a clear chain of command and well-defined expectations and duties for the staff, you can achieve anything. Those who play by the rules and live up to your exacting standards are rewarded in fair measure.

You see your role as reliably providing for your organization's practical needs. You are accurate, decisive, and know how to get things done.

Your decision-making style is to absorb and assess as many facts as possible. Then you measure the cost of each possible solution before choosing the optimal one.

## As a Team Player

Your positive contributions are many. Getting to the core of problems quickly; clarifying issues, obstacles, and goals; bringing logic to the table; preventing important details from falling through the cracks; ensuring needed resources are available; acting as a reality check about costs . . . no team functions optimally without a Gold/Blue Introvert as one of its members.

You feel both responsible and loyal to your teammates. You know how important your contributions are, and you work hard not to let others down. However, you may irritate team members by not sharing information until too late in the process and/or being rigid about how things should be done.

Look at Figure 22–1 for a list of your natural work-related strengths.

Now see how some Gold/Blue Introverts use these strengths in very different fields.

---

### Figure 22–1   Natural Work-Related Strengths

Approximately 80 percent of these attributes will apply to you. Check off those that do and use them in your resume and interviews. This will set you apart from the canned responses of others. You:

☐ Naturally adapt to the role assigned to you, be it leader or follower.

☐ Are accurate about all parts of a task.

☐ Create and enforce policies, procedures, and schedules that keep everyone effective and on track.

☐ Are fair with others and earn their respect.

☐ Are decisive, organized, and get things done.

☐ Have deep powers of concentration and can work alone for long periods of time.

# Senior Investment Officer, Private Bank

Sergio I. de Araujo has the classic Gold/Blue Introvert resume, with clear corporate loyalty and few career changes. He has been with his current company, U.S. Trust Company, for almost eighteen years and today is a Managing Director and Senior Investment Officer for the Southeast region.

His Gold management skills are put to active use overseeing regional investment activities and directing portfolio managers in several Florida offices. Says Serge, "among my responsibilities is to see that we adhere to investment policy, develop strategies for dealing with concentrated positions, and follow agreed-upon client objectives." Golds follow established policies to the letter, an important characteristic in high-level financial positions.

Client relationship initiatives such as wealth advice, planning, and relationship reviews are Serge's strengths, drawing on his attention to detail and organizational skills. He also directly handles several portfolios for individual clients. Previously, he worked for the Rothschild family and helped found Citigroup's International Private Banking Division in 1971, where he spent the other half of his career.

Early on, Serge realized how to make himself indispensable in an industry where there are always younger, brighter, better-educated, and cheaper managers waiting to step into one's shoes. "I enjoy working with the clients," he says, "and soon realized they are the anchor of one's career."

He also enjoys making a major contribution to his firm's bottom line. "At Citibank or JP Morgan Chase, the trust and investment business never represented a significant percent of revenue and profits," he says. "Here, I am in an institution where 100 percent of its profits come from the wealth management business, and the firm has a long history of success and commitment."

Managing people, Sergio says, is simply one aspect of his demanding job. In addition to his managerial role, he must balance the myriad of daily challenges that often include providing superior client service and competitive investment performance, keeping up with technological and professional advances, and implementing compliance initiatives.

Working for an organization that has had low turnover, however, is particularly satisfying to this Color group. At U.S. Trust many people have been around for thirty to forty years, and this satisfies a Gold's need for continuity, tradition, and stability.

Sergio's top three strengths have attracted a large book of business for him to manage, but he has had to pare it down in order to handle his duties as regional Senior Investment Officer. "I am a good listener," he says. "I am able to empathize with people, and I'm decisive."

### case study three

## Chemical Engineer, Manufacturing Company Owner

In Germany, all little Martin Deeg wanted to do was play in the dirt. The family had different ideas. "I grew up with parents who were both technically trained," says Martin. "It was an environment that discouraged anything other than being a scientist; an engineer was marginal, but nevertheless acceptable." His family moved to the United States in the 1960s when his father took a job as Director of Materials Research at the American Optical Corporation in Southbridge, Massachusetts.

Martin's adolescent rebellion led to a college major in archeology. "I would have loved to have been an archeologist. I like digging in the dirt." But parental expectations prevailed. After studying Chemical Engineering in college, Martin worked in product development for Celanese Corporation. He began as a Process Development Engineer and ultimately attained the position of Staff Scientist. He holds more than ten patents in the fields of high-performance composite materials and PET/PBT melt spinning.

Martin branched out when he joined Scott Paper Company. Starting there as Technology Manager, Martin eventually expanded into Director of Business Development–World Wide and concentrated on the marketing side. Following Scott Paper's merger with Kimberly Clark, he was given the title Senior Research Fellow.

In 1999, he established and became president of Icarus West, Inc., a niche business manufacturer handling supplies for the polysilicon industry: "We make very clean, very pure, very expensive, extremely specialized polyethylene gloves," he says. Martin is involved in all parts of the business, handling all customer contact. "We have no competition," he says. Other companies "have not been able to meet the same kind of quality standards," he says. No doubt his Gold/Blue process skills keep those standards high.

Being company president has its down side, however. "Bookkeeping, dealing with suppliers . . . taxes are downright stressful!" he says. "But probably the most stressful thing is dealing with ongoing requests to decrease price. I hate negotiating—I like things black and white, nice and straightforward."

Martin doesn't define what he's doing now as success. "I'll have success once I retire. The definition of success for me is being able to wake up in the morning and feel good about whatever it is I'm going to do for the day." To accomplish this, Martin plans to go back to his roots. "Doing relatively basic clearing, constructing, excavating . . . something outside, pushing dirt around, seems to be potentially a fun thing to do . . . it justifies buying big mechanical toys."

## Ideal Work Environment

For both Dr. Kathleen Waldron and Sergio de Araujo, a stable and well-respected institution with a predictable future is their chosen environment; Martin Deeg owns his own business and frequently works at home.

When a job offer is made, leverage as much as you can from the list in Figure 22–2.

### Figure 22–2    The Ideal Gold/Blue Introvert Work Environment

Compare your current work environment to the description below. Don't be deceived if these descriptions seem "obvious." It confirms you've tested your individual color correctly. Other Colors, especially Greens and Reds, would find this environment uncomfortable and unproductive. The optimal Gold/Blue Introvert work environment:

☐ Has clear rules and expectations. It wastes valuable time try-ing to make up rules as you go along. You don't want to be bothered by this.

☐ Includes hard-working co-workers who pride themselves on doing things right. It's much easier when everyone is on the same page about how to get things done. You see crises and emotionalism as unnecessary weakness, even slacking, on the part of others.

☐ Is a stable and well-respected institution with a predictable fu-ture. You work hard and want to be rewarded with money and respect. Small, growing companies or distressed companies can't offer this. You are a quintessential corporate worker.

☐ Rewards dependability and precision. You're on time, have a well-planned schedule and do your job with consistency. No company runs well for long without a Gold/Blue Introvert on staff. You deserve recognition.

☐ Involves concrete and practical projects and products. Intangi-ble services are tough for you to quantify and measure. Stick with the things you can touch and see.

☐ Is results-oriented. You are frankly a bit skeptical of any work that can't be evaluated with a spreadsheet.

☐ Has a clear hierarchy. Structure gives you comfort and frees you to concentrate on the task at hand.

☐ Values loyalty and commitment. These are a deep and natural part of the core of who you are. In today's workplace, they are less valued, and that's unfortunate for us all. Today, you are better off choosing to place your loyalty with a mentor rather than a company.

☐ Allows for private space. As an Introvert, your batteries get drained when dealing with people, even if your people skills are superb. You recharge your batteries by being alone. If you have to share your work space with others, you will feel a lot more fatigue at the end of the day. You think and perform bet-ter in a private space where you can reflect in-depth on proj-ects; insist on one as a condition of employment if at all possible.

A corporate culture integrating the above elements is fertile soil for your career advancement.

The WORST type of work culture for a Gold/Blue Introvert is loose and open-ended with regard to goals and measures of success. "You're only as good as your last (fill in the blank)" describes a work environment that would make you tear out your hair.

You also hate working with people who take things too personally. You want to stay focused on task; emotional situations are cloudy and distracting. Never work for a company that values intuition over hard data. You need facts, bottom-line costs, and rules in order to feel comfortable at work.

When Gold/Blue Introverts work in nonideal corporate cultures, productivity is stunted and career achievements become an uphill climb.

## The Introverted Gold/Blue's Ideal Boss

Even a great job can be frustrating under the wrong boss; a mediocre job under a wonderful boss is pretty hard to leave. Gold/Blues get along especially well with other Golds. But bosses of other Color types who possess the characteristics in Figure 22–3 also can be good mentors.

## Careers That Attract Gold/Blue Introverts

Like Sergio de Araujo, you want to find a place to call home, where you can work comfortably for many years under the guidance of clear rules, procedures, and expectations. You require predictability and stability to be at your best. You are happiest upon reaching a high level of responsibility, like Dr. Kathleen Waldron, in a culture where there's a clear chain of command. Like Martin Deeg, you particularly need to be rewarded for your abilities to be accurate and get things done.

*Please note that not all* the following careers will appeal to you, but recognize that each, in some way, draws on the strengths of your style and appeals to a significant number of your Color group. This is not a comprehensive list, but it will show underlying patterns of preference. If unlisted careers offer similar patterns, your chances of success increase. Copy in parentheses highlights the Color style characteristics that create success.

---

### Figure 22–3    The Gold/Blue Introvert's Ideal Boss

Check off if your boss:

- ☐ Is highly respected personally and professionally.
- ☐ Values your experience, thoroughness, and hard work.
- ☐ Gives you clear overall directions.
- ☐ Does not micromanage.

In addition, two codes indicate those jobs that are currently predicted to have an above-average salary and growth potential. This information is based on the continuously revised data provided by the U.S. Department of Labor and Bureau of Labor Statistics available on the O*NET website, *http://online.onetcenter.org/*.

**Bold** indicates that the career is considered to be among the top **100 best-paying jobs** based on the average or median salary paid to individuals *with five years of experience.* Excluded are jobs where salary statistics are not available, such as "business owner," or not indicative, such as "actor."

*Italics* identifies the jobs that are predicted to benefit from an above-average growth rate over the next several years.

***Bold and italics*** indicates jobs that will benefit from both **higher pay** and *high growth potential.*

Note there are successful people of all Color styles in all occupations. In nonideal jobs you can still shine by creating your own niche.

## Business/Finance

*accountant* ◆ *auditor* ◆ bank officer (all types) ◆ **budget/financial analyst** ◆ credit analyst ◆ *financial advisor* ◆ financial examiner ◆ *investment banker* ◆ *stockbroker* ◆ **treasurer/chief financial officer** ◆ **venture capitalist** (efficiency, observant of details, moral certitude and appropriateness, low tolerance for unconventionality).

## Business/Management/Insurance/Manufacturing

actuary ◆ *administrative services manager* ◆ *auditor* ◆ *chief information officer* ◆ *compensation and benefits manager* ◆ efficiency expert ◆ **executive** ◆ insurance claim examiner/underwriter ◆ *human resources specialist* ◆ *management consultant* ◆ *managers of all types* [construction, database, factory, financial institution, hospital, hotel, industrial production, office, sales, etc.] ◆ **insurance agent/broker** ◆ project manager ◆ **purchasing manager**/agent ◆ real estate agent/appraiser ◆ sales [tangible products] (accurate memory of details, bottom line and cost-oriented, well-developed administrative skills, need for order, give clear directions).

## Computer/Information Technology

*computer analyst/security specialist* ◆ *information system manager* ◆ *network administrator* ◆ *web editor* (good memory for details, efficient, solid administrative skills, keep things orderly and on track).

## Education

*athletic coach/trainer* ◆ *professor* ◆ **school principal/administrator** ◆ **university president** ◆ vocational teacher (administrative skills, respect for "the system," common sense, thoughtfulness, practical experience).

## Health Science

*anesthesiologist* ◆ clinical technician ◆ **dentist** ◆ *medical and health service manager/technician* ◆ *pharmacist* ◆ *optometrist* ◆ *primary care physician* ◆ *radiologic technician* (accuracy, keen observation of details, practical and measurable work, organizational skills).

## Law/Law Enforcement/Government

compliance officer ◆ *corrections officer* ◆ **division manager** ◆ firefighter ◆ *investigator* ◆ IRS agent ◆ **judge** ◆ **lawyer** [particularly administrative, antitrust, bankruptcy, real estate, securities, taxation, transportation] ◆ military officer ◆ **pilot** ◆ *police officer* ◆ security consultant/guard (respect for rules and procedures, good administrative skills, observant of details, fact-oriented, boldness, ability to make tough decisions).

## Science Research, Engineering, Mathematics

**engineer** [civil, chemical, *environmental*, health and safety, industrial, mechanical, nuclear] ◆ **geologist** ◆ meteorologist (good memory for details, efficient, ability to work with tangible things and projects, keep things orderly and on track).

## Other

carpenter ◆ electronic repair ◆ general contractor ◆ mechanic ◆ plumber ◆ surveyor.

case study four

### When a Career Isn't Working

Brad Gunter was fed up, and the good money he was making wasn't enough compensation for the daily aggravations. Worse yet, he felt trapped. His uncle Phil, who was a partner in a major Los Angeles advertising firm, had gotten him this high-paying job as an account executive. Brad desperately wanted to quit, but he could not let the family down.

Even weaving his way through LA traffic in his new Porsche Carrera wasn't cheering him up as it once had. The day had been especially grueling when it should have been triumphant. Brad had just landed a major airline account. Today, it seemed as if his private office had been stormed by everyone in the firm. The Creative Department wanted ideas and brainstorming, which Brad hated. The back office needed lots of hand-holding as they established an account larger than any they had ever seen. Brad was assigned to three new teams, and working on teams was something he dreaded. All he had wanted to do was sift through demographic information about potential airline customers and memo the right people. Instead, his reference materials had gone untouched all day, and Brad was suffering from the serious Introvert's overexposure to people.

Finally, a pleasant thought entered his crowded mind—Michelle, the lovely young woman he had just met. They had had a wonderful lunch conversation several days ago about her work as a real estate appraiser. Convinced at first he would be bored out of his skull, Brad had been surprised by how interested he was in Michelle's work. The factual data-gathering, the comparisons to similar properties, the long hours alone with papers to be interpreted . . . right now, Michelle's job seemed like heaven to Brad. It certainly was a job for which Gold/Blue Introvert Brad felt well suited.

Fast forward two years. Brad finally found the courage to give up his stressful account executive position despite family opposition. Using the money he made from his commissions (which ran well into six figures), Brad supported himself while studying to become a real estate appraiser. When Brad married Michelle, she quit so the two of them could form their own appraisal firm. Energized daily, Brad loves his new career and is about to hire several people.

## Your Personality's Challenges

Gold/Blue Introverts have a unique set of potential work related blind spots. Some you have, others you don't. No one has them all. Tone down a blind spot by focusing on it, then choose more productive actions and make them habits. (Suggestions for doing so are in parentheses below.) You:

- May prematurely dismiss new ideas. (Dismiss nothing until you know the who, what, where, when, why, and cost of a new idea.)
- May focus too much on the flaws in the efforts of others and not give credit where credit is due. (Make a discipline of giving some sort of affirmation to a colleague after listing flaws. Acknowledge those who deserve it; say when the flaws are outweighed by the good work.)
- Stress immediate results and overlook long-range implications. (Invest some time in long-range planning and get more comfortable with it as a tool. Ask a willing Blue to help.)
- Are fixed in supporting established ways of doing things. (The tried-and-true contribute much to efficiency. But they won't keep your company alive when the market is moving or changing. Also, established ways can be improved. Focus on the who, what, where, when, why, and cost of changing a procedure so you can take some of the credit.)
- Are rigid about how others should perform their responsibilities. (This book reveals the strengths of other Colors; strengths you may be lacking. Results are the priority, not necessarily the efficiencies of getting there. Grant the wisdom of others some benefit of the doubt while awaiting proven results. If their way proves better than yours, you don't want to look stupid.)

## Your Job Search—the Good, the Bad, and the Ugly

Gold/Blue Introverts need to process information. With some interviewers, particularly Golds and Blues, you will feel a comfortable rapport. But with other Colors, you need to prepare and rehearse responses outside your comfort zone. Many human resource people are Greens; make a study of how to communicate effectively with this Color group before your first interviews.

Your natural strengths easily allow you to:

- Set realistic goals and timelines.
- Adequately research prospective employees.
- Be well prepared for interviews and come across as hard-working and competent.
- Logically consider pros and cons of every offer.
- Be patient with delays and obstacles.
- Show confidence in your ability to deal with bottom-line issues.

In order to tone down your blind spots, you need to:

- Go beyond your circle of friends to expand networking circle.
- Prepare questions to ask interviewers.

- Do some brainstorming with a willing Blue or Green to consider alternative careers.
- Be more assertive about selling yourself.
- Do some thinking about a prospective company's future direction (ask a willing Blue to help).
- Resist the urge to be overly cautious about change.
- Step back to reflect for a day or two about a job's impact on you and your family when tempted to make a snap decision

## The Gold/Blue Introvert's Interviewing Style

With an interviewer whose Color is close to your own, you will feel immediate rapport. However, if your interviewer seems to have a significantly different style (and it's statistically likely that they will have a Green component), use the suggestions in parentheses.

In following your natural style, you:

- Are calm and composed. (This can look like disinterest—most interviewers expect a certain amount of nervousness. Make sure to speak more than you normally do, especially at first.)
- Document your experience well, in an easy-to-follow manner.
- Prefer written communications before face-to-face meetings. (Practice interview questions before the meeting. This will boost your confidence.)
- Share few feelings with people. (A Green interviewer relies on his or her emotional response to you as a big part of the decision-making process. If your interviewer asks you questions like "How did you get along with previous co-workers?" he or she may be Green. Prioritize building a personal rapport with such an interviewer by answering emotion-based questions at length. Role-play with a willing Green.)
- Focus on the present. (Especially if interviewing for a senior level position, you will need to prepare a position on future planning. Take a Blue colleague to lunch and run a few ideas by him or her before an interview. At least research public statements about the company's future direction prior to an interview.)
- Follow through with all details; respect deadlines and commitments. (Interviewers respect that you send requested items, call to follow up, show up on time, and send thank-you notes.

Okay, go do something purposeful now. Later, check out Chapter 15, Blues Overall, first, then carefully read Chapter 4, A Tour of the Prism Company, and Chapter 25, Adjusting to the Styles of Others, to learn about the strengths of other Colors. Like all Colors, you need the strengths of others. You can put them to work for you if you know where to look and how to ask. If you invest time learning how to recognize the Colors who can best assist you, it will make everyone more effective and productive. You can do this by quickly reading the Blue, Red, and Green "Overall" chapters.

If you are actively engaging in a job search, jot notes in the Roadmap in Chapter 28. Recording your strengths and strategies is a concrete and results-oriented way to navigate the minefields of a job search.

# CHAPTER 23

# Gold/Green Extroverts

**YOU'RE NOT ONLY A GOLD,** you also have strong secondary characteristics of the Green personality. And you have tested as a Color Q Extrovert, which means you recharge your batteries by being with people, rather than being alone. Your Color group values efficiency, accuracy, predictability, tradition, and social responsibility. Affirming others is a strong inner drive. These core tendencies should ring true with you, since they've been researched worldwide for well over half a century. (If not, return to your Self-Assessment and follow the directions for re-evaluating yourself.) It's important that you read the exact right profile, since you can significantly enhance your professional and personal relationships as well as your job search with the information that follows.

## You Overall

Ensuring welfare of those around you, whether family or colleagues, is the focus of your energy and has been since you were a child. You affirm others and put them at ease. People in your Color group have continuous curiosity about people and keen observational skills.

Testing new ideas makes you uncomfortable; you favor working with real things and sticking with what you've experienced. Since few details escape your notice, you may feel you've "seen it all." Preferring the here-and-now, you shun change and minimize future thinking.

One of your best qualities is your highly developed work ethic. Commitments and obligations are undertaken with utmost seriousness. Your follow-through is unwavering; you easily mobilize others when help is needed. Strengths of your group include anticipating what needs to be done, getting involved in details, and organizing resources and procedures. Along the way you create harmony and stability, always aware of how you might serve both people and goals. You are a consummate volunteer or service career worker.

Straightforward yet diplomatically is how you prefer to communicate with others. The people who irritate you most are those who do not share your personal warmth and work ethic—the discourteous, the unreliable, and the unprepared.

Here's how all these qualities combine in a real-life Gold/Green Extrovert.

case study one

## Union Executive

Linda Chavez-Thompson grew up working the cotton fields of Texas. During the back-breaking days of those hot summer months, young Extroverted Linda dreamed of a sales job at Sears, "where I could dress up for work, be in air-conditioning, and work eight instead of ten hours a day."

Today, still mindful of her roots, she has reached far beyond this dream. Her work as Executive Vice President of the American Federation of Labor and Congress of Industrial Organizations (AFL-CIO) helps thousands of field, factory, and retail laborers attain better working conditions. With a Gold's single focus, she says, "I never really considered another career." While her Green secondary supports her caring, human concern side, her Gold primary leads the way to organize real changes in the world.

She has been most energized by restructuring state federations and central labor councils of the AFL-CIO in six states. With typical Gold organizational skills, she recrafted internal structures and strengthened the work of each body. Her Gold ability to focus clearly on short- and long-term goals "helped build their organizations into more powerful voices on issues affecting working families." The positive human impact this makes fulfills her Green side, while her Extroverted self enjoys the many people with whom she interacts.

# You on the Job

## As a Leader

"Getting the right things to the right people, in the right amounts, to the right place at the right time" is the crux of your talent. Outstanding logistical skills are the hallmark of Gold/Green Extroverts in leadership roles. Providing clear guidelines and instructions, you build productive teams on which all are kept well-informed.

You welcome responsibility as a tool for instituting sensible rules and procedures. You feel accountable for proper use of all resources and are vigilant to prevent their misuse.

You are suspicious of the agendas of those who question authority, believing they are slackers or troublemakers. You are loyal and expect loyalty in return. The personal attention you give your people gains you not only loyalty, but also goodwill.

## As a Team Player

You encourage your teammates to share viewpoints and ideas. But when goals have been set, you're the one who provides clear and practical ideas to achieve them. Getting things accomplished on time and on budget is the only acceptable way. You keep the agreed agenda on track, keep progress records for everyone, get the needed resources, and respect rules and procedures.

While other team members may not realize what resource they need until they need it, you've already anticipated and supplied it. Your contribution to

## Figure 23-1  Natural Work-Related Strengths

Approximately 80 percent of these attributes will apply to you. Check off those that do and use them in your resume and interviews. This will set you apart from the canned responses of others. You:

- ☐ Have a strong need to be of service to others.
- ☐ Acknowledge and respect the chain of command.
- ☐ Can easily repeat and sequence tasks.
- ☐ Deal well with details.
- ☐ Apply common sense.
- ☐ Motivate others to cooperate in achieving goals.
- ☐ Stay with the job until it's done.
- ☐ Get things done on time and under budget.

the team is immense. However, you may irritate others by talking too much. If nobody else has said anything for a while, solicit opinions. You also may hamper your efforts by sulking over disagreements you tend to take too personally.

Look at Figure 23–1 on page 219 for a list of your natural work-related strengths.

Here is another Gold/Green Extrovert using her strengths in a very different way.

case study two

## Philanthropist, Historical Documents Preservationist

On many hot days of an earlier era, two little girls played in the gardens of the Ibrahim palace, an architectural jewel set on the outskirts of Cairo, Egypt. One was a Hungarian who had escaped her native land several years before; the second was Princess Fazilé Ibrahim, member of the Egyptian royal family and great-granddaughter of the last Turkish sultan.

Then, on what is still known today as "Black Saturday," political turmoil struck. Thousands of religious fundamentalists, communists, and radical students began gathering in the streets. Within twenty-four hours, many of the symbols that had given Cairo its glamour had been burned down. Guests were thrown out of their windows at the Shepherd Hotel. We could see the mobs pulling people out of their cars and stoning them to death. It is a memory that will remain forever, for this is the author's story as well.

The two families fled rapidly—one going to the United States and the other settling in France. It would be thirty years before we would meet again.

Today Princess Fazilé Ibrahim is President of The Ibrahim Pasha of Egypt Fund, affiliated with the London-based Royal Asiatic Society. The organization is dedicated to encouraging the development of Ottoman studies internationally by publishing Ottoman documents and manuscripts of historical importance from the classical period up to 1839. A true Extrovert, she is an active, hands-on executive, traveling to elevate awareness of her Fund's mission and encourage submission of manuscripts. "I was clear about the fact that I intended to involve myself in all the proceedings in order to reach the precise goal of my foundation," she said. Her focus and determination are very much Gold/Green characteristics.

Making scholars familiar with the work of the Fund is a not a quick process, but Princess Fazilé continues the quest to find important Ottoman-era documents that will underpin historical research. "The Fund is small, not well-known for the present, and nothing compels people to come to us," she says. "We have to smile and encourage . . . and be patient." She has traveled to Turkey to meet with historians at two major universities and has visited the Centre of Istanbul Archives.

When manuscripts of great historical importance do come to her notice, "then it is a blessed moment for me, when I no longer question the validity of my project," she says. She finds these discoveries most energizing. Golds have a reverence for history and its preservation.

The Princess defines success as "doing something I care for and that some other people care for, too." When pushed about her strengths, she reluctantly says, "Maybe I am very stubborn; the fact is that I never got anything I wanted without giving a fierce fight." She claims she is not a businesswoman, but these Gold/Green Extroverted characteristics serve her well.

## Ideal Work Environment

A stable, organized institution with a predictable future is where Gold/Green Extroverts feel most at home. When a job offer is made, leverage as much as you can from the list in Figure 23–2 on page 222.

The WORST type of work culture for a Gold/Green Extrovert is impersonal and highly competitive. Constant change makes you feel that your great administrative and organizational strengths are valueless. You need rules, stability, and positive personal interactions in order to feel comfortable at work.

When Extroverted Gold/Greens work in nonideal corporate cultures, productivity is stunted and career achievements become an uphill climb.

## The Extroverted Gold/Green's Ideal Boss

Even a great job can be frustrating under the wrong boss; a mediocre job under a wonderful boss is pretty hard to leave. Gold/Greens get along especially well with other Golds. But bosses of other Color types who possess the characteristics in Figure 23–3 on page 223 also can be good mentors.

## Figure 23–2   The Ideal Gold/Green Extrovert Work Environment

Compare your current work environment to the description below. Check all that ring true for you. Don't be deceived if these descriptions seem "obvious." It confirms you've tested your individual Color correctly. Other Colors, especially Blues, would find this environment uncomfortable and unproductive. The optimal Gold/Green Extrovert work environment:

☐ Is a stable, well-recognized entity with a solid reputation in your community. You gravitate to established organizations; start-ups don't appeal to you.

☐ Involves concrete and practical projects and products. Intangible services are tough for you to quantify and measure. Stick with the things you can touch and see.

☐ Has clear rules, reporting lines, and expectations. Valuable time is wasted trying to make up rules as you go along. You don't want to be bothered by this.

☐ Allows you to work within a group or team. You need people to stay energized.

☐ Contains trustworthy co-workers.  You take an interest in the well-being of both colleagues and clients and prefer that it's reciprocated.

☐ Is service-oriented. You are by nature service-oriented and want to work in a place that honors those values.

☐ Rewards reliable people. It's rare that you fail to meet your deadlines.

☐ Provides financial security. You take pride in being competent and expect to be compensated appropriately.

☐ Makes you feel like part of a big family. You thrive in collegial places.

☐ Allows you to factor in the needs of your family. Since you make sure goals are achieved at work, you expect to be able to take time for significant family needs.

A corporate culture integrating the above elements is fertile soil for your career advancement.

**Figure 23–3   The Gold/Green Extrovert's Ideal Boss**

Check off if your boss:

☐ Shows appropriate personal concern for each staff member.
☐ States clearly what needs to be done.
☐ Sets achievable goals.
☐ Is reliable about providing needed resources.
☐ Holds to firm completion dates.

# Careers That Attract Gold/Green Extroverts

Gold/Green Extroverts like Princess Fazilé Ibrahim and Linda Chavez cluster in fields that provide professional respect, require high levels of competence, and contribute in a meaningful way to society (especially in well-known institutions). You need predictability and stability to be at your best. Upon reaching a high level of responsibility, you assemble a competent and loyal staff.

*Please note that not all* the following careers will appeal to you, but recognize that each, in some way, draws on the strengths of your style and appeals to a significant number of your Color group. This is not a comprehensive list, but it will show underlying patterns of preference. If unlisted careers offer similar patterns, your chances of success increase. Copy in parentheses highlights the Color style characteristics that create success.

In addition, two codes indicate those jobs that are currently predicted to have an above-average salary and growth potential. This information is based on the continuously revised data provided by the U.S. Department of Labor and Bureau of Labor Statistics available on the O*NET website, *http://online.onetcenter.org/*.

**Bold** indicates that the career is considered to be among the top **100 best-paying jobs** based on the average or median salary paid to individuals *with five years of experience.* Excluded are jobs where salary statistics are not available, such as "business owner," or not indicative, such as "actor."

*Italics* identifies the jobs that are predicted to benefit from an above-average growth rate over the next several years.

***Bold and italics*** indicates jobs that will benefit from both **higher pay** and *high growth potential.*

Note there are successful people of all Color styles in all occupations. In nonideal jobs you can still shine by creating your own niche.

## Business/Management/Promotion/Sales

*compensation and benefits manager* ◆ *convention planner* ◆ customer service manager ◆ *human resources manager/specialist* ◆ insurance underwriter/agent ◆ land developer ◆ *labor relations specialist* ◆ lobbyist ◆ *marketing executive* [radio, television] ◆ office manager ◆ private banker ◆ performing arts administrator ◆ *public relations specialist* ◆ real estate agent/*manager* ◆ salesperson [tangible products] ◆ service sales representatives (human interaction, organizational skills, straightforward and diplomatic communication, service career orientation).

## Education

*athletic coach* ◆ *principal* ◆ teacher [*preschool, elementary,* home economics, *special education*] (meaningful contribution to society, respect for rules, professional respect, service career orientation).

## Health Science

*biomedical technologist* ◆ *chiropractor* ◆ *dental hygienist* ◆ **dentist** ◆ dietitian ◆ *exercise physiologist* ◆ *hospice nurse* ◆ *hospital administrator* ◆ *nurse*/nursing instructor ◆ **optometrist** ◆ *pediatrician* ◆ *pharmacist* ◆ *pharmaceutical sales rep* ◆ *primary care/family physician/physician assistant* ◆ public health educator ◆ *speech pathologist* ◆ *radiologic technologist* ◆ *therapists of all types* [*occupational, physical, radiation, respiratory, speech*] ◆ *veterinarian/vet assistant* (high levels of competence, professional respect, service career orientation, observant of details, curious about people, put people at ease, ensuring welfare of others).

## Human Services

advocacy leader ◆ *childcare center director* ◆ community welfare worker ◆ counselor [career, *child welfare, employee assistance, family, substance abuse*] ◆ fundraiser ◆ religious leader [clergy, rabbi, religious educator] ◆ *social worker* (service career orientation, human interaction, affirming of others, help stabilize others, professional respect, contribute meaningfully to society, respect for tradition).

## Law/Hospitality/Small Business

hotel/restaurant owner ◆ innkeeper ◆ **lawyer** [limited interest in but include children, consumer affairs, domestic and healthcare] ◆ *retail owner/manager* (service career orientation, interaction with people, diplomatic, observant of details, ensuring welfare of others).

## Other Services

caterer ◆ cosmetologist ◆ court reporter ◆ fashion designer ◆ flight attendant ◆ fundraiser ◆ hairdresser ◆ interior designer ◆ landscape designer ◆ museum conservator ◆ *paralegal* ◆ personal trainer/exercise instructor ◆ travel agent (service career orientation, eye for detail, interaction with people, affirming of others, keen aesthetic sense).

case study three

### When a Career Isn't Working

Gold/Green Extrovert Dawson Perkins got his nice, practical MBA under pressure from his parents and promptly settled in to work at a leading investment bank in his city. He was pleased with life until the realities of the job settled in. The number crunching was endless, and client negotiations were tense to the point of exhaustion after typical 70-hour work weeks. Because he was really good interacting with clients (typical of a Gold/Green Extrovert), his boss frequently sent him on business trips to pitch ideas to prospective clients. After months on the road and one too many pre-closing all-nighters, his marriage was in serious trouble.

Typical of Gold/Greens, Dawson liked the money, prestige, and solid future he had at the firm. But he was desperately unhappy and burned out. The long hours of financial analysis and projecting the futures of client companies did not feed his Gold/Green need to work on tangible products with immediate results.

Gold/Green Extroverts can do quite well in private banking where the focus is on high-level client relationship-building. Otherwise, the financial world often does not afford the concrete and practical projects Gold/Greens prefer.

Dawson was offered a job with a client firm that sold home healthcare products. This allowed him to sell real, tangible products, have frequent daily interactions with others, and minimize the number-crunching and future-thinking he disliked. The move saved his marriage, and he is now overseeing a national sales staff.

## Your Personality's Challenges

Gold/Green Extroverts have a unique set of potential work-related blind spots. Some you have, others you don't. No one has them all. Tone down a blind spot by focusing on it, then choose more productive actions and make them habits. (Suggestions for doing so are in parentheses below.) You:

- ◆ Get too involved with details, ignore the big picture. (Find a willing Blue and lunch with that person twice a month. Occasionally emulate his or her long-term strategic thinking so it's a tool when you need it, but it will never feel natural.)
- ◆ Need significant praise and appreciation and get dispirited when there is none. (Not all Colors verbalize appreciation. It's there, but not evident. Either ask, "How am I doing?" or give yourself a pep talk. You know how you're doing, and you're usually doing very well.)
- ◆ Don't handle competitive situations well. (When you cannot turn the tide to cooperation, or calm things down, step back and disengage. Refuse to play the game. Most of the time, this is the only way to defuse the pressure.)
- ◆ Tend to stick to what has worked in the past. (There are many paths to the same place. All have their strengths and advantages. Yes, your way is the right way . . . one of many. Ignore your discomfort once or twice a year and examine the advantages of another way.)
- ◆ Do not naturally see new possibilities. (If your experience isn't addressing a new situation well, you get discouraged and hopeless, sometimes giving up. Get help—talk to someone, preferably a Blue or Red, to see beyond the now. Resist insisting on procedures just for their comfort value.)
- ◆ Make up your mind too quickly. (Even if you receive new information, it's difficult for you to reverse a position. Often in life you have felt stuck with a position not in your best interest in order to get something done. Throw a cog in the machine when you feel the need [ESPECIALLY if you have doubts about a marriage or having a child!]. Believe it or not, it will be good for everyone.)

## Your Job Search—the Good, the Bad, and the Ugly

Gold/Green Extroverts are better than most Colors at drumming up informational interviews and getting referrals to job leads. Your strengths and blind spots below apply equally to both informational and formal interviews.

With some interviewers, particularly Golds and Greens, you will feel a comfortable rapport. But with those of other Colors, you need to prepare and rehearse responses outside your comfort zone. Many human resource people are Greens; make a study of how to communicate effectively with this Color group before your first interviews.

Your natural strengths easily allow you to:

◆ Have a clear action plan for your search and proceed in an orderly fashion.
◆ Have measurable, realistic, and well-defined goals and meet them.
◆ Be patient with job application rules and procedures.
◆ Have a wide network of friends and colleagues upon which to draw for job leads.
◆ Adequately research a company before the interview.
◆ Follow through on details of job search, like writing appropriate thank-you notes.
◆ Create time lines, daily status reports, and budgets that reduce stress on both you and the family.

In order to tone down your blind spots, you need to:

◆ Balance networking and research.
◆ Be willing to consider less obvious career opportunities and ways to get interviews.
◆ Resist getting depressed and gloomy about turndowns; they're not personal rejections.
◆ Plan a "think-through session"; reflect for a day or two about long-term implications of a job for both you and your family before deciding.

# The Gold/Green Extrovert's Interviewing Style

With an interviewer whose Color is close to your own, you will feel immediate rapport. However, if your interviewer seems to have a significantly different style, use the suggestions in parentheses. Mercilessly exploit these natural abilities of yours, and get more job offers!

In following your natural style, you:

◆ Have an accurate and well-presented resume. (Accurate may not mean intriguing. Write descriptions that invite the interviewer to delve deeper; ask a willing Green for assistance.)
◆ Focus on the present. (Especially if interviewing for a senior level position, you will need to prepare a position on future planning.

Take a Blue colleague to lunch and run a few ideas by him or her before an interview. At least read public statements about company direction.)

◆ Come across as stable, hard working, warm, and with solid past accomplishments. (Good foot in the door, but not enough. Awareness of bottom-line considerations is just as important. Adjust some of your language to address cost management if applicable.)

◆ Demonstrate enthusiasm for the job. (This becomes a negative if you "gush." Keep sentences short, body language under control, hand gestures below neck.)

◆ May not think outside the box. (Your orderly mind knows what your next career step should be, but tends to close off other potentials. You prefer established fields, but there are always those you haven't considered that may allow you to move higher and faster than your planned career path.)

Take a break now to socialize. Later, read the Chapter 15, Greens Overall, first, then carefully read Chapter 4, A Tour of the Prism Company, to learn about the strengths of other Colors. In certain key areas, you need their strengths. You can put them to work for you if you know where to look and how to ask. If you invest time reading Chapter 25, Adjusting to the Styles of Other Colors, you'll learn how to recognize the Colors who can best assist you. This will make you more effective and productive.

If you are actively engaging in a job search, jot notes in the Roadmap in Chapter 28. Recording your strengths and strategies is a concrete and results-oriented way to navigate through the discouraging parts of a job search. It also will help capture what you learn on informational interviews and remember who to thank when you land your new job.

# CHAPTER 24

# Gold/Green Introverts

**YOU'RE NOT ONLY A GOLD,** you also have strong secondary characteristics of the Green personality. And you have tested as a Color Q Introvert, which means you recharge your batteries by being alone, rather than being with people. Your Color group has gentle and supportive people who value tradition and have strong follow-through skills. It's helpful to know your strengths so you can maximize them and your weaknesses so you can delegate or ask for help with them. Suggestions follow for all of this.

## You Overall

Quiet and reflective, the focus of your energy is to ensure the welfare of those under your care. This core tendency surfaces early in your life. Very few people get to see your rich inner world because you always are more focused on the needs of others.

At work this translates to a highly developed work ethic where commitments and obligations are undertaken with seriousness and given top priority. A practical, detail-oriented, and thorough person, you can always see and address what needs to be done at each phase of a project.

Your warmth, sense of responsibility, and desire to create stability and harmony lead you to service careers and volunteer activities. But you don't last long in hectic and ambiguous environments; stable organizations that provide ample private time to plan will better support your ambitions.

Authority, history, and tradition are things you respect. So is the conservation of any kind of resource, natural or man-made. You find change, abstract concepts, and untested theories irritating. When you start imagining things, it's usually worst-case scenarios that fill you with doom, gloom, and self-doubt. Pulling yourself back to the real world makes you feel better, and you prefer staying here. Imagination is not your friend, and the vivid imaginations of Greens in particular make you uncomfortable.

If you have co-workers who are discourteous, unreliable, noisy, or unprepared, it drives you crazy. Conflicts are problematic for you and avoided wherever possible, allowing bad behaviors to continue unchecked.

At cocktail parties or business functions, you just enjoy blending in. Controlling the attention or taking a dominant role isn't something you want or need. You leave the starring roles to others. One-on-one is the way you prefer to communicate, and you listen attentively. Putting others at ease is a talent you've acquired through your natural curiosity about people and your keen powers of observation.

case study one

## Psychologist and Teacher

Eric Nichols, Ph.D., is a gentle personality who wants to retire to a cabin with enough land to raise chickens and sheep. He suspects that's a pipe dream, but it keeps him going in his roles as a licensed psychologist and teacher of graduate counseling students. Eric sees patients 10 to 12 hours a week in therapy. The rest of the time he runs graduate courses at the University of Vermont's College of Education and Social Services in diversity, family counseling, testing, counseling theory, and internship.

His Gold personality is well-suited to his administrative tasks—scheduling, interviewing prospective students, and serving on University committees. "As for the administrative stuff, I love organizing and attending to the details of the program," he says, a typical Gold. "I like being helpful."

His passions are sharing stories with his students and listening to people's life stories. "They intrigue me," Eric says. His Green side gives him a natural strength for the emotional aspects of his therapeutic work. It's important for him to feel needed. "I worry about what it will be like for me when I retire next year from the University," he says. He plans to continue his therapy practice.

In his top strengths he includes kindness, persistence, loyalty, attention to detail, and follow-through. "As I get older, I am more and more willing to take calculated risks," he says. "I like that."

Eric's definition of success is being happy with what he does and having enough money to live comfortably, responsibly, and generously (his Gold side talking). If the cabin of his dreams doesn't pan out at retirement, he wants to cook either professionally or for his own pleasure, and travel more, especially to Mexico (his Green side talking). "I started studying Spanish two years ago, and I want to get good at speaking that," he says.

## You on the Job

### As a Leader

"Getting the right things to the right people, in the right amounts, to the right place, at the right time" is the crux of your talent. Outstanding logistical skills are the hallmark of Gold/Green Introverts in leadership roles. You supply clearly defined guidelines and instructions for your staff, and you often jump in and share the work.

You see your role as providing for the organization's practical needs, to which you attend as if providing for a family. You welcome responsibility, feel keenly accountable, and prevent misuse of key resources. Everyone is kept informed, reaping goodwill and productivity.

When making important decisions, you go step-by-step, avoiding all foreseeable risks. As much factual information as possible is absorbed and assessed. You are uncomfortable "going with your gut."

### As a Team Player

You rarely seek to lead but encourage others to express their ideas, provide positive feedback, and usually are modest about your own contributions. When a team needs a practical reality check, you're the one to provide it. Dependable and reliable, you do thorough work, meet deadlines, respect rules and procedures, and don't understand the motivations of others who behave differently.

If you speak up about the less productive actions of team members and they argue with you, you are apt to take it too personally.

Look at Figure 24–1 for a list of your natural work-related strengths.

Now see how one Gold/Green Introvert uses these strengths in a different field.

## Figure 24-1    Natural Work-Related Strengths

Approximately 80 percent of these attributes will apply to you. Check off those that do and use them in your resume and interviews. This will set you apart from the canned responses of others. You:

☐ Can organize people to accomplish well-defined goals.
☐ Observe the needs of others and supply them whenever you can.
☐ Are practical about what needs to be done and how to do it.
☐ Support and encourage others.
☐ Work well on a team.
☐ Are not ego-driven.
☐ Follow the rules.

case study two
_____

## Small Business President

Mary Waite's dream of a career in agriculture took some twists and turns. Growing up in a small rural town in Connecticut, Mary watched her parents run a feed, grain, and dairy business on their family farm. "The secretaries sat at our dining room table," she says. "I learned a lot about the business by osmosis."

In college, she majored in agricultural economics and got married. After graduation, she began work as an agricultural loan officer. "That involved two things I enjoyed," she recalls. "Banking and agriculture."

She had to quit as her husband's corporate career took off, with moves to metropolitan areas up and down the East Coast. "Not where you find agricultural lending agencies!" Mary says. She worked as a straight loan officer, "which I still found enjoyable, because you get to see what works and what doesn't financially for different businesses." When her children were born, Mary left the business world to raise them.

She inherited her childhood farm when her parents passed away. She and her husband made one final move back to it. "It was extremely gratifying to move back here," says Mary. "The kids seemed to appreciate their roots, the ones my parents worked so hard to put down here." Golds value traditions and family history. One thing Mary especially values here is the ability to keep cows, sheep, goats, rabbits, and ducks and re-claim her desire for an agriculturally based life.

When her children were in high school, Mary and her hus-band acquired two niche businesses in the industrial safety garment industry. She became president of the smaller of the two, in Texas. "I do everything, minus the actual production," she says, including bookkeeping, purchase orders, payroll, purchase checking, and customer relations. They have a dozen clients. "I said upfront to my husband, this is what I can do," says Mary. "I didn't want or need the challenges of trying to run or expand a business. But my strengths are detail work, the nit-picking, the follow-through. In our business, there's a right way and a wrong way, it's very clear cut, important that it's done a certain way, and that you follow through." Mary's Gold side is ideally suited for these demands.

The most stressful aspect of the work for Mary is the highly technical customer contact, not unusual for an Introvert.

Mary's Green side finds working with animals during off time on the farm most energizing and satisfying. She also enjoys making personal connections with people. "I like finding the strengths of others, figuring out what they might need, and connecting them with the right person, place, or thing." Caring for others is typical of a Gold/Green Introvert.

Soon to retire, Mary looks forward to "doing more for my community. I'd love to develop some sustainable agriculture that utilizes all our land, and maybe get four or five llamas."

## Ideal Work Environment

You, like Eric Nichols, gravitate to stable, recognized entities with solid rep-utations in the community. When a job offer is made, leverage as much as you can from the list in Figure 24–2 on page 234.

The WORST type of work culture for an Introverted Gold/Green is highly competitive and rewards intuition over factual accuracy. Environ-ments of constant change, like start-up or distressed companies, can stress you to the point of physical illness.

When Introverted Gold/Greens work in nonideal corporate cultures, productivity is stunted and career achievements become an uphill climb.

## Figure 24–2    The Ideal Gold/Green Introvert
##                  Work Environment

Compare your current work environment to the description below. Don't be deceived if these descriptions seem "obvious." It confirms you've tested your individual color correctly. Other Colors, especially Reds, would find this environment uncomfortable and unproductive. The optimal Gold/Green Introvert work environment:

☐ Is a stable and well-respected institution with a predictable future. You work hard and want to be rewarded with money and respect. New or distressed companies can't offer this. You are a quintessential corporate worker and, unless you are the boss, you want to ally yourself with a firm that stands behind its people and products.

☐ Involves concrete and practical projects and products. Intangible services are tough for you to quantify and measure. Stick with the things you can touch, see, and immediately evaluate.

☐ Is oriented to serving both customers and staff. You have a deeply rooted principle of serving others. If your company disregards that, you will not work there long.

☐ Values and returns loyalty and commitment. These are a deep and natural part of the core of who you are. In today's workplace, few companies can afford to offer their employees the loyalty they once did. Today, you are better off choosing to place your loyalty with a mentor rather than a company; but there are still a few good firms around.

☐ Has a work/life balance program that respects the family needs of staff. Family is your first priority, and you are too good a worker not to be allowed time for family needs.

☐ Is quiet, orderly, and calm. The one situation you are weakest at coping with is chaos.

☐ Allows for private space. As an Introvert, your batteries get drained when dealing with people, even if your people skills are superb. You recharge your batteries by being alone. If you have to share your work space with others, you will feel a lot more fatigue at the end of the day. You think and perform better in a private space where you can reflect in-depth on projects; insist on one as a condition of employment if at all possible.

A corporate culture integrating the above elements is fertile soil for your career advancement.

## Figure 24-3    The Gold/Green Introvert's Ideal Boss

Check off if your boss:

- ☐ Is organized and sets clear objectives.
- ☐ Is reliable and trustworthy.
- ☐ Takes a personal interest in each employee.
- ☐ Is loyal.
- ☐ Provides needed resources.

# The Gold/Green Introvert's Ideal Boss

Even a great job can be frustrating under the wrong boss; a mediocre job under a wonderful boss is pretty hard to leave. Gold/Greens get along especially well with other Golds. But bosses of other Color types who possess the characteristics in Figure 24–3 also can be good mentors.

# Careers That Attract Gold/Green Introverts

The company you'll call home is one where you can work in a secure career path for many years under the guidance of clear rules, procedures, and expectations. As with Mary Waite, predictability and stability bring out your best work. You particularly need to be rewarded for your abilities to be accurate and get things done. Financially well-managed companies are what you instinctively prefer.

*Please note that not all* the following careers will appeal to you, but recognize that each, in some way, draws on the strengths of your style and appeals to a significant number of your Color group. This is not a comprehensive list, but it will show underlying patterns of preference. If unlisted careers offer similar patterns, your chances of success increase. Copy in parentheses highlights the Color style characteristics that create success.

In addition, two codes indicate those jobs that are currently predicted to have an above-average salary and growth potential. This information is based on the continuously revised data provided by the U.S. Department of Labor and Bureau of Labor Statistics available on the O*NET website, *http://online.onetcenter.org/*.

**Bold** indicates that the career is considered to be among the top **100 best-paying jobs** based on the average or median salary paid to individuals *with five years of experience*. Excluded are jobs where salary statistics are not available, such as "business owner," or not indicative, such as "actor."

*Italics* identifies the jobs that are predicted to benefit from an above-average growth rate over the next several years.

***Bold and italics*** indicates jobs that will benefit from both **higher pay** and *high growth potential*.

Note there are successful people of all Color styles in all occupations. In nonideal jobs you can still shine by creating your own niche.

## Business/Management/Promotion/Sales

bookkeeper ◆ *convention planner* ◆ customer service manager ◆ *human resources specialist* ◆ insurance underwriter/agent ◆ lobbyist ◆ ***marketing executive*** [radio, television] ◆ office manager ◆ private banker ◆ performing arts administrator ◆ *public relations specialist* ◆ real estate agent/*manager* ◆ salesperson [tangible products] ◆ service sales representatives ◆ small business owner (human interaction, organizational skills, straightforward and diplomatic communication, service career orientation).

## Creative/Other Services

antique dealer ◆ caterer ◆ cosmetologist ◆ court reporter ◆ *desktop publisher* ◆ fashion designer ◆ flight attendant ◆ hairdresser ◆ interior designer ◆ jeweler ◆ librarian ◆ landscape designer ◆ museum conservator ◆ *paralegal* ◆ personal trainer/exercise instructor ◆ proofreader ◆ travel agent (service career orientation, eye for detail, interaction with people, affirming of others, keen aesthetic sense).

## Education

**school administrator** ◆ *guidance counselor* ◆ teacher [*preschool, elementary,* home economics, *special education, some postsecondary*] (meaningful contribution to society, respect for rules, professional respect, service career orientation).

## Health Science

***anesthesiologist*** ◆ *biomedical technologist* ◆ ***chiropractor*** ◆ *dental hygienist/lab technician* ◆ **dentist** ◆ dietitian ◆ *exercise physiologist* ◆ *hospice nurse* ◆ *hospital administrator* ◆ *nurse*/nursing instructor ◆ **optometrist** ◆ *pedi-*

*atrician* ◆ *pharmacist* ◆ *primary care/family physician/physician assis-tant* ◆ public health educator ◆ *speech pathologist* ◆ *radiologic technologist* ◆ *therapists of all types* [*occupational, physical, radiation, respiratory, speech*], *veterinarian/vet assistant* (high levels of competence, professional respect, service career orientation, observant of details, curious about people, put people at ease, ensuring welfare of others).

## Human Services

advocacy leader ◆ *childcare center director* ◆ community welfare worker ◆ counselor [career, child welfare, employee assistance, family, substance abuse] ◆ fundraiser/institutional solicitor ◆ religious leader [clergy, rabbi, religious educator] ◆ *social worker* (service career orientation, human interaction, af-firming of others, help stabilize others, professional respect, contribute meaningfully to society, respect for tradition)

## Law/Hospitality/Small Business

innkeeper/motel manager ◆ **lawyer** [limited interest in but include children, consumer affairs, domestic and health care] ◆ *retail owner/manager* (serv-ice career orientation, interaction with people, diplomatic, observant of de-tails, ensuring welfare of others)

case study three

### When a Career Isn't Working

Bertie Feldman learned a lot by doing his cousin Tom a favor. Tom decided to run for State Treasurer and asked Bertie to man-age his campaign. Bertie was deeply flattered; his cousin compli-mented him on his superior abilities to tune in to people's needs, handle details, and complete follow-through tasks. "Bertie," his cousin said, "no one is better at these things than you!"

It probably helped that Bertie recently had been laid off from his middle management job with a big enough severance package to see him through the four-month campaign. But Bertie also knew it wouldn't just be his cousin getting expo-sure. Introverted Bertie was determined to use the experience to get his resume around and meet people with whom he would never otherwise come in contact.

The cramped campaign quarters did not allow Bertie a private office. Over time, this would become a major fatigue factor, with volunteers dropping in to ask questions or talking too loudly on their phones. Gold/Green Bertie much preferred the stability and predictability of his old job; by contrast, the campaign was uncomfortably fluid, with candidate plans changing constantly. Concrete-thinking Bertie was at a loss during strategy sessions, when as campaign manager he should have been leading the discussion. But strategies and theories stymied Bertie's factually oriented, Gold/Green character.

He was great, however, at managing the volunteer staff. No task ever lacked a competent person, and even the media noted how well his cousin's campaign was organized. Tom won the election, and Bernie knew what he wanted to do and where.

Two weeks after the elections, Bertie was offered the job of his dreams—managing the volunteer staff at the National Historical Museum two towns away from his home. Half of his time would be spent doing research in a private (hallelujah!) office. The salary was identical to his old job, with superior benefits. Bertie's family was especially happy when he came home revved up at the end of each day.

## Your Personality's Challenges

Gold/Green Introverts have a unique set of potential work-related blind spots. Some you have, others you don't. No one has them all. Tone down a blind spot by focusing on it, then choose more productive actions and make them habits. (Suggestions for doing so are in parentheses below.) You:

◆ Don't see the forest for the trees. (Details, rather than the big picture, are your preferred focus. Without an overview, your detail decisions may be flawed. Keep in mind the end result and the details become clearer.)

◆ Need approval and get dispirited if it's not expressed. (Myth: If they don't express it, they don't feel it. Fact: More than one Color feels appreciation without expressing it. Sometimes, you just have to reward yourself.)

◆ Overreact to competition and infighting. (When you can't avoid conflict, you become cold, snappy, and overly negative. Be proactive; nipping it in the bud will drain you less. You'll beat competitors with your tireless follow-through; don't be afraid of them. They have something to prove; you don't.)

- May be overly cautious about new ways. (Focus on whether the new is practical; that's your strength. Support pilot projects and trial periods before saying no.)
- Can be less assertive and direct than needed. (You prefer to blend in; but occasionally you have to step up and share your knowledge. This is what it takes sometimes to get the job done. Do it without reservation.)

## Your Job Search—the Good, the Bad, and the Ugly

Gold/Green Introverts have the advantage of being best one-on-one. With some interviewers, particularly Golds and Greens, you will feel a comfortable rapport. But with those of other Colors, you need to rehearse responses outside your comfort zone.

Your natural strengths easily allow you to:

- Assemble a close and supportive network.
- Construct an accurate and compelling resume.
- Create a clear action plan.
- Have measurable and well-defined short- and long-term goals.
- Research and collect facts on prospective employers.
- Proceed through the interview process in an orderly way.
- Come across as hard-working, warm, and prepared.
- Be patient with what needs to be done and job application rules.
- Follow through on all details of the search. Are decisive when the right opportunity turns up.

In order to tone down your blind spots, you need to:

- Not take delays and obstacles as rejections.
- Prevent stress by organizing time lines, status reports, and a job search budget to track how well you are meeting your goals.
- Stretch yourself socially to broaden your network.
- Drill down to bottom-line implications and be tough when focusing on that aspect of a job.
- Role-play uncomfortable salary negotiations (get a willing Blue or Red to assist).
- Refuse to give in to depression after being turned down.

## The Gold/Green Introvert's Interviewing Style

With an interviewer whose Color is close to your own, you will feel immediate rapport. However, if your interviewer seems to have a significantly different style, use the suggestions in parentheses.

In following your natural style, you:

- Listen more than you speak. (This can look like disinterest. Make sure to speak more than you normally do, especially at first.)
- Prefer written communications before face-to-face meetings. (Read several back issues of pertinent trade journals if necessary. Gather facts from all sources—Internet, library, annual reports. Such preparation will boost your confidence.)
- Prefer to talk about specific details, schedules, and deadlines. (A Green interviewer relies on his or her emotional response to you as a big part of the decision-making process. If your interviewer asks you questions like "How did you get along with previous co-workers?" he or she may be Green. Prioritize building a personal rapport with such an interviewer. Role-play with a willing Green.)
- Focus on the present. (Especially if interviewing for a senior level position, you will need to prepare a position on future planning. Take a Blue or Green colleague to lunch and run a few ideas by him or her before an interview. At least read public statements about the company's future direction prior to an interview.)

Okay, go do something valuable to your community now. Later, check out Chapter 15, Greens Overall, first, then carefully read Chapter 4, A Tour of the Prism Company, and Chapter 25, Adjusting to the Styles of Others, to learn about the strengths of other Colors. Like all Colors, you need the strengths of others. You can put them to work for you if you know where to look and how to ask. If you invest time learning how to recognize the Colors who can best assist you by reading Figure 3 in each of the "Overall" Color chapters, it will make everyone more effective and productive.

If you are actively engaging in a job search, jot notes in the Roadmap in Chapter 28. Recording your strengths and strategies is a concrete and results-oriented way to assess the progress of your job search.

# GETTING THE JOB

# CHAPTER 25

# Before I Do Something Stupid . . . Adjusting to Other Styles

**PEOPLE LEAVE JOBS BECAUSE** they dislike the people more often than because they dislike their tasks. "If it weren't for my boss, I'd really love my job." "If Mary would just stay out of my hair, I'd be able to complete my projects on time." Certain Color Q personalities clash with others because they don't recognize each other's strengths. Believe it or not, your boss and your co-worker Mary can actually make your work easier . . . if you learn their strengths. In this chapter, you'll learn how to do this using Color Q. Start by identifying the Colors of others (see Figure 3 in each of the "Overall" Color chapters), and then determine what they can do for you. Finally, there are tips on how to speak their languages.

Giving someone the Self-Assessment in Chapter 2 often is not feasible. So here's how to do Color Q detective work. Follow the steps in Figure 25–1 to assess someone else's Color. (These tips work outside the office, too; for example, on dates or when trying to improve relations with your spouse or parents.)

Once you have an idea about a person's personality Color, you can begin to change the tone of your interactions. Two things will happen. You will get more help from your adversaries, and they will respect you more. You will come to appreciate their strengths, too (perhaps to the point of even liking them . . . a little!).

**Figure 25–1**

Figuring out someone's Color is not easy. It takes time and close observation to figure out someone's full Color type. But if you can assess any part of their Color makeup, it will go a long way toward improving communications.

Everyone has a Gold OR Red component, AND a Blue OR Green component. In this section, we will concentrate on identifying these components. If you can recognize these pieces, whether they are primary or backup, you're already ahead of the game. In addition, everyone is either an Extrovert or an Introvert.

There are three steps to revealing these components.

1)  First, look at his or her workspace. Try to look at it in the morning, at noon, and after he or she has gone home for the day.

    He's A GOLD IF: The desk is usually uncluttered, has no piles, and everything is neatly filed. Golds begin and end projects before starting new ones. Other clues: Golds tend to be serious and formal and always on time.

    She's A RED IF: The desk is a mess of files, papers, and piles. Usually everything is a work in progress. Other clues: Reds are loose and relaxed (may even have their feet up on the desk) and often time-pressured or late.

2)  The second piece of this detective work is the Blue/Green component. Start a conversation and talk about any comfortable subject, but notice:

    Green vs. Blue: How much does he personalize the relationship with you? Greens will, Blues won't.

    She's A GREEN IF: There's a lot of small talk, an effort to personalize the relationship even if it is business focused, an effort to put you at ease.

    He's A BLUE IF: There is limited chitchat, a sense of distance, a desire to keep the relationship on a professional basis; if he is brief and terse, gets to the point, imparts a sense that he is appraising you.

3)  Finally, everyone is either an Introvert or an Extrovert. Both may have good people skills, but they express themselves in different ways.

    EXTROVERTS are more talkative, speak in a louder voice, and gesticulate more. They may even speak before thinking and later change their mind.

**Figure 25–1    Continued**

INTROVERTS listen more, tend to have more subdued energy, and gesticulate less. They think before answering and
will rarely change their minds.

You can observe people's style while they are speaking and adjust your behavior accordingly. The benefit is that all will be more
comfortable in your presence and listen to what you have to say.

# Getting Along with the Other Colors at Work

Whether you are managing, selling to, motivating, or working with others,
Color Q helps hone your approach. Use the tips below to change the tone
of your communications with troublesome bosses and co-workers, and note
the results. If you've accurately assessed their primary Color, the effects will
be significant.

# Communicating Smoothly with Golds

When you are MANAGING a Gold, give him or her precise expectations,
and then provide a stable environment with clear channels of communication and authority. You need to come across as decisive and organized, emphasizing firm procedures and deadlines. Then get out of the way and
respect Golds' unique ability to "get things done."

When SELLING, PERSUADING, or WORKING WITH a Gold, make
sure you first have you own act together and any presentation or meeting
runs smoothly. Be reliable enough to arrive at your meeting on time. At all
costs, avoid vague information and abstract theories; stick with being factual,
accurate, precise, and down-to-earth. Make your points sequentially. Avoid
words like "feel" and "believe." Use words like "tradition," "respected," and
"proven." Follow whatever procedures the gold has requested. Respect the
hierarchy of Golds' department or company; if they say you have to talk to
someone else, they mean it and are not blowing you off.

# Communicating Smoothly with Blues

When you are MANAGING a Blue, you need to be visionary in order to
capture his or her interest. Explain how what you're doing will have an impact in the future—even have global consequences. Establish demanding
goals or Blues will get bored and distracted. Debate with the Blue and don't

take challenges personally; it's a sign you've got Blue's interest. Be open to making changes based on his or her insights and analytical skills. Above all, provide Blues an autonomous environment with minimal guidelines. They won't disappoint you.

When SELLING, PERSUADING, or WORKING WITH a Blue, it is imperative to come across as competent or he or she will not respect you or your message. Present the "big picture" first and limit the facts, which dampen their interest. Show the long-term potential of new solutions. Don't become personally offended by anything Blues say. Respond with ingenuity and logic. Avoid words like "feel" and "believe;" use words like "think" and "know."

## Communicating Smoothly with Reds

When MANAGING a Red, face-to-face is always better. Memos and emails do not engage Reds. They need stimulation, fun, freedom, and independence to be on top of their game, so provide them with the most flexible and self-paced environment possible. Reds not only enjoy crises, they will create them if they are bored; so avoid meetings, rules, and memos where possible. Use a Red to solve problems and crises, and allow him or her to follow instincts. Reds are difficult to control and impossible to micromanage, but they will not disappoint you if you provide them the above conditions.

When SELLING, PERSUADING, or WORKING WITH a Red, be brief and use action verbs like "stimulate," "liven up," "challenge," "enjoy," or "confront." Hands-on demonstrations are way better than computer slideshows. For Reds, timing is everything, so don't continue if they're distracted. Acknowledge the distraction and ask to meet again later that day. Get to the point, avoid theories and frameworks, and stress the immediacy of your solutions. Be very flexible, open-ended, and ready for "fly by the seat of your pants" decisions and fast closes.

## Communicating Smoothly with Greens

When MANAGING a Green, provide him or her a harmonious environment and stress opportunities for personal growth. Greens become troubled and distracted by undue competition and personal conflict; minimize this among co-workers. Personalize your working relationship—ask about their families and pets in appropriate ways.

Be inspiring and positive. Work with them to establish a mutually accepted vision and allow them creative freedom to address it. Give frequent feedback, but keep it diplomatic; they are turned off by harsh criticism or fear tactics. They prefer to work collaboratively, so imposing strict hierarchies on Greens reduces productivity rather than increasing it, as with Golds.

When SELLING, PERSUADING, or WORKING WITH a Green, above all personalize the relationship. Ask what he or she needs, then listen empathetically to the answer. Expect the Green's discussion to be nonsequential, but know that he or she will return to the original point. When presenting your product or solution, give the big picture and limit support facts, unless they communicate the impact on people. Use words like "feel," "believe," "value," and "like." Be insightful, idea-driven, and stress innovative and future-driven solutions.

## Introvert versus Extrovert

Often you will be communicating with someone who is your opposite. If you find conversations getting cut short, this may be the reason. If you are an Extrovert speaking with an Introvert, just bring your energy level down a notch. NEVER jump in to fill an Introvert's silence, no matter how uncomfortable it makes you. One time, I let an Introvert think silently for seven minutes on the phone; he had constructed an entire conference panel for me with topic, speakers, and copy!

If you are an Introvert speaking with an Extrovert, raise your energy level a little, make eye contact, and ask questions to keep the dialogue going.

## Taking Control of Your Work Environment

If you have assessed correctly the primary Color of your boss or co-worker, you will see a dramatic and immediate improvement in your communications using these Color Q guidelines. Relationships will improve, tasks will be accomplished more smoothly, and teams will get less bogged down in conflict.

If following these tips does not produce much result, you need to reassess that person's primary Color OR avoid behaviors typical of your own Color that create communication irritants. (One example: Trying to force a sequential conversation on a nonsequential-thinking Color.) The "Overall" Color chapters, and Chapter 4, A Tour of the Prism Company, can assist.

Before you quit your job, try changing your approach to those who irritate you at work. At least you will add to your people skills. You may even get a promotion, salary increase, or find you already have the job of your dreams.

# CHAPTER 26

# Would I Make a Good Entrepreneur?

There are three answers to the question, "Would I make a good entrepreneur?"

1. All Colors can be entrepreneurs.
2. All Colors need the help of other Colors to succeed in their new venture.
3. Some Colors make better natural entrepreneurs than others (see Figure 26–1 on page 248).

The reason you need the other Colors on your entrepreneurial team is that natural entrepreneurs have their weaknesses, and less natural entrepreneurs have their strengths. So it's not where you start as an individual—it's the team you assemble that ultimately will make or break your venture.

Here are the innate entrepreneurial styles of the four primary Colors. You also will have some of the strengths of your backup Color as well.

## The Gold Entrepreneurial Style
### How Golds Set Goals

You are one of the best of all Colors at setting goals and making plans to achieve them. You prioritize, follow through, and evaluate progress effortlessly. What you are not good at is modifying your well-laid plans to adapt to changing circumstances.

**Figure 26–1    Colors as Entrepreneurs**

Colors that make the best entrepreneurs, starting with the most naturally gifted:

Reds

Blues

Golds

Greens

Remember, ALL Colors can be entrepreneurs because all need the help of the other Colors to succeed. Golds and Greens should partner with Reds and Blues to provide a balance of talent.

Before casting your business plan in stone, run it by people you respect who are of other personality Colors. Ask them what additional options to consider, especially involving a work team or your family. Don't rush into it, even if you are excited and energized.

Then, schedule reevaluations at specific points along the way. Mark your calendar to sit back and reflect whether your goals are being met or you need to readjust them. You may be tempted to avoid this uncomfortable task; inviting a Blue or Green to help prevents procrastination. This one exercise could spell the difference between success and failure.

## Golds at the Start of the Venture

You are not one of the world's "dreamers and schemers," but many Golds have come up with brilliant business ideas and gotten rich from them. At your core, you are driven to be a responsible overseer of people and resources, and this makes you a cautious risk-taker. In your favor, you are not likely to be diverted by other opportunities, as Reds and Blues often are. You will rely on tried-and-true methodology to move predictably from one milestone to the next.

Once in business, your first priority is establishing order. Systems and procedures are in place virtually from Day One. The sooner you can create predictability in your business, whether in sales, manufactured inventory, or cash flow, the more comfortable you are.

Foreseeing and responding to changes in the marketplace will never be your forte, and handling unexpected crises is downright stressful to you. Make sure you have a Blue or Green on board to identify future trends that might impact your business. Get a Red to buffer you from the normal crises to which all young firms are subjected.

## The Rooneys—Father and Daughter Entrepreneur Team

At age 36 Trisha Rooney Alden is President of R4 Services, LLC, a leading records management company she formed thirteen years ago. She always wanted to be an entrepreneur and has let little get in her way. This includes marriage, having two babies, and joining her husband in another city while keeping her business headquartered in Chicago. Shuttling between clients and family in some fifty trips a year utilizes all her Gold organizational skills. She needed help.

Enter her father, Phil, former CEO of a public company who of late had been enjoying a stress-free life managing his investments. Today he comes into R4 Services at 5:30 AM every morning without getting paid. Why so early? "That's when the day starts operationally," he explains. "By 8 AM clients have urgent needs and we need to respond to them in a timely fashion."

For Golds, family is key, and Phil truly enjoys the opportunity of helping his daughter fulfill her dreams (even in the early hours of dawn!). Of course, he is quick to point out that she makes all the decisions. "R4 Services was a multimillion dollar business when I came aboard," he stresses, "I just provide support and advice where needed."

Trish and Phil are both Gold backup Greens, and the firm's culture reflects this. For instance, Trish has a small cubicle rather than a large corner office. "I love it that way," she says. "I am out of the office a lot with clients; this way I get to hear everything that is going on," she adds, reflecting the Green need for connectivity.

In order to succeed in a business that handles intricate records management and destruction issues for some 600 clients, collaboration between father and daughter is key. So is listening to, and cultivating the opinions of, the service and warehouse staff. Phil picks up donuts each morning to ensure that the early arriving staff has something to eat.

Both father and daughter take great pride in the low turnover of their staff, noting 60 percent have been with the company for over ten years. "One of our goals," they say, "is to help employees have really good lives and a great place to work." This is a classic example of how Gold/Greens attend to the practical needs of others.

Trish sees her top strengths as working well with people, listening deeply to clients to discover needs, communicating clearly, and always delivering what has been promised. All these strengths express her Gold/Green components. Clients are highly energizing to her. "I like to organize them," she says, "and to call them often to talk about present and future needs. They are my passion!"

What about stress areas? Pricing services and having clients negotiate downward are stressful, as are doing budgets and focusing on the financials of the business. These reflect her Green side, which dislikes confrontation and excessive work in the area of numbers. Here she relies on her father's thirty-plus years of business experience.

As two Gold/Greens, father and daughter have established an easy work relationship. He oversees operations, she focuses on new business development. The mutual respect is evident and contributes to the firm's steady growth.

Meanwhile, they are also actively involved in a wide range of philanthropic organizations involving children, museums, universities, and hospitals. In true Gold fashion, they welcome opportunities to take care of their community.

# The Red Entrepreneurial Style

## case study two

## Helen Glunz

Helen Glunz is president of the Glunz Family Winery and Cellars and arranges the importation of wines into the Louis Glunz Wines, Inc. warehouse. Since they were first married, she and her husband Joseph B. Glunz, president of Louis Glunz Wines, Inc., have worked in the wine business together. Ten children later, "I am starting to fade now . . . I try to take

Mondays off." Helen admits to accomplishing this goal only four or five times a year.

The company produces draft wine for the restaurant market, varietals, fortified wines, and what Helen refers to as "fun" wines. These are family favorites like May wine, Glogg, and Sangria, which are sold through high-end retail outlets like Marshall Fields and Whole Foods. Reds are naturally attracted to working with fine wines and good foods.

Putting ten children through college placed big demands even on this successful couple's budget. Helen's husband Joe, a Green/Red Introvert, decided to meet the challenge by purchasing ten acres across the street from their family farm and establishing a raspberry "U-Pick" operation. "Every time I hear Joe say, 'I have an idea,' I get nervous," Helen admits. "But almost always I go along with him, because he is usually right." Helen's Red spontaneity helps her here, and the fact that her husband is a Green means he has outstanding ability to create product brands. In 2004 Glunz Raspberry Wine, a fortified dessert wine made from part of their ten-acre crop, won five gold medals in international tastings.

## How Reds Set Goals

Reds don't plan, they evolve. "Planning" is an ongoing process of flexible decisions. You set goals by instinct, always ready to turn on a dime. The ability to change direction based on market needs is a very real strength. But setting real goals that others must work on is a challenge. Set short-term targets; your people will have a clearer direction, and immediate successes energize you.

## Reds at the Start of a Venture

Reds are the born entrepreneurs of the world, but need the right circumstances to thrive. You are natural risk-takers, negotiators, and crisis managers, skills that are critical in the start-up phase of a venture. You excel as long as what you are doing is in demand and business is brisk. When a venture ceases to be fun and stimulating, your attention wanders. However, in crisis mode you excel, coolly managing the situation long after others have caved in.

Reds are impatient with formal education and prefer practical knowledge. These "street smarts" serve you well in new ventures. When interested, you become a real specialist in your field, with or without formal training. You see rules and procedures as guidelines only and never feel particularly bound by them (to the chagrin of any Gold partners).

Your freedom of thought lets you "surf" the marketplace with fresh ideas and new ways of responding to customer desires. A Green will help you market those terrific ideas and get your promotional tasks done quickly. Conventional ways are the last thing on your mind when beginning a new project. Strategic thinking and organizational skills ultimately are needed, however. Bring a Blue on board to help with strategy and a Gold to organize your office.

## The Blue Entrepreneurial Style
### How Blues Set Goals

You're a natural at strategizing, creating plans, and refining them along the way. Too much complexity is your goal-setting blind spot. Be sure to add practical details and concrete steps to your business plan. You won't enjoy it, but it will help keep you realistic about your plans.

---

case study three

### Nordhal Brue

Nordhal ("Nord") Brue is the 60-year-old founder of the Bruegger's Bagels chain. Like many Blues, he excels at combining passion, good ideas, and financial business acumen into single entrepreneurial ideas. Others see him as both intense and playful. "He is a deep thinker," says Chris Dutton, CEO of Green Mountain Power, "who can analyze issues on several different levels."

Recognizing the many skills required to run a successful venture, Nord always partners with someone whose talents balance his own. Always a few steps ahead of national trends, in the early 1980s he saw the potential of turning bagels—then a niche, urban product—into a "quick service" food concept that would appeal to a national audience. Brue's strategy was to start in secondary and suburban markets, far away from metropolitan centers like New York, Philadelphia, and Chicago where bagels were well-known, in order to test the economic feasibility while educating his customers' tastes.

Brue was right. By the mid-1990s Brueggers had grown into almost 500 stores throughout the country and ushered in the first "healthy alternative" quick food concept. He sold the company in 1996 for a stock trade worth $123 million, rebought the company for $45 million a year later, and resold it again for an undisclosed amount in 2000.[20]

Brue has since founded Franklin Foods, a soft unripened cheese manufacturer. While excited about its potential, he's not wedded to it, or any company he builds. "If Kraft says we have to have it, if it's worth more to them than to me, then I'll do a new thing," he told *Vermont Business Magazine* in January 2004.[21] Brue is also chairman of four boards, which he thoroughly enjoys. "I am always better at dealing with the big picture," he says, "which is another way of saying I am not great at the details. My mission is to get these companies to articulate a vision that will take them to the next level—find that very exciting," he says in typical Blue fashion.

## Blues at the Start of a Venture

Many a Blue has launched a successful business off limited information or a hunch. It's the ideas that excite you, and you're at the peak of your talents when creating and refining them. You understand and accept that risks are part of the deal, and you are well able to cope with them.

Daily routine makes you restless; your style is to handle many projects at once. Seeing new trends in the marketplace is an entrepreneurial strength. But it can be a weakness in attempting to actually get things done.

Fortunately, Blues delegate freely and rely on other Colors instinctively. You're the idea person, and you want others to handle the people, procedures, and controls. Make sure you get a Green on board to tap substantial people and promotional skills, a Red to move things along, and a Gold to set up those needed procedures.

# The Green Entrepreneurial Style
## How Greens Set Goals

For you goals and plans are changeable, depending on whatever is exciting to you at the moment. Prioritizing is problematic for you, especially when

[20]Joyce Marcel, "Profiles in Business," *Vermont Business Magazine* (January 2004) p. 17.
[21]*Ibid.*, pg 23

two or more exciting things compete for your attention. The process and the people you meet along the way are of more importance to you than final outcomes.

You will stick to a goal if it helps you find your deepest possible satisfaction. If you can stick to a (relatively) permanent core goal, especially one that reflects your personal values, underlying goals will be more achievable and less of a distraction.

Other Colors will criticize and pressure you into making rigid, financially oriented plans "to keep your business on the right track." You will not complete these plans and will frustrate those who are dependent on you to set direction. You must have the ability to make legitimate detours while keeping sight of the ultimate destination. More than any other Color, you need to partner with a friend, preferably a Gold or Red, who can ground you in the present when needed. You do best when collaborating with other Colors.

## case study four

## Carla Hall

Carla Hall formed the successful Carla Hall Design Group, a marketing communications firm, in 1980. Though she has tried, she has never been able to complete a formal business plan. Most stressful yet is to formally market herself. "If I follow my natural style, I find the right long-term clients," she says.

Carla's clients are some of the world's top financial firms for whom she helps create a brand or image, expressing it through logos, marketing materials, websites, advertising, presentations, events, and trade shows. Her strength, Carla says, "is to provide creative clarity and interpretations to complex messages that result in a fresh and emotional experience for her clients' audiences."

Defining an organization's essence, then directing the internal team of marketers, designers, writers, and legal and performance measurement specialists to execute its outward expression is Carla's greatest talent. It is a very natural one for a Green to possess and makes Carla Hall a highly successful entrepreneur.

## Greens at the Start of a Venture

Greens are less motivated by material gain than other Colors. You prefer to provide value and express your creative energies in whatever business situation stimulates you. Sometimes that will be an entrepreneurial venture, most often prompted by a change in employment status, a disagreement with the practices of an employer, or the need for a family-oriented work schedule.

The ability to create value is both your strength and your blind spot. You will build an extremely loyal clientele, but often think little of sacrificing profit margin to achieve a certain quality of product or service. This loyal clientele, however, is the heart of your business success. High customer loyalty and low staff turnover often get a Green enterprise through rough times when other companies fail.

Your superior abilities to promote and market get you noticed quickly. A Green company often takes off fast, but then needs the tough negotiating skills of Reds and the business systems implemented by Golds to survive in the fast lane. You also have the added frustration that your considerable people and communications skills are underestimated by other Colors, who want you to focus on the balance sheet rather than the customer base.

# CHAPTER 27

# Money and Compensation

**FOR ALL COLOR Q PERSONALITIES,** money itself is either a mirror of self-worth or a means to an end. But how we negotiate our salaries, manage our budgets, and save for important goals is very much driven by our primary and secondary Color Q personalities. Each Color has a different and unique competence when handling this all-important aspect of life. Your natural Color Q salary negotiating and investment styles have been researched by author Shoya Zichy for seven years with close to a thousand people. Some of her proprietary results are being made available for the first time, and only in this book.

## Greens and Money

Given a choice, Greens prefer to deal with other things in life. When supporting just yourself, you see money as a tool to further your own personal development and create aesthetic surroundings. The rabid pursuit of riches usually turns you off. If you are the breadwinner, however, your attitude and involvement change rapidly. People you care about depend on you, and you will learn what it takes to provide for them.

Greens approach money in one of two predictable ways—you are either focused or spontaneous. Focused Green/Golds take a disciplined approach to saving for significant life goals like retirement. Spontaneous Green/Reds are sporadic savers and planners at best and innately high-risk takers when investing. While Green/Reds seem unlikely ever to accumulate enough to retire, you are supported by your almost psychic ability to predict investment trends.

Both types of Greens develop warm, trusting relationships with advisors or financial planners, serving as excellent sources of referrals.

You want to hear how a company impacts people more than about its analytics before investing in its stock. Social investments are of particular interest to you.

## Green/Golds

**Compensation**   When negotiating a compensation package, usually you do not push hard enough. If you like the job and the people and a reasonable number is offered, you'll take it. This often means you have folded too early in the negotiation. You may even accept a salary lower than you want just to get the job.

**Tips**   Don't be so nice. Research what you are worth and practice negotiating, preferably with a Red friend. You have a right to expect reasonable compensation for the value you provide. The other side expects you to play the game, and you'll leave money on the table if you don't. It will never feel natural, but you can learn the game and play it well.

## Green/Reds

**Compensation**   The money a job pays is not your top priority. Does the job help you grow? Does it allow you to express your creativity? Then lucky you, you've hit the jackpot, and whatever it pays you is icing on the cake. You expect people to notice your good work and increase your salary accordingly. Of all the Colors, you need the most practice before walking into a salary negotiation because you truly hate to argue, especially about money.

**Tips**   As with the Green/Golds above, PRACTICE PRACTICE PRACTICE with a tough-minded friend how to play the chess game of salary negotiations. Don't accept the first amount they offer. Have a well-researched counter offer in mind. THIS IS THE ONE TIME IN YOUR LIFE WHEN IT'S OKAY NOT TO BE NICE. Make a list of things you could buy with the extra money you negotiate; this will provide incentive. If the salary remains low, suggest extra time off, a company vehicle, a private office, or free health insurance for your family instead. Use phrases like, "With my qualifications, I am expecting X." You deserve to be compensated in a way that means something to you for the value you provide.

# Reds and Money

Reds are the risk-takers of the investment world, especially when you feel you have sufficient knowledge and disposable income. As in other areas of life, you like to operate by your own rules. You can become quite adept at dealing in the stock (and other) markets.

Your strength is picking up investment cues others miss. You'll benefit from your acute powers of observation and the broad storehouse of practical knowledge you've accumulated since birth. These, combined with your above-average flexibility, create opportunities you pounce on with good timing.

More than other Colors, you prefer to invest in individual stocks rather than mutual funds unless handling family money. Advisors to you are a source of research, execution, and recordkeeping. Detailed planning just gets in the way of plunging into interesting investments.

Your savings account, if it exists, is likely to be starved for attention. You tend not to save. You simply don't obsess about money and figure it will be earned as needed.

## Red/Blues

**Compensation**    For you, tomorrow is another day to earn another dollar. It's likely you have been through both rich and lean times. Your aggressive negotiating style works well in compensation discussions. In fact, other Colors come to you for advice before walking into salary negotiations.

## Red/Greens

**Compensation**    You are a good negotiator, but your style is more relaxed than that of Red/Blues. You also feel tomorrow is another day to earn another dollar, and you can live on a lot of money or a little. You won't, however, leave any money or benefits on the table during salary negotiations.

# Blues and Money

Blues use money as proof of competence. The higher your salary, the more competent the world sees you. More than other Colors, you understand money in the abstract as a flow rather than a stagnant resource. But Blue/Golds and Blue/Reds differ in their approach to money. Where Blue/Golds are disciplined savers, Blue/Reds typically are not.

In your favor, you are intrigued by complex asset allocation strategies that determine how much to invest in stocks, bonds, and other vehicles. You will benefit in real returns from this ability. Against you is your overconfidence. Because you are more likely than most to research and understand all the components of your portfolio, you forget that markets are not always rational.

## Blue/Golds

**Compensation**    You know exactly how much you are worth before you walk in the door to interview. You will drive compensation negotiations to their highest possible level, leaving no money or benefit issue unexplored. Other Colors come to you for advice before their salary negotiations.

## Blue/Reds

**Compensation**    You know what you're worth, what's available, and how to get it. You relax into the process and enjoy the give-and-take of it. Often the people with whom you've negotiated give you far more than they were intending and come away feeling good about it! You are perhaps the smoothest negotiator of all the Colors, leaving nothing on the table and agreeably removing the chairs as well!

# Golds and Money

There's a reason your group was named the Golds! Money is extremely important to your sense of security. You are highly focused on saving and long-term planning and fully in control of your cash flow at all times. You abhor the misuse of money and rarely go into debt or squander the assets you have.

Your investments have to be well-researched, backed by a solid track record, and fully documented with concrete facts. As long as investments meet these criteria, you'll invest directly in the market; but mutual funds are a popular option for Golds. You want your portfolio to be your passport to a worry-free future, and you are likely to achieve this goal early in life.

You have a limited tolerance for risk and volatility, favoring time-tested strategies. Fixed-income instruments like bonds and GICs make you comfortable in a portfolio balanced with blue chip stocks.

Financially, you are a meticulous record keeper. You can reconcile the accuracy of your accounts without the assistance of intermediaries. You prefer working with well-established firms, insisting upon advisors who are organized, consistent, and produce predictable results.

---

### case study one

## Betsy Howie

Betsy Howie is a Gold who boasts major successes in fields where most Golds fear to tread. She wrote and starred in the Off-Broadway play "*Cowgirls*"; she has acted in television soap operas and done numerous commercials for such corporate giants as American Express, Clorox, Monster.com, and Wendy's. She also has done financial humor commentaries for National Public Radio.

Her Gold financial talents come through best however, in her most recent novel, *Callie's Tally*, a humorous accounting of each and every cost of the first year of her daughter Callie's life.

## Gold/Blues

**Compensation**   You are a focused and tough negotiator, having researched what you're worth well in advance. Gold/Blues can be prone to "bag person syndrome," the fear you will wind up penniless on the streets. Because you feel your security is on the line, you accept nothing less than everything there is to get.

## Gold/Greens

**Compensation**   Although you, too, have the "bag person syndrome" suffered by your Gold/Blue cousins, it doesn't drive your negotiation process as strongly. Typically, you won't push the envelope as hard at salary negotiations. Consequently, you may leave the bargaining table with a sinking feeling that you will not be making the money you deserve, unable to allay the lurking bag person in your mind.

**Tip**   You are organized enough to have researched what the market pays for your skills, but are likely to accept a lesser amount after one counter offer. Role-play with a willing Gold/Blue, or any Red, to help you find strategies and phrases with which you are comfortable. A Red/Green is particularly likely to have a style you can emulate.

# PART 7

# CREATING A CUSTOMIZED ROADMAP FOR YOUR PROFESSIONAL LIFE

**CHAPTER 28**
A Roadmap for Putting It All Together

# A Roadmap for Putting It All Together

This is a diary area for those who want to record notes on the material provided in this book. You can collect the ideas you want to revisit here, so you don't have to go looking through the chapters again. It's an excellent place to centralize the information collected during a job search.

**List your top three work-related strengths here** (choose from Figure 1 in your personality's chapter).

1.
2.
3.

**List your top three ideal work environment conditions** (choose from Figure 2 in your personality's chapter).

1.
2.
3.

**List your top three characteristics of an ideal boss** (choose from Figure 3 in your personality's chapter).

1.
2.
3.

**List five careers that you would like to research.** (If you are already in the work force, include at least one that is different than what you are doing now. If you are a student, choose one that is out of the pattern of your proposed career path. Eliminate all careers you feel you OUGHT to pursue and include only those you'd ENJOY pursuing.)
1.
2.
3.
4.
5.

## For Each of the Five Careers You Chose Above, Do the Following Steps:

1. Look up that career on the government's website http://online.onet-center.org
2. Print out the functions and skills required for that career.
3. Compare these functions and skills against your profile's description of the ideal job—how well do they match?
4. Are you an Introvert or an Extrovert? Does the level of people contact seem energizing or draining to you?
5. What are the educational requirements? Do you need more schooling?
6. Look at the bottom of the webpage for the salary. Could you live comfortably on it?
7. Identify several companies you'd like to work for, listing pros and cons.
8. Make a contact list—call or ask people you know for the name and number of the right person to contact at your preferred companies, and if possible research job openings before inquiring. Usually within six random inquiries you will find someone who can make an introduction.

## Review Your Desire to be an Entrepreneur:

1. List your top three entrepreneurial strengths as defined in your primary Color section of Chapter 26, Would I Make a Good Entrepreneur?
2. List your top three concerns about being an entrepreneur. Do a reality check. Talk to several entrepreneurs in your community and ask how they addressed these concerns. Most will be happy to talk with you.
3. List here the skills you DON'T have as an entrepreneur. Next to each, make notes on how you would get help with these. List the Colors with whom you would need to partner (check your Entrepreneurial Style, Bottom Line).

## If You Don't Have a Clue What You Want to Do:

THINK OF A TIME YOU HAD A PEAK EXPERIENCE—WHAT WERE YOU DOING AND WHY WERE YOU SUCCESSFUL?

WHAT TOPICS OF CONVERSATION DO YOU FIND FASCINATING?

TO WHAT KIND OF MAGAZINES AND ARTICLES ARE YOU DRAWN?

WHAT RECREATIONAL ACTIVITIES/HOBBIES DO YOU ENJOY MOST OR HAVE THOUGHT ABOUT STARTING?

WHERE ARE YOU ON THE STABILITY VS. CHANGE AND RISK SCALE? Place an X at the appropriate point on the scale.

Want/Need Security //_____0_____//Will Take Risks

CHOOSE THREE CAREERS THAT INCORPORATE THESE INTERESTS AND SKILLS. (If you're good at something, like acting, don't think you just have to be an actor. Presenting skills and high ability to focus are skills used in teaching, sales, corporate training, etc.)

JOB SEARCH HIGHLIGHTS

NETWORKING NOTES

PEOPLE TO THANK/ACKNOWLEDGE

COMPANY RESEARCH NOTES

RESUME REALITY CHECK
1. Run your resume by friends or family of different Color groups.
2. Go to the Resource section at the back of this book for helpful websites.

LIST YOUR TOP FIVE INTERVIEWING STRENGTHS HERE AND READ BEFORE YOUR APPOINTMENT FOR ENCOURAGEMENT (select from "Interviewing Style" section of your personality's chapter).

LIST YOUR TOP THREE INTERVIEWING WEAKNESSES HERE AND IDEAS FOR ADDRESSING THEM (select from "Interviewing Style" section of your personality's chapter).

COMPENSATION RESEARCH NOTES

COMPENSATION NEGOTIATION STRATEGIES TO EMPLOY (READ BEFORE YOUR APPOINTMENT)

. . . AND FINALLY, WAYS TO HAVE FUN WHILE JOB HUNTING. CREATIVE STRATEGIES, REWARDS FOR DOING SOMETHING DIFFICULT, CONTACTING OLD FRIENDS . . .LIST (AND DO) IT ALL!

We leave you with the Ladder of Success; use Color Q to help you climb to the top!

| WORK DRAWS ON MY NATURAL STRENGTHS |
| --- |
| BOSS I LIKE OR RESPECT |
| IDEAL WORK ENVIRONMENT FOR MY PERSONALITY |

Having the above will make you successful. Later, if you can tap into your passion or compelling interest as well, you will be truly outstanding. Enjoy your journey!

| MY PASSION OR COMPELLING INTEREST |
| --- |

# Bibliography
# and Resources

## Bibliography
### General Career Books

Baber, Anne, and Waymon Lynne. 2007. *Make your contacts count: Networking know-how for business and career success.* New York: AMACOM.

Bernstein, Alan B., and the Staff of the Princeton Review. 2003. *Guide to your career.* New York: Random House.

Citrin, James, and Richard Smith, 2005. *The 5 patterns of extraordinary careers.* New York: Three Rivers Press.

Craddock, Maggie. 2004. *The authentic career.* Novato, CA: New World Library.

Enelow, Wendy, and Shelly Goldman. 2004. *Insider's guide to finding a job: Expert advice from America's top employers and recruiters.* Indianapolis, IN: Jist Publishing.

Farr, Michael, and Laurence Shatkin. 2006. *200 best jobs for college graduates.* Indianapolis, IN: Jist Publishing.

Jansen, Julie. 2003. *I don't know what I want, but I know it's not this.* New York: Penguin Books.

Love, Nicholas. 1998. *The pathfinder.* New York: Fireside/Simon & Schuster.

Nierenberg, Andrea. 2002, 2005. *Nonstop networking, million dollar networking: The sure way to find, grow and keep your business.* Sterling, VA: Capital Books.

Shapiro, Cynthia. 2005. *Corporate confidential: 50 secrets your company doesn't want you to know—and what to do about them.* New York: St. Martin's Griffin.

Wendleton, Kate. 1999, 2000. *Building a great resume, getting interviews, interviewing and salary negotiation.* Franklin Lakes, NJ: The Five O'Clock Club/The Career Press.

Yate, Martin. 2005. *Knock em dead.* Avon, MA: Adams Media Corp.

# Books on the Myers-Briggs and Temperament Models

Berens, Linda V. 2001, 2003. *Understanding yourself and others: Introduction to temperament: Quick guide to the 16 personality types in organizations.* Huntington Beach, CA: Telos Publications.

Demarest, L. 1997. *Looking at type in the workplace.* Gainesville, FL: Center for Application of Type.

Dunning, Donna. 2001. *What's your type of career?* Mountain View, CA: Davies-Black Publishing.

Hammer, Allen. 1993, 1996. *Introduction to type and careers, Career management and counseling.* Mountain View, CA: Davies-Black Publishing.

Hammer, Allen, and J. M. Kummerow. 1996. *Strong and MBTI® career development guide* (Rev. ed). Palo Alto, CA: Davies-Black Publishing.

Hammer, Allen, and G. Macdaid. 1994. *MBTI career report.* Mountain View, CA: Consulting Psychologist Press.

Isachsen, Olaf. 1996. *Joining the entrepreneurial elite.* Palo Alto, CA: Consulting Psychologists Press.

Hirsh, Sandra, and Jean Kummerow. 1998. *Introduction to type in organizations.* Palo Alto, CA: Davies-Black Publishing.

Keirsey, David. 1998. *Please understand me II.* Del Mar, CA: Prometheus Nemesis Book Co.

Kroeger, Otto, and Janet Thuesen. 2002. *Type talk: Type talk at work.* New York: Dell Publishing.

Martin, Charles R. 2005. *Quick guide to the 16 personality types and career mastery.* Huntington Beach, CA: Telos Publications.

Myers, Isabel Briggs, with Peter Myers. 1980, 1995. *Gifts differing.* Mountain View, CA: Davies-Black Publishing.

Myers, Katharine D., and Linda K. Kirby. 1987, 1998. *Introduction to type: Introduction to type dynamics and development.* Palo Alto, CA: Davies-Black Publishing.

Quenk, Naomi. 2002. *Was that really me?* Palo Alto, CA: Davies-Black Publishing.

Tieger, Paul D., and Barbara Barron-Tieger. *Do what you are.* Boston: Little, Brown.

Zichy, Shoya. 2001. *Women and the leadership Q.* New York: McGraw-Hill.

For additional books and resources on the MBTI and temperaments, check out:

## Center for Application of Psychological Type (CAPT)
*www.capt.org*
CAPT offers training, consulting services for professionals and the public, and publishes Type-related materials; compiles research to advance the understanding of Type and maintains the Isabel Briggs Myers Memorial Library.

## Consulting Psychologist Press (CPP)
*www.cpp-db.com*
CPP is the publisher and distributor of the MBTI instrument and related materials. CPP also provides reports including Allen Hammer's *MBTI Career Reports,*

based on research with more than 92,000 working adults who have taken the MBTI and reported levels of work satisfaction. The reports cover 22 job families and 282 specific occupations that can be linked to the O*NET national occupational database. They cover career choice, career exploration, and career development and are available for use by qualified Type practitioners.

**16types.com**
*www.16types.com*
16types.com provides training and resources related to the Keirseyan Temperaments, Berens's Interaction Styles, Jung's Cognitive Processes, and other models that can be integrated with the 16 Personality Types.

**Keirsey Temperament Theory**
*www.keirsey.com*
Publishes and represents the work of David Keirsey and others specializing in temperament theory.

**OKA**
*www.typetalk.com*
A management consulting firm that offers a variety of training programs, materials, and books based on Personality Type and the MBTI.

**PersonalityType.com**
*www.Personalitytype.com*
Consulting group that provides training for individuals and professional trainers interested in using the MBTI in a variety of practical ways.

**Canada—Career/Lifeskills Resources Inc.**
*www.career-lifeskills.com*
Offers a wide range of assessments, training programs, and books.

# Resources
## Assessments, General Counseling, and Information Centers

*www.ColorQProfiles.com* to check out the author's newsletter and other resources.

*online.onetcenter.org/* **The U.S. Department of Labor & the National O*NET Consortium** provide information on an extensive range of careers including job functions, required skills, related subfields, median salary, projected growth rate, and more.

*www.CareerMatchWebsite.com* To take **the Myers-Briggs Type Indicator and/or Strong Interest Inventory,** click on the appropriate assessment and organize a telephone or in-person counseling session.

*www.hcgroup.org* **The Highlands Consulting Group (HCG)** administers **The Highlands Potential Indicator (THPi™)** a comprehensive personal assessment process that identifies and objectively measures natural strengths from among nineteen abilities and helps individuals link these to specific careers and suitable roles within those careers. HCG also uses the ability battery to help identify leadership strengths and areas of challenge. These serve as the foundation for a leader's professional development plan.

*www.careercc.org.* **Career Counselors Consortium** is an organization of professional career counselors who work with clients on job search, resume development, assessment, career change, and performance coaching. Nationwide consultations are by phone or in person in the New York tri-state area.

*www.fiveoclockclub.com* **The Five O'Clock Club** combines individual and group coaching. Local branches meet weekly in the United States and Canada. Different price levels.

*www.acpinternational.org* **Association of Career Professionals International** is a global nonprofit organization with members in over 30 chapters in the United States and abroad who provide lifelong career coaching related services.

*www.jocrf.org* **The Johnson O'Connor Research Foundation** is a nonprofit scientific research and educational organization that administers a proprietary battery of tests to measure people's natural aptitudes in eleven different areas to help them make decisions about school and work. These measured traits are highly stable over long-term periods. For information about locations in eleven cities, check the website.

## College/First Job Entry Level Sites

*www.campuscareercenter.com; www.collegejobboard.com*
*www.experience.com; www.planetedu.net*

## General Job Banks

*www.ajb.org* America's Job Bank (AJB). Click link on Career Infonet. Then click resources.

*www.bestjobsusa.com* A comprehensive site.

*www.careerbuilder.com* Recruitment center for over thirty-five newspapers in the United States.

*www.careercity.com*

*www.careermag.com* Career magazine with industry-specific career channels.

*www.compuserve.com*

*www.flipdog.com* Uses a special crawler technology to search jobs on company sites.

*www.hotjobs.com* Central resume database where companies search.

*www.interbiznet.com/hunt/companies* Useful when checking the job site pages of individual companies.

*www.jobbankusa.com*

*www.monster.com* The largest job/resume bank.

*www.mkt10.com* A recruiting service that functions like an online "headhunter." Uses technology to match candidate's core capabilities with open positions. Free to job candidates.

*www.nationjob.com*
*www.netshare.com, www.6figurejobs.com* Job boards for executives making $100K+.
*www.nydailynews.com New York Daily News* want ads.
*www.nytimes.com/yr/mo/day/jobmarket New York Times* want ads.
*www.truecareers.com* Includes a contest that wipes away your student loan.
*www.worktree.com* Connects to 300 major job sites.

## Specific Niche Job Sites

Advertising, PR, and graphic arts: *www.creativehotlist.com*; *www.prweek.net*; *www.adage.com*
Home employment: *www.homejobstop.com*; *http://ahbwa.com/html2/index.php*
Engineering: *www.engineerjobs.com*
Freelance professional services online: *www.elance.com*; *www.freelance.com*
Freelance writers: *www.freelancing4money.com*
Financial services: *www.BankJobSearch.com*
Healthcare: *www.healthjobsusa.com*
Hotel management: *www.hospitalityonline.com*
Human resources: *www.HR.com*
IT: *www.nytechjobs.com*
Legal: *www.legalstaff.com*
Non-for-profit: *www.idealist.com*
Pharmaceuticals: *www.RXcareerCenter.com*
Older Age Workers: *www.aarp.org*; *www.seniorjobbank.com*
Retail: *www.retailjobnet.com*
Sales professional: *www.jobs4sales.com*; *www.NASP.com*
Teaching: *www.higherEdjobs.com*
Women only: *www.careerwomen.com*

## Industry/Company Research

*www.bigbook.com* Good source for company information.
*www.carolworld.com* Corporate annual reports.
*www.corporationinformation.com*
*www.downside.com* Direct access to latest company financials including 10K and 10Q.
*www.Hoovers.com*
*www.Vault.com* Well-presented reports on different sectors.
*www.virtualpet.com/industry/mfg/mfg.htm* Comprehensive collection of industry portals.
*www.wetfeet.com* Industry profiles plus much more.

## Salary Information

*www.salary.com*
*www.wageweb.com*

## Career Search Tools and Strategies

*www.acinet.org* Site includes information on general outlook of occupations, wages, trends and has a resource library.

*www.bls.gov/oco* Labor bureau occupational outlook handbook.

*www.careerroadblocks.com* Focus on career blocks.

*www.careerjournal.com Wall Street Journal* articles.

*www.myreferences.com* Will check your references for you.

*www.nycareerzone.org* Supported by New York State Department of Labor.

*www.oalj.dol.gov/libdot.htm Dictionary of Occupational Titles* (DOT)

*www.onecenter.org* Occupational information network.

*www.rileyguide.com/jobs.html* Should visit at least once for advice on job search.

*www.stats.bls.gov/emphome.htm* Site for projections for the fastest growing occupations and industries, labor force statistics, and contact information for your state.

## Resume Preparation

*www.10minuteresume.com*
*www.jobstar.org/tools/resume/index.htm*
*www.nycareerzone.com*
*www.provenresumes.com*
*www.winway.com*

## Other Resources

*www.asaenet.org* Find your associations here. Select "Directories," "Associations," "Gateway," then type in your search criteria.

*www.fastcompany.com* Go to the "Guides" section, which contains some great articles about careers and succeeding in your job.

*www.idealist.org* Jobs and volunteer opportunities at nonprofits.

*www.volunteermatch.org* Find out about volunteer opportunities; could jump-start your next career.

*www.fortune.com* The magazine's website; find lists of the best companies to work for. May need to subscribe, but inexpensive.

*www.quarterlifecrisis.com* Focused on the "twentysomethings" who wish they had a guidebook to help them navigate life after school.

# Index

# About the Authors

**Shoya Zichy** has made five career changes within the teaching, journalism, private banking, commercial real estate, and training industries in order to find the work that draws on her most natural skills and best fulfills her needs. She finds that by following your passion, you create a unique brand that, in turn, effortlessly attracts the attention of others. Her work has been featured in *Fortune, Barron's, Newsday,* the *Chicago Sun-Times, US 1,* and on CNN. A frequent speaker and seminar leader, her client list includes ABN/LaSalle Bank, Deloitte & Touche, Merrill Lynch, Northern Trust, Prudential, UBS, and the U.S. Treasury. She lives in New York City and is the author of **Women and the Leadership Q** (McGraw-Hill, 2001); also available in Chinese and Korean.

For more information visit the author's website at *www.ColorQProfiles.com*

**Ann Bidou** has published hundreds of articles and written regularly for publications such as the **Chicago Tribune.** She has long been a student of Zichy's Color Q system, and it has changed her life from Wall Street executive to small business owner in the Berkshires. She has written previously on the Color Q system for application by financial executives who manage pension plans. She lives in Falls Village, Connecticut.

# Advance praise for *Career Match*

"Spot-on advice for anyone involved in career management—either for themselves or coaching others. One of the best books on the subject."
—*Joseph F. Weldon, Managing Director, Global Director, Learning & Development, Citigroup Corporate and Investment Banking*

"This is the indispensable guide we've all been looking for. It takes all the guesswork out of trying to find the career path and job that's the best match for you. 'Bloom where you're planted' takes on a whole new meaning when you can choose your best soil!"
—*Cynthia Shapiro, Job Search Consultant and Author of* Corporate Confidential: 50 Secrets Your Company Doesn't Want You to Know – And What to Do About Them

"*Career Match* gives you the tools to help guide you to decisions and careers that are right for you. Or if you are a parent, you may often feel you know what is best for your children....This book can help you be right and make your recommendations more effective."
—*Barbara Bartilson, Senior Vice President, LaSalle Bank Corporation*

"Shoya's assessment and book makes 'climbing a ladder of success' easy and fun. Like a laser beam, she goes to the heart of the issue, provides deep and insightful feedback, and tools that enable people to move forward."
—*Marianna Lead, Ph. D., President, International Coach Federation, NYC Chapter; Adjunct Faculty, New York University; Life/Executive Coach & Hypnotherapist*

"Using the *Career Match* personality model definitely helped our team appreciate one another's strengths. Applying these principles to career decisions would, I think, allow individuals to make even better choices—for themselves and for their colleagues."
—*E. M. Reynolds, Senior Vice President, The Segal Company*